A-Level Year 1 & A

Exam Board: AQA

What's your favourite element? Ours is magnesium. No, argon. Or maybe cobalt? It's just too hard to decide.

One thing's for sure, though — when it comes to AQA AS Chemistry revision, this CGP book is the only choice. (And it's perfect for Year 1 of the A-Level course too.)

It's packed with crystal-clear study notes explaining every topic, plus plenty of realistic exam questions (with detailed answers at the back). And if you're tired of lugging all this paper around, there's even a free Online Edition you can read on your computer or tablet!

How to access your free Online Edition

This book includes a free Online Edition to read on your PC, Mac or tablet.
You'll just need to go to **cgpbooks.co.uk/extras** and enter this code:

0297 2402 9967 0004

By the way, this code only works for one person. If somebody else has used this book before you, they might have already claimed the Online Edition.

A-Level revision? It has to be CGP!

Contents

Unit 3: Section 3 — Alkenes and Alcohols

Unit 3: Section 4 — Organic Analysis

Practical Skills

Published by CGP

Editors:
Emily Forsberg, Charles Kitts, Andy Park and Sarah Pattison.

Contributors:
Vikki Cunningham, Ian H. Davis, John Duffy, Max Fishel, Emma Grimwood,
Lucy Muncaster, David Paterson, Derek Swain, Louise Watkins and Chris Workman.

ISBN: 978 1 78908 027 8

With thanks to Alex Billings, Katie Burton, Barrie Crowther and Mary Falkner for the proofreading.
With thanks to Jan Greenway for the copyright research.

Cover Photo **Laguna Design**/Science Photo Library

With thanks to Science Photo Library for permission to reproduce the photograph used on page 60.

Clipart from Corel®
Printed by Elanders Ltd, Newcastle upon Tyne.

Based on the classic CGP style created by Richard Parsons.

The Atom

This stuff about atoms and elements should be ingrained in your brain from GCSE. You do need to know it perfectly though, if you are to negotiate your way through the field of man-eating tigers that is Chemistry.

Atoms are made up of **Protons, Neutrons** and **Electrons**

All elements are made of **atoms**. Atoms are made up of 3 types of particle — **protons**, **neutrons** and **electrons**.

Electrons

1) Electrons have **–1** charge.
2) They whizz around the nucleus in **orbitals**. The orbitals take up most of the **volume** of the atom.

Nucleus

1) Most of the **mass** of the atom is concentrated in the nucleus.
2) The **diameter** of the nucleus is rather titchy compared to the whole atom.
3) The nucleus is where you find the **protons** and **neutrons**.

The mass and charge of these subatomic particles is **really small**, so **relative mass** and **relative charge** are usually used instead.

Subatomic particle	Relative mass	Relative charge
Proton	1	+1
Neutron	1	0
Electron, e^-	$\frac{1}{2000}$	–1

The mass of an electron is negligible compared to a proton or a neutron — this means you can usually ignore it.

Nuclear Symbols Show Numbers of **Subatomic Particles**

You can figure out the **number** of protons, neutrons and electrons in an atom from the **nuclear symbol**.

$$^{A}_{Z}X$$

Mass number — This tells you the **total** number of **protons** and **neutrons** in the nucleus.

Element symbol

Atomic (proton) number

1) This is the number of **protons** in the nucleus — it identifies the element.
2) **All** atoms of the same element have the **same** number of protons.

Sometimes the atomic number is left out of the nuclear symbol, e.g. ^{7}Li. You don't really need it because the element's symbol tells you its value.

1) For **neutral** atoms, which have no overall charge, the number of electrons is **the same as** the number of protons.
2) The number of neutrons is **mass number minus atomic number**, i.e. 'top minus bottom' in the nuclear symbol.

Nuclear symbol	Atomic number, Z	Mass number, A	Protons	Electrons	Neutrons
$^{7}_{3}Li$	3	7	3	3	7 – 3 = 4
$^{79}_{35}Br$	35	79	35	35	79 – 35 = 44
$^{24}_{12}Mg$	12	24	12	12	24 – 12 = 12

"Hello, I'm Newt Ron..."

Ions have **Different** Numbers of **Protons** and **Electrons**

Atoms form ions by losing or gaining electrons. **Negative** ions have **more electrons** than protons...

E.g. Br^- — The negative charge means that there's 1 more electron than there are protons. Br has 35 protons (see table above), so Br^- must have 36 electrons. The overall charge = +35 – 36 = –1.

...and **positive** ions have **fewer electrons** than protons. It kind of makes sense when you think about it.

E.g. Mg^{2+} — The 2+ charge means that there are 2 fewer electrons than there are protons. Mg has 12 protons (see table above), so Mg^{2+} must have 10 electrons. The overall charge = +12 – 10 = +2.

The Atom

Isotopes are Atoms of the Same Element with Different Numbers of Neutrons

Make sure you **learn** this definition and totally **understand** what it means:

Isotopes of an element are atoms with the same number of protons but different numbers of neutrons.

Chlorine-35 and chlorine-37 are examples of isotopes.

35 – 17 = 18 neutrons ← **Different** mass numbers mean different numbers of neutrons. → 37 – 17 = 20 neutrons

$^{35}_{17}Cl$ The **atomic numbers** are the same. **Both** isotopes have 17 protons and 17 electrons. $^{37}_{17}Cl$

1) It's the **number** and **arrangement** of electrons that decides the **chemical properties** of an element. Isotopes have the **same configuration of electrons**, so they've got the **same** chemical properties.
2) Isotopes of an element do have slightly different **physical properties** though, such as different densities, rates of diffusion, etc. This is because **physical properties** tend to depend on the **mass** of the atom.

Here's another example — naturally occurring **magnesium** consists of 3 isotopes.

^{24}Mg (79%)	^{25}Mg (10%)	^{26}Mg (11%)
12 protons	12 protons	12 protons
12 neutrons	13 neutrons	14 neutrons
12 electrons	12 electrons	12 electrons

The periodic table gives the atomic number of each element. The other number by an element's symbol in the periodic table isn't the mass number though — it's the relative atomic mass (see page 5).

Warm-Up Questions

PRACTICE QUESTIONS

Q1 Draw a diagram showing the structure of an atom, labelling each part.

Q2 Where is the mass concentrated in an atom, and what makes up most of the volume of an atom?

Q3 Draw a table showing the relative charge and relative mass of the three subatomic particles found in atoms.

Q4 Using an example, explain the terms 'atomic number' and 'mass number'.

Q5 Define the term 'isotopes' and give examples.

Exam Questions

Q1 Hydrogen, deuterium and tritium are all isotopes of each other.

a) Identify one similarity and one difference between these isotopes. [2 marks]

b) Deuterium can be written as $^{2}_{1}H$. Determine the number of protons, neutrons and electrons in a deuterium atom. [1 mark]

c) Write the nuclear symbol for tritium, given that it has 2 neutrons. [1 mark]

Q2 This question relates to the atoms or ions A to D: A $^{32}_{16}S^{2-}$ B $^{40}_{18}Ar$ C $^{30}_{16}S$ D $^{42}_{20}Ca$

a) Identify the similarity for each of the following pairs, justifying your answer in each case.

i) A and B. [1 mark]

ii) A and C. [1 mark]

iii) B and D. [1 mark]

b) Which two of the atoms or ions are isotopes of each other? Explain your reasoning. [2 marks]

Got it learned yet? — Isotope so...

This is a nice page to ease you into things. Remember that positive ions have fewer electrons than protons, and negative ions have more electrons than protons. Get that straight in your mind or you'll end up in a right mess. There's nowt too hard about isotopes neither. They're just the same element with different numbers of neutrons.

Models of Atomic Structure

The model of the atom on the previous pages is darn useful for understanding loads of ideas in chemistry. You can picture what's happening in your mind really well. But it is just a model. So it's not completely like that really.

The **Accepted Model** of the **Atom** Has **Changed** Throughout History

The model of the atom you're expected to know (the one on page 2) is one of the **currently accepted** ones. But in the past, **completely different** models were accepted, because they fitted the evidence available at the time. As scientists did more experiments, **new evidence** was found and the models were **modified** to fit it.

1) At the start of the 19th century **John Dalton** described atoms as **solid spheres**, and said that different spheres made up the different elements.

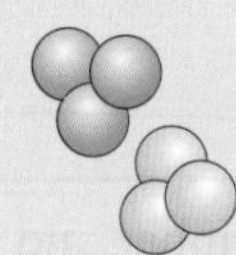

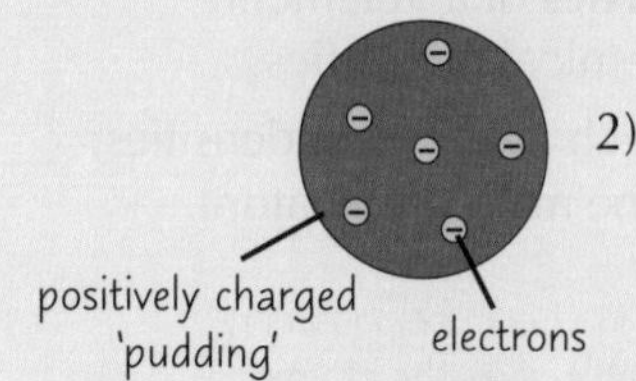

2) In 1897 **J. J. Thomson** discovered the electron. This showed that atoms **weren't** solid and indivisible. The 'solid sphere' idea of atomic structure had to be changed. The new model was known as the **'plum pudding model'**.

3) In 1909 **Ernest Rutherford** and his students **Hans Geiger** and **Ernest Marsden** conducted their famous **gold foil experiment**. They fired positively charged **alpha particles** at a very thin sheet of gold. The plum pudding model suggested that **most** alpha particles would be **slightly** deflected by the positive 'pudding' that made up most of the atom. In fact, most of the particles passed **straight through** the gold with only a small number being deflected **backwards**. The plum pudding model **couldn't be right**, so Rutherford developed the **nuclear model** of the atom. In this, a **tiny positively charged nucleus** is surrounded by a **'cloud'** of **negative electrons** — most of the atom is **empty space**.

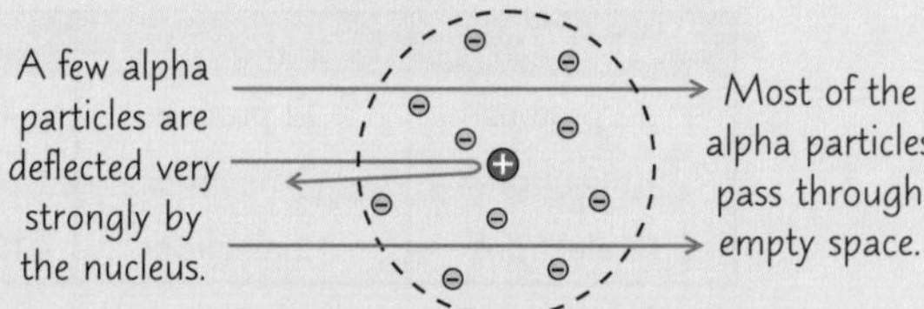

A few alpha particles are deflected very strongly by the nucleus.
Most of the alpha particles pass through empty space.

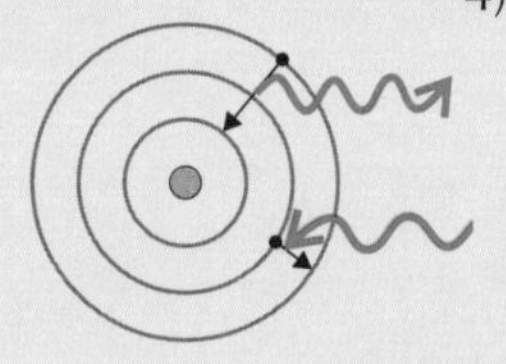

4) Scientists realised that electrons in a **'cloud'** around the nucleus of an atom, as Rutherford described, would quickly **spiral down** into the nucleus, causing the atom to **collapse**. **Niels Bohr** proposed a new model of the atom where electrons exist in **shells** or **orbits** of **fixed energy**. When electrons move between shells, **electromagnetic radiation** (with **fixed** energy or **frequency**) is **emitted** or **absorbed**. The Bohr model **fitted experimental observations** of the radiation emitted and absorbed by atoms.

5) Scientists later discovered that not all the electrons in a shell have the same energy. This meant that the Bohr model wasn't quite right. So, they **refined** it to include **sub-shells**. The refined Bohr model isn't perfect — more accurate models exist today, but it's a useful model because it's **simple** and explains many **experimental observations**, like bonding and ionisation energy trends.

Warm-Up Questions

Q1 Why did Rutherford think that a new model of the atom was needed?

Q2 Who developed the 'nuclear' model of the atom?

Q3 Why is Bohr's model thought to be a truer description of the atom than Rutherford's?

Q4 Describe the model of the atom first proposed by Niels Bohr. How was it later refined?

Q5 More accurate models of the atom have been developed since the Bohr model. Explain why the Bohr model is still used today.

These models are tiny — even smaller than size zero, I reckon...

The process of developing a model to fit the evidence available, looking for more evidence to show if it's correct or not, then revising the model if necessary is really important. It happens with all new scientific ideas. Even really long standing theories get changed or ditched sometimes in response to a new piece of evidence that someone has uncovered...

Relative Mass and the Mass Spectrometer

Relative mass...What? Eh?...Read on...

Relative Masses are Masses of Atoms Compared to Carbon-12

The actual mass of an atom is **very**, **very tiny**. Don't worry about exactly how tiny for now, but it's far **too small** to weigh. So, the mass of one atom is compared to the mass of a different atom. This is its **relative mass**. Here are some definitions to learn:

The **relative atomic mass**, A_r, is the **average mass** of an atom of an element on a scale where an atom of **carbon-12** is 12.

Relative isotopic mass is the mass of an atom of an **isotope** of an element on a scale where an atom of **carbon-12** is 12.

Relative atomic mass is an average, so it's not usually a whole number. Relative isotopic mass is usually a whole number. E.g. a natural sample of chlorine contains a mixture of ^{35}Cl (75%) and ^{37}Cl (25%), so the relative isotopic masses are 35 and 37. But its relative atomic mass is 35.5.

The **relative molecular mass**, M_r, is the average mass of a **molecule** on a scale where an atom of **carbon-12** is 12.

To find the relative molecular mass, just add up the relative atomic mass values of all the atoms in the molecule, e.g. $M_r(C_2H_6O) = (2 \times 12.0) + (6 \times 1.0) + 16.0 = 46.0$

Relative formula mass is used instead for compounds that are ionic (or giant covalent). To find the relative formula mass, just add up the relative atomic masses (A_r) of all the atoms in the formula unit. E.g. $M_r(CaF_2) = 40.1 + (2 \times 19.0) = 78.1$

"All those pies have made me relatively massive."

Relative Masses can be Measured Using a Mass Spectrometer

You can use a **mass spectrometer** to find out loads of stuff. It can tell you the **relative atomic mass**, **relative molecular mass**, **relative isotopic abundance** and your **horoscope** for the next fortnight.

There are **4** things that happen when a sample is squirted into a **time of flight (TOF) mass spectrometer**.

① **Ionisation** Two ways of ionising your sample are:
Electrospray ionisation — the sample is dissolved and pushed through a small nozzle at high pressure. A high voltage is applied to it, causing each particle to **gain an H⁺** ion. The sample is turned into a **gas** made up of **positive ions**.
Electron impact ionisation — the sample is vaporised and an 'electron gun' is used to fire high energy electrons at it. This knocks one electron off each particle, so they become **+1 ions**.

② **Acceleration** — the positively charged ions are accelerated by an **electric field** so that they all have the **same kinetic energy**. (This means that the lighter ions will end up moving faster than the heavier ions.)

③ **Ion Drift** — the ions enter a region with no electric field, so they just **drift** through it. Lighter ions will drift through faster than heavier ions.

④ **Detection** — because ions that have a **lower mass/charge ratio** travel at **higher speeds** in the drift region, they reach the detector in **less time** than ions with a higher mass/charge ratio. The detector detects **charged** particles and a **mass spectrum** (see next page) is produced.

vacuum

lower mass/charge ion

higher mass/charge ion

ion detector

The detectors used in mass spectrometers detect charged particles. An electrical current is produced in the detector when a charged particle hits it.

Relative Mass and the Mass Spectrometer

A **Mass Spectrum** is **Mass/Charge** plotted against **Abundance**

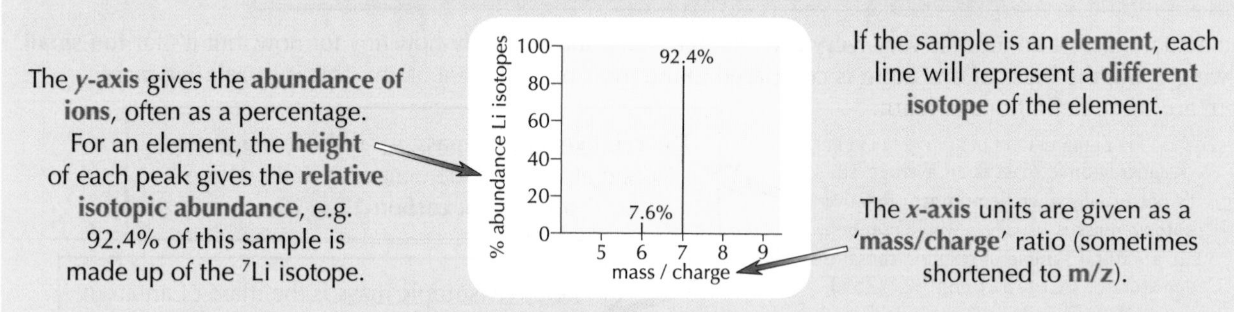

The *y*-axis gives the **abundance of ions**, often as a percentage. For an element, the **height** of each peak gives the **relative isotopic abundance**, e.g. 92.4% of this sample is made up of the ^{7}Li isotope.
% abundance Li isotopes
100
80
60
40
20
0
92.4%
7.6%
5 6 7 8 9
mass / charge
If a sample being analysed contains magnesium, this isotopic distribution will show up in the mass spectrum.
If the sample is an **element**, each line will represent a **different isotope** of the element.
The *x*-axis units are given as a '**mass/charge**' ratio (sometimes shortened to **m/z**).

The spectrum above was produced using **electron impact ionisation**. One **electron** has been **knocked off** each particle to turn them into **+1 ions** — so the mass/charge ratio of each peak is the same as the **relative mass** of that isotope. (If **electrospray ionisation** had been used instead, an H^+ **ion** would have been **added** to each particle to form **+1 ions** — so the mass/charge ratio of each peak would be **one unit greater** than the relative mass of each isotope.)

All of the spectra shown in this topic have been produced using electron impact ionisation.

You Can Work Out **Relative Atomic Mass** from a **Mass Spectrum**

You need to know how to calculate the **relative atomic mass** (A_r) of an element from the **mass spectrum**. Here's how to calculate A_r for magnesium, using the mass spectrum below:

1) For each peak, read the **% relative isotopic abundance** from the y-axis and the **relative isotopic mass** from the x-axis. **Multiply** them together to get the total mass for each isotope: 79 × 24 = 1896; 10 × 25 = 250; 11 × 26 = 286
2) **Add** up these totals: 1896 + 250 + 286 = 2432
3) **Divide by 100** (as percentages were used): A_r(Mg) = 2432 ÷ 100 = 24.32 = **24.3 (3 s.f.)**

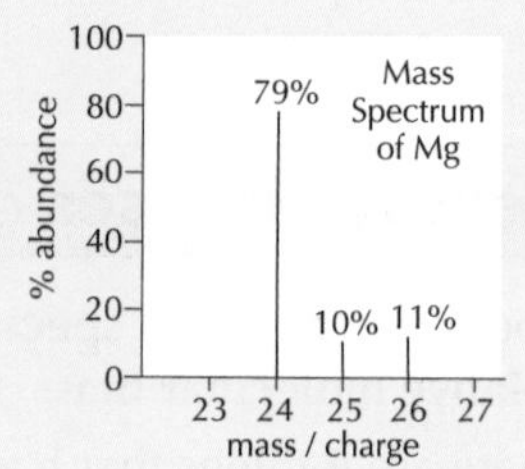

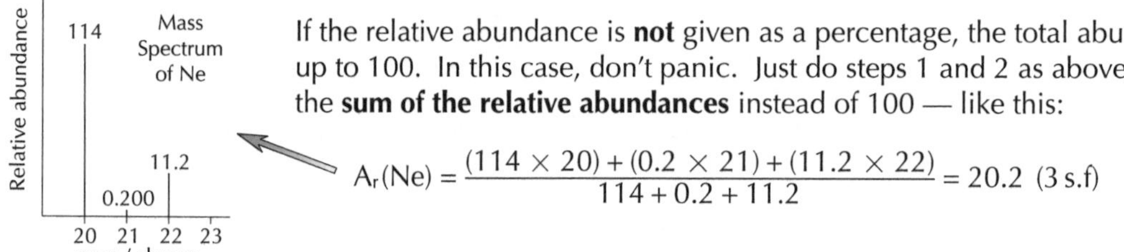

If the relative abundance is **not** given as a percentage, the total abundance may not add up to 100. In this case, don't panic. Just do steps 1 and 2 as above, but then divide by the **sum of the relative abundances** instead of 100 — like this:

$$A_r(\text{Ne}) = \frac{(114 \times 20) + (0.2 \times 21) + (11.2 \times 22)}{114 + 0.2 + 11.2} = 20.2 \text{ (3 s.f)}$$

Mass Spectrometry can be used to **Identify Elements**

Elements with different **isotopes** produce more than one line in a mass spectrum because the isotopes have **different masses**. This produces characteristic patterns which can be used as '**fingerprints**' to **identify** certain **elements**.

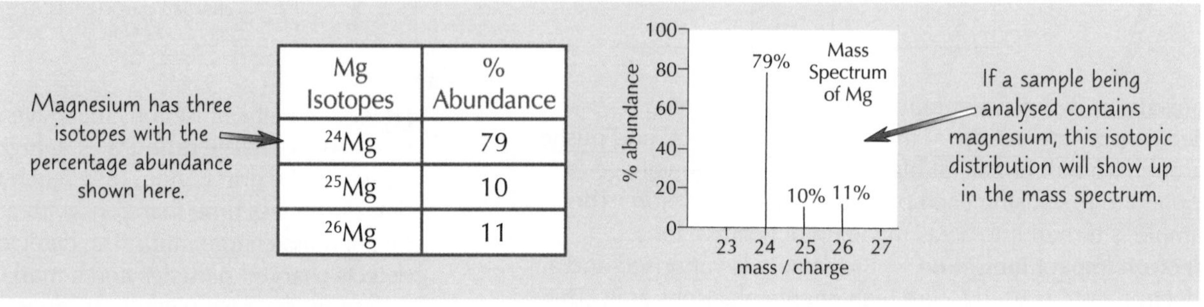

Magnesium has three isotopes with the percentage abundance shown here.

Mg Isotopes	% Abundance
^{24}Mg	79
^{25}Mg	10
^{26}Mg	11

Many elements only have one stable isotope. They can still be identified in a mass spectrum by looking for a line at their **relative atomic mass**.

Relative Mass and the Mass Spectrometer

Mass Spectrometry can be used to Identify Molecules

You can also get a mass spectrum for a **molecular sample**.

1) A **molecular ion**, M^+, is formed in the mass spectrometer when one electron is removed from the molecule.
2) This gives a peak in the spectrum with a mass/charge ratio equal to the **relative molecular mass** of the molecule.
3) This can be used to help **identify** an unknown compound.
   There's more about using mass spectrometry to identify compounds on page 99.

Example: A sample of a straight-chain alcohol is analysed in a mass spectrometer. The mass/charge ratio of its molecular ion is 46.0. Identify the alcohol.

The table on the right shows the **M_r** of the first three straight-chain alcohols. The mass/charge ratio of the molecular ion must **equal** the M_r of the alcohol in the sample. So the alcohol must be **ethanol, C_2H_5OH**.

Alcohol	M_r
methanol CH_3OH	32.0
ethanol C_2H_5OH	46.0
propanol C_3H_7OH	60.0

If you have a mixture of compounds with different M_r values, you'll get a peak for the molecular ion of each one.

Warm-Up Questions

Q1 Explain what relative atomic mass (A_r) and relative isotopic mass mean.

Q2 Explain the difference between relative molecular mass and relative formula mass.

Q3 Describe how electrospray ionisation works.

Q4 Explain how a mass spectrum can be used to determine relative molecular mass.

Exam Questions

Q1 Copper, Cu, exists in two main isotopic forms, ^{63}Cu and ^{65}Cu.

a) Calculate the relative atomic mass of Cu using the information from the mass spectrum on the right. [2 marks]

b) Explain why the relative atomic mass of copper is not a whole number. [2 marks]

Mass Spectrum of Cu

Relative abundance: 120.8 (mass/charge 63), 54.0 (mass/charge 65)

mass / charge: 61 63 65 67

Q2 The percentage make-up of naturally occurring potassium is 93.11% ^{39}K, 0.12% ^{40}K and 6.77% ^{41}K.

a) What method is used to determine the mass and abundance of each isotope? [1 mark]

b) Use the information to determine the relative atomic mass of potassium. [2 marks]

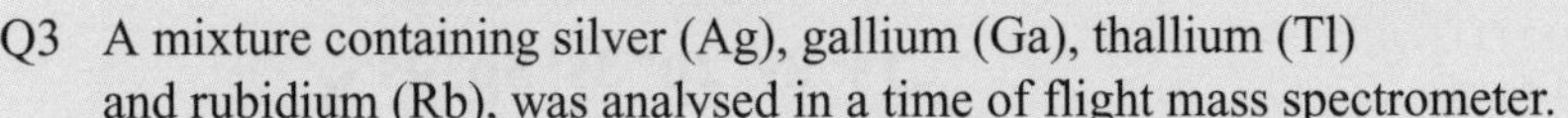

Q3 A mixture containing silver (Ag), gallium (Ga), thallium (Tl) and rubidium (Rb), was analysed in a time of flight mass spectrometer.

a) Why do samples need to be positively charged in time of flight mass spectrometry? [2 marks]

b) Explain how time of flight mass spectrometry distinguishes between ions with different masses. [4 marks]

c) The abundance of the isotopes of the elements in the mixture are shown below. Which element is responsible for the part of the spectrum on the right?

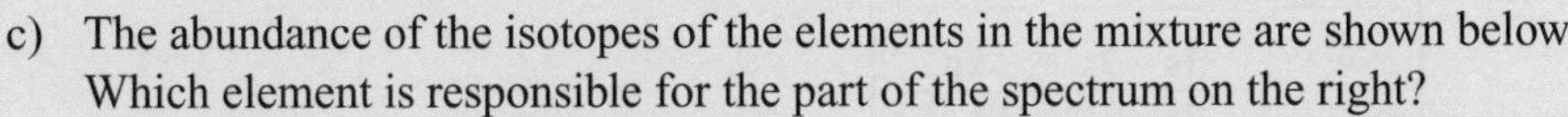
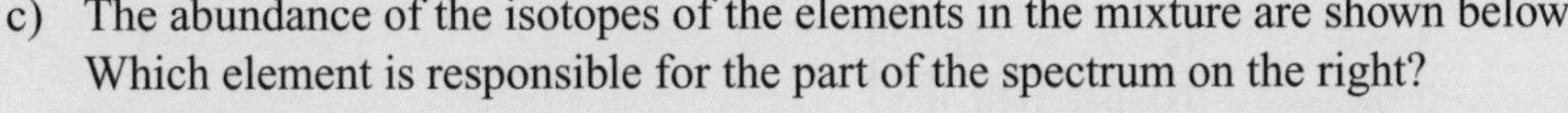
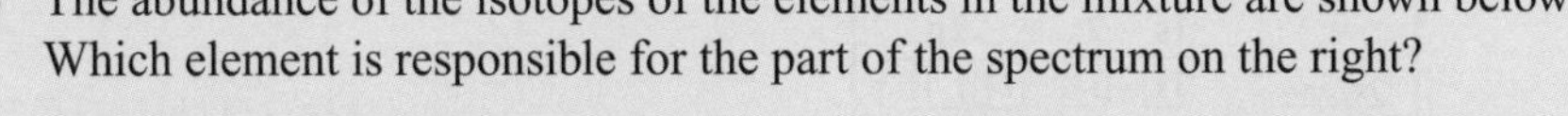

A Silver: 51.8% ^{107}Ag, 48.2% ^{109}Ag

B Gallium: 60.1% ^{69}Ga, 39.9% ^{71}Ga

C Thallium: 29.5% ^{203}Tl, 70.5% ^{205}Tl

D Rubidium: 72.2% ^{85}Rb, 27.8% ^{87}Rb

[1 mark]

% abundance: 0, 20, 40, 60, 80, 100

mass / charge

You can't pick your relatives — you just have to calculate them...

All this mass spectrometry stuff looks a bit evil, but it really isn't that bad once you get your head round it. Make sure you've done the practice and exam questions, cos they cover all the stuff you need to be able to do, and if you can get them right, you've nailed it. Then you can go and do something much more fun, like cutting the lawn with nail scissors...

Electronic Structure

Those little electrons prancing about like mini bunnies decide what'll react with what — it's what chemistry's all about.

Electron Shells are Made Up of **Sub-Shells** and **Orbitals**

1) In the currently accepted model of the atom, electrons have **fixed energies**.
They move around the nucleus in certain regions of the atom called **shells** or **energy levels**.
2) Each shell is given a number called the **principal quantum number**.
The **further** a shell is from the nucleus, the **higher** its energy and the **larger** its principal quantum number.
3) **Experiments** show that not all the electrons in a shell have exactly the same energy.
The **atomic model** explains this — shells are divided up into **sub-shells** that have slightly different energies.
The sub-shells have different numbers of **orbitals** which can each hold up to **2 electrons**.

This table shows the number of electrons that fit in each type of sub-shell.

Sub-shell	Number of orbitals	Maximum electrons
s	1	$1 \times 2 = 2$
p	3	$3 \times 2 = 6$
d	5	$5 \times 2 = 10$
f	7	$7 \times 2 = 14$

And this one shows the sub-shells and electrons in the first four energy levels.

Shell	Sub-shell	Total number of electrons
1st	1*s*	2
2nd	2*s* 2*p*	$2 + (3 \times 2) = 8$
3rd	3*s* 3*p* 3*d*	$2 + (3 \times 2) + (5 \times 2) = 18$
4th	4*s* 4*p* 4*d* 4*f*	$2 + (3 \times 2) + (5 \times 2) + (7 \times 2) = 32$

4) The two electrons in each orbital spin in **opposite directions**.

Work Out **Electron Configurations** by Filling the **Lowest** Energy Levels First

You can figure out most electron configurations pretty easily, so long as you know a few simple rules —

1) Electrons fill up the **lowest** energy sub-shells first.

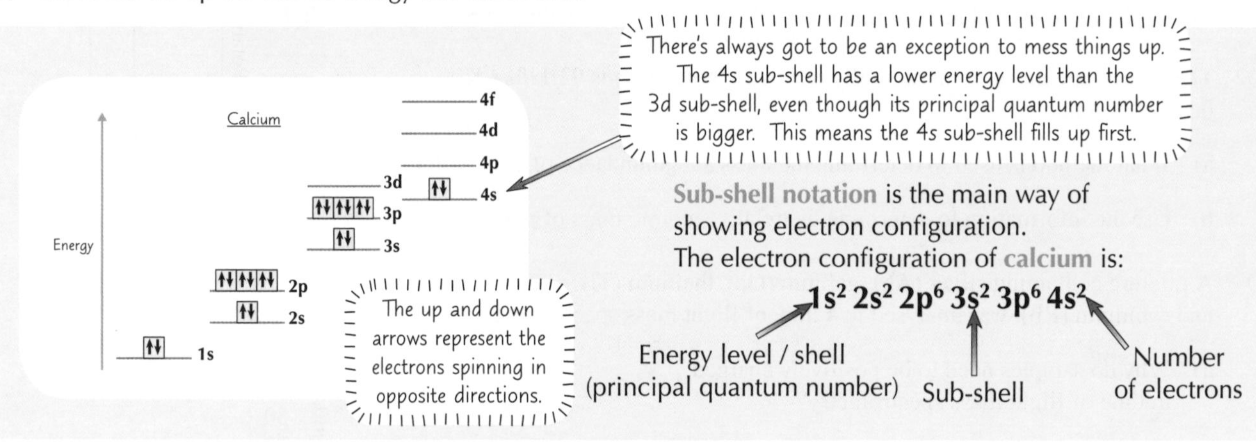

Calcium
Energy
4f
4d
4p
3d
4s
3p
3s
2p
2s
1s
There's always got to be an exception to mess things up. The 4s sub-shell has a lower energy level than the 3d sub-shell, even though its principal quantum number is bigger. This means the 4s sub-shell fills up first.
The up and down arrows represent the electrons spinning in opposite directions.
Sub-shell notation is the main way of showing electron configuration.
The electron configuration of calcium is:
$1s^2\ 2s^2\ 2p^6\ 3s^2\ 3p^6\ 4s^2$
Energy level / shell (principal quantum number)
Sub-shell
Number of electrons

2) Electrons fill orbitals **singly** before they start sharing.

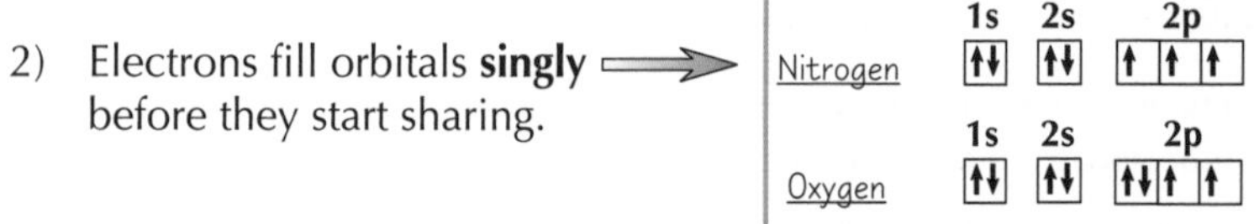

See the next page for more on the s and p blocks.

3) For the configuration of **ions** from the **s** and **p** blocks of the periodic table, just **remove or add** the electrons to or from the highest energy occupied sub-shell.
E.g. Mg = $1s^2\ 2s^2\ 2p^6\ 3s^2$, so Mg^{2+} = $1s^2\ 2s^2\ 2p^6$. Cl = $1s^2\ 2s^2\ 2p^6\ 3s^2\ 3p^5$, so Cl^- = $1s^2\ 2s^2\ 2p^6\ 3s^2\ 3p^6$.

Watch out — **noble gas symbols**, like that of argon (Ar), are sometimes used in electron configurations. For example, calcium ($1s^2\ 2s^2\ 2p^6\ 3s^2\ 3p^6\ 4s^2$) can be written as $[Ar]4s^2$, where $[Ar] = 1s^2\ 2s^2\ 2p^6\ 3s^2\ 3p^6$.

Electronic Structure

Transition Metals Behave Unusually

1) **Chromium** (Cr) and **copper** (Cu) are badly behaved. They donate one of their **4s** electrons to the **3d sub-shell**. It's because they're happier with a **more stable** full or half-full d sub-shell.
   Cr atom (24 e^-): $1s^2\ 2s^2\ 2p^6\ 3s^2\ 3p^6\ 3d^5\ 4s^1$ Cu atom (29 e^-): $1s^2\ 2s^2\ 2p^6\ 3s^2\ 3p^6\ 3d^{10}\ 4s^1$
2) And here's another weird thing about transition metals — when they become **ions**, they lose their **4s** electrons **before** their 3d electrons.
   Fe atom (26 e^-): $1s^2\ 2s^2\ 2p^6\ 3s^2\ 3p^6\ 3d^6\ 4s^2 \rightarrow$ Fe^{3+} ion (23 e^-): $1s^2\ 2s^2\ 2p^6\ 3s^2\ 3p^6\ 3d^5$

It's OK to write the 3d and 4s sub-shells the other way round if you prefer.

Electronic Structure Decides the **Chemical Properties** of an Element

The number of **outer shell electrons** decides the chemical properties of an element.

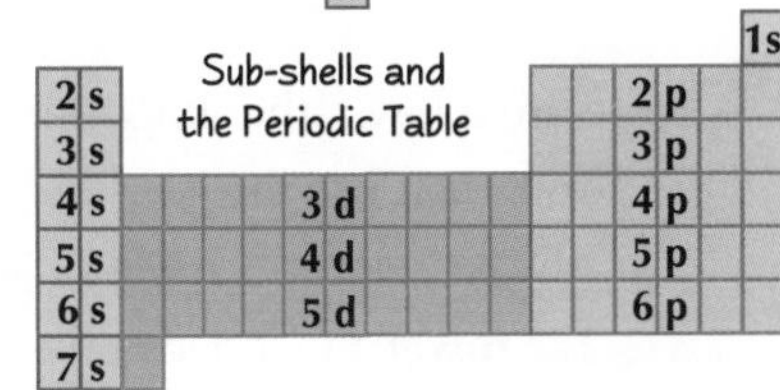

1) The **s block** elements (Groups 1 and 2) have 1 or 2 outer shell electrons. These are easily **lost** to form positive ions with an **inert gas configuration**.
   E.g. Na: $1s^2\ 2s^2\ 2p^6\ 3s^1 \rightarrow Na^+$: $1s^2\ 2s^2\ 2p^6$
   (the electronic configuration of neon).
2) The elements in Groups 5, 6 and 7 (in the p block) can **gain** 1, 2 or 3 electrons to form negative ions with an **inert gas configuration**.
   E.g. O: $1s^2\ 2s^2\ 2p^4 \rightarrow O^{2-}$: $1s^2\ 2s^2\ 2p^6$.
   Groups 4 to 7 can also **share** electrons when they form covalent bonds.
3) Group 0 (the inert gases) have **completely filled** s and p sub-shells and don't need to bother gaining, losing or sharing electrons — their full sub-shells make them **inert**.
4) The **d block elements** (transition metals) tend to **lose** s and d electrons to form positive ions.

Warm-Up Questions

Q1 Write down the sub-shells in order of increasing energy up to 4p.

Q2 How many electrons would each of these types of sub-shell contain when full: a) s, b) p, c) d?

Q3 Chromium and copper don't fill up their shells in the same way as other atoms. Explain the differences.

Q4 Which groups of the Periodic Table tend to gain electrons to form negative ions?

Exam Questions

Q1 Potassium reacts with oxygen to form potassium oxide, K_2O.

a) Give the full electron configurations of the K atom and K^+ ion. [2 marks]

b) Using arrow-in-box notation, give the electron configuration of the oxygen atom. [2 marks]

Q2 This question concerns the electron configurations in atoms and ions.

a) What is the full electron configuration of a manganese atom? [1 mark]

b) Using arrow-in-box notation, give the electron configuration of the Al^{3+} ion. [2 marks]

c) Identify the element with the electron configuration $1s^2\ 2s^2\ 2p^6\ 3s^2\ 3p^6\ 3d^{10}\ 4s^2\ 4p^2$. [1 mark]

d) Suggest the identity of an atom, a positive ion and a negative ion with the configuration $1s^2\ 2s^2\ 2p^6\ 3s^2\ 3p^6$. [3 marks]

She shells sub-shells on the sheshore...

The way electrons fill up the orbitals is like how strangers fill up seats on a bus. Everyone tends to sit in their own seat till they're forced to share. Except for the huge, scary, smelly man who comes and sits next to you. Make sure you learn the order the sub-shells are filled up, so you can write electron configurations for any atom or ion they throw at you.

Ionisation Energy

This page gets a trifle brain-boggling, so I hope you've got a few aspirin handy...

Ionisation is the **Removal** of One or More **Electrons**

When electrons have been removed from an atom or molecule, it's been **ionised**.
The energy you need to remove the first electron is called the **first ionisation energy**.

You might see 'ionisation energy' referred to as 'ionisation enthalpy' instead.

The **first ionisation energy** is the energy needed to remove 1 electron from **each atom** in **1 mole** of **gaseous** atoms to form 1 mole of gaseous 1+ ions.

You have to put energy in to ionise an atom or molecule, so it's an **endothermic process** — there's more about endothermic processes on page 36.

You can write **equations** for this process — here's the equation for the **first ionisation of oxygen**:

$O_{(g)} \rightarrow O^{+}_{(g)} + e^{-}$ **1st ionisation energy = +1314 kJ mol⁻¹**

Here are a few rather important points about ionisation energies:

1) You **must** use the gas state symbol, **(g)**, because ionisation energies are measured for gaseous atoms.
2) Always refer to **1 mole** of atoms, as stated in the definition, rather than to a single atom.
3) The **lower** the ionisation energy, the **easier** it is to form an ion.

The **Factors** Affecting Ionisation Energy are...

Nuclear Charge — The **more protons** there are in the nucleus, the more positively charged the nucleus is and the **stronger the attraction** for the electrons.

Distance from Nucleus — Attraction falls off very **rapidly with distance**. An electron **close** to the nucleus will be **much more** strongly attracted than one further away.

Ways in which bears are like electrons #14 — the more warm apple pies there are cooling on a window sill, the tastier the window sill smells and the stronger the attraction for the bears.

Shielding — As the number of electrons **between** the outer electrons and the nucleus **increases**, the outer electrons feel less attraction towards the nuclear charge. This lessening of the pull of the nucleus by inner shells of electrons is called **shielding (or screening)**.

A **high ionisation energy** means there's a **high attraction** between the **electron** and the **nucleus** and so **more energy** is needed to remove the electron.

Successive Ionisation Energies Involve Removing **Additional** Electrons

1) You can remove **all** the electrons from an atom, leaving only the nucleus. Each time you remove an electron, there's a **successive ionisation energy**.
2) The definition for the **second ionisation energy is** —

The **second ionisation energy** is the energy needed to remove 1 electron from **each ion** in **1 mole** of **gaseous** 1+ ions to form 1 mole of gaseous 2+ ions.

And here's the equation for the **second ionisation of oxygen**:

$O^{+}_{(g)} \rightarrow O^{2+}_{(g)} + e^{-}$ **2nd ionisation energy = +3388 kJ mol⁻¹**

3) You need to be able to write equations for **any** successive ionisation energy. The equation for the ***nth* ionisation energy** is....

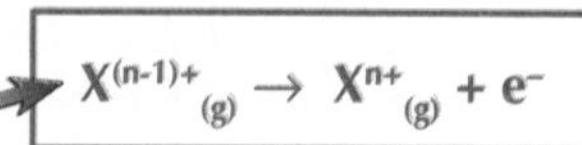

$X^{(n-1)+}_{(g)} \rightarrow X^{n+}_{(g)} + e^{-}$

Ionisation Energy

Successive Ionisation Energies Show **Shell Structure**

A **graph** of successive ionisation energies (like this one for sodium) provides evidence for the **shell structure** of atoms.

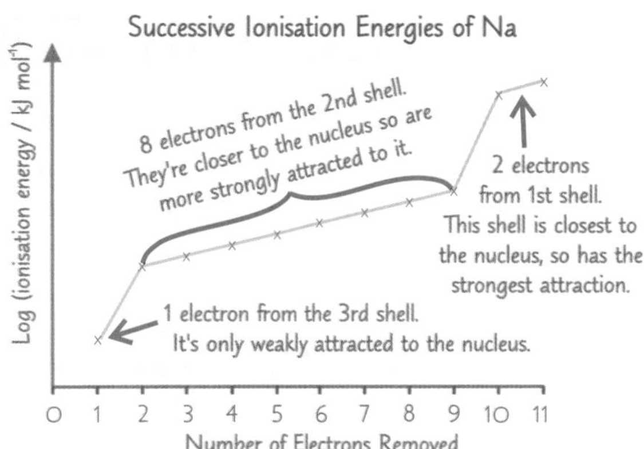
Successive Ionisation Energies of Na
Log (ionisation energy / kJ mol⁻¹)
8 electrons from the 2nd shell. They're closer to the nucleus so are more strongly attracted to it.
2 electrons from 1st shell. This shell is closest to the nucleus, so has the strongest attraction.
1 electron from the 3rd shell. It's only weakly attracted to the nucleus.
0 1 2 3 4 5 6 7 8 9 10 11
Number of Electrons Removed

1) **Within each shell**, successive ionisation energies **increase**. This is because electrons are being removed from an **increasingly positive ion** — there's **less repulsion** amongst the remaining electrons, so they're **held more strongly** by the nucleus.
2) The **big jumps** in ionisation energy happen when a new shell is broken into — an electron is being removed from a shell **closer** to the nucleus.

1) Graphs like this can tell you which **group** of the periodic table an element belongs to. Just count **how many electrons are removed** before the first big jump to find the group number.

   E.g. In the graph for sodium, **one electron** is removed before the first big jump — sodium is in **group 1**.

2) These graphs can be used to predict the **electronic structure** of elements. Working from **right to left**, count how many points there are before each big jump to find how many electrons are in each shell, starting with the first.

   E.g. The graph for sodium has **2 points** on the right-hand side, then a jump, then **8 points**, a jump, and **1 final point**. Sodium has **2 electrons** in the first shell, **8** in the second and **1** in the third.

Warm-Up Questions

PRACTICE QUESTIONS

Q1 Define first ionisation energy and give an equation as an example.

Q2 Describe the three main factors that affect ionisation energies.

Q3 How is ionisation energy related to the force of attraction between an electron and the nucleus of an atom?

Exam Questions

Q1 This table shows the nuclear charge and first ionisation energy for four elements.

Element	B	C	N	0
Charge of Nucleus	+5	+6	+7	+8
1st Ionisation Energy (kJ mol^{-1})	801	1087	1402	1314

a) Write an equation, including state symbols, to represent the first ionisation energy of carbon (C). [2 marks]

b) In these four elements, what is the relationship between nuclear charge and first ionisation energy? [1 mark]

c) Explain why nuclear charge has this effect on first ionisation energy. [2 marks]

Q2 This graph shows the successive ionisation energies of a certain element.

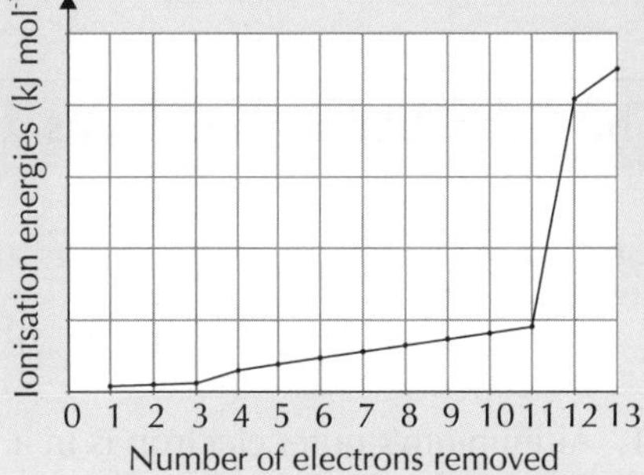
Ionisation energies (kJ mol⁻¹)
0 1 2 3 4 5 6 7 8 9 10 11 12 13
Number of electrons removed

a) To which group of the periodic table does this element belong? [1 mark]

b) Why does it takes more energy to remove each successive electron? [2 marks]

c) What causes the sudden increases in ionisation energy? [1 mark]

d) What is the total number of electron shells in this element? [1 mark]

Shirt crumpled — ionise it...

When you're talking about ionisation energies in exams, always use the three main factors — shielding, nuclear charge and distance from nucleus. Recite the definition of the first ionisation energies to yourself until you can't take any more.

Trends in First Ionisation Energy

Let joy be unconfined — it's another two pages about ionisation energy. This time though it's all about trends in first ionisation energies and what they can tell you about the structure of atoms.

There are **Trends** in **First Ionisation Energies**

1) The first ionisation energies of elements **down a group** of the periodic table **decrease**.
2) The first ionisation energies of elements **across a period generally increase**.
3) You need to know **how** and **why** ionisation energy **changes** as you go down **Group 2** and across **Period 3**. Read on to discover all...

Ionisation Energy **Decreases** Down Group 2

This graph shows the first ionisation energies of the elements in **Group 2**. It provides **evidence** that electron shells **REALLY DO EXIST** and that successive elements down the group have **extra**, **bigger**, **shells**...

1) If each element down Group 2 has an **extra electron shell** compared to the one above, the extra inner shells will **shield** the outer electrons from the attraction of the nucleus.
2) Also, the extra shell means that the outer electrons are **further away** from the nucleus, so the nucleus's attraction will be greatly reduced.

It makes sense that both of these factors will make it **easier** to remove outer electrons, resulting in a **lower ionisation energy**.

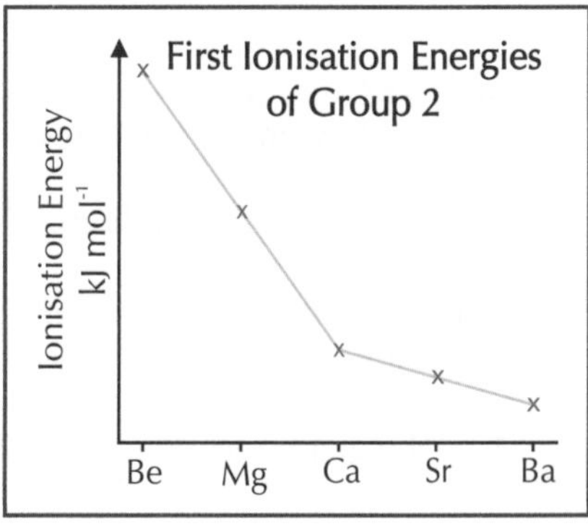

Ionisation Energy **Increases** Across a Period

The graph below shows the first ionisation energies of the elements in **Period 3**.

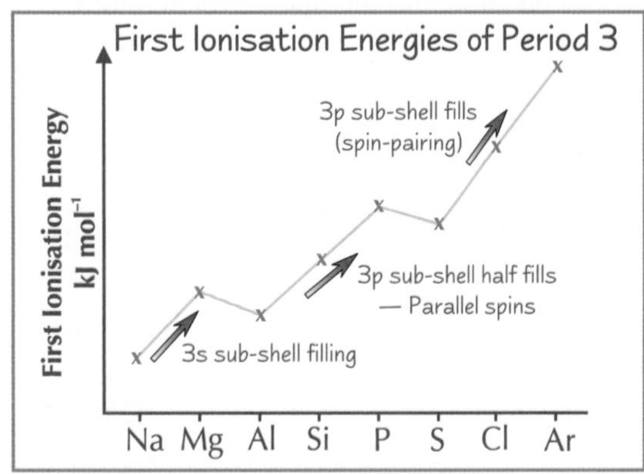

1) As you **move across** a period, the general trend is for the ionisation energies to **increase** — i.e. it gets harder to remove the outer electrons.
2) This can be explained because the number of protons is increasing, which means a stronger **nuclear attraction**.
3) All the extra electrons are at **roughly the same** energy level, even if the outer electrons are in different orbital types.
4) This means there's generally little **extra shielding** effect or **extra distance** to lessen the attraction from the nucleus.
5) But, there are **small drops** between Groups 2 and 3, and 5 and 6. Tell me more, I hear you cry. Well, alright then...

The Drop between Groups 2 and 3 Shows **Sub-Shell Structure**

Example

Mg $1s^2 2s^2 2p^6 3s^2$ 1st ionisation energy = 738 kJ mol^{-1}
Al $1s^2 2s^2 2p^6 3s^2 3p^1$ 1st ionisation energy = 578 kJ mol^{-1}

1) Aluminium's outer electron is in a **3p orbital** rather than a 3s. The 3p orbital has a **slightly higher** energy than the 3s orbital, so the electron is, on average, to be found **further** from the nucleus.
2) The 3p orbital has additional shielding provided by the **$3s^2$ electrons**.
3) Both these factors together are strong enough to **override** the effect of the increased nuclear charge, resulting in the ionisation energy **dropping** slightly.
4) This pattern in ionisation energies provides **evidence** for the theory of electron sub-shells.

Trends in First Ionisation Energy

The Drop between Groups 5 and 6 is due to Electron Repulsion

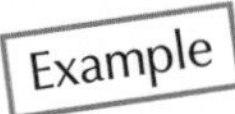

P $1s^2 2s^2 2p^6 3s^2 3p^3$ 1st ionisation energy = 1012 kJ mol^{-1}
S $1s^2 2s^2 2p^6 3s^2 3p^4$ 1st ionisation energy = 1000 kJ mol^{-1}

1) The **shielding is identical** in the phosphorus and sulfur atoms, and the electron is being removed from an identical orbital.
2) In phosphorus's case, the electron is being removed from a **singly-occupied** orbital. But in sulfur, the **electron** is being **removed** from an orbital containing two electrons.

   Phosphorus: [Ne] 3s [↑↓] 3p [↑][↑][↑]   Sulfur: [Ne] 3s [↑↓] 3p [↑↓][↑][↑]

   The **repulsion** between two electrons in an orbital means that electrons are **easier to remove** from shared orbitals.
3) Yup, yet more **evidence** for the electronic structure model.

Ways in which bears are like electrons #23 — the repulsion between two bears in a river means that bears are easier to remove from shared rivers.

Warm-Up Questions

Q1 Describe the trend in ionisation energy as you go down Group 2.

Q2 Why do ionisation energies change down a group?

Q3 Which electron is easier to remove, a lone electron in an orbital or one in a pair?

Exam Questions

Q1 The first ionisation energies of the elements lithium to neon are given below in kJ mol^{-1}:

Li	Be	B	C	N	O	F	Ne
519	900	799	1090	1400	1310	1680	2080

a) Explain why the ionisation energies show an overall tendency to increase across the period. [3 marks]

b) Explain the irregularities in this trend for:

i) boron [2 marks]

ii) oxygen [2 marks]

Q2 First ionisation energy decreases down Group 2.

Explain how this trend provides evidence for the arrangement of electrons in levels. [3 marks]

Q3 a) Which of these elements has the highest first ionisation energy?

A Krypton B Lithium C Potassium D Neon [1 mark]

b) Explain your reasoning for the answer given in part a). [2 marks]

Q4 a) Which of these elements has the largest jump between its first and second ionisation energies?

A Sodium B Magnesium C Argon D Chlorine [1 mark]

b) Explain your reasoning for the answer given in part a). [3 marks]

First ionisation energies are so popular, they're trending...

If all these trends across and up and down the periodic table get confusing, just think back to basics — it's all about how strongly the outer electron is attracted to the nucleus. THAT depends on shielding, nuclear charge and distance from the nucleus and THEY depend on which shell, sub-shell and orbital the electron is in.

The Mole

It'd be handy to be able to count out atoms — but they're way too tiny. You can't even see them, never mind get hold of them with tweezers. Luckily, you can use the idea of moles to figure out how exactly much stuff you've got.

A **Mole** is Just a (Very Large) **Number of Particles**

In formulas, number of moles is often given the symbol n.

1) Amount of substance can be measured using a unit called the **mole** (**mol** for short).
2) One mole contains **6.02×10^{23} particles** — this number is known as **Avogadro's constant.**
3) It **doesn't matter** what the particles are. They can be atoms, molecules, electrons, ions, penguins — **anything**.

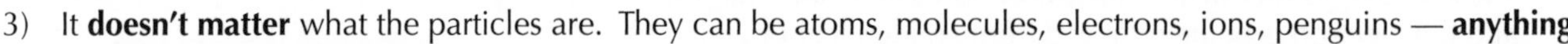

1 mole of **carbon** (C) contains **6.02×10^{23} atoms.** 1 mole of **methane** (CH_4) contains **6.02×10^{23} molecules.**
1 mole of **sodium ions** (Na^+) contains **6.02×10^{23} ions.** 1 mole of **electrons** contains **6.02×10^{23} electrons.**

4) You can use Avogadro's constant to convert between number of particles and number of moles.

   Just remember this formula: **Number of particles = Number of moles × Avogadro's constant**

Example: How many atoms are in 0.450 moles of pure iron?

Number of atoms = $0.450 \times (6.02 \times 10^{23})$ = **2.71×10^{23}**

The Amount of a Substance in **Moles** can be Calculated from **Mass** and **M_r**

1) **1 mole** of any substance has a **mass** that's the same as its **relative molecular mass** (M_r) in **grams**. For example, the M_r of water (H_2O) is $(1 \times 2) + 16 = 18$, so 1 mole of water has a mass of 18 g.
2) This means that you can work out how many **moles** of a substance you have from the **mass** of the substance and its **relative molecular mass** (M_r). Here's the formula you need:

$$\textbf{Number of moles} = \frac{\textbf{mass of substance}}{\mathbf{M_r}}$$

Example: How many moles of aluminium oxide are present in 5.10 g of Al_2O_3?

M_r of Al_2O_3 = $(2 \times 27.0) + (3 \times 16.0) = 102.0$

Number of moles of Al_2O_3 = $\frac{5.10}{102.0}$ = **0.0500 moles**

If you need to find M_r or mass instead, you can re-arrange the formula using this formula triangle:

mass
moles × M_r

The **Concentration** of a Solution is Measured in **mol dm^{-3}**

1) The **concentration** of a solution is how many **moles** are dissolved per **1 dm^3** (that's 1 litre) of solution. The units are **mol dm^{-3}**.
2) Here's the formula to find the **number of moles**:

   Number of moles = Concentration (mol dm^{-3}) × Volume (dm^3)

This one can go in a handy formula triangle too:

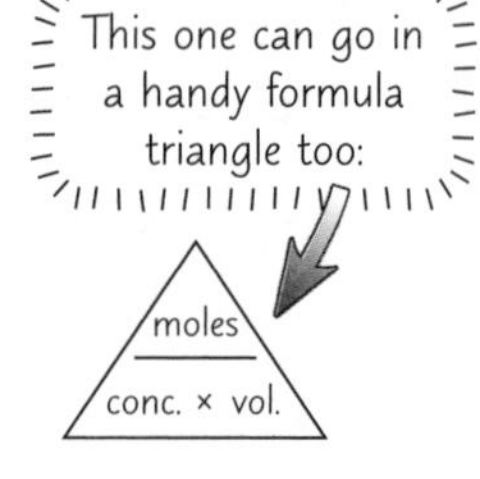

3) Watch out for the units — you might be given the volume in cm^3 rather than dm^3. If that's the case, you'll have to convert it to dm^3 first.

Example: What mass of sodium hydroxide (NaOH) needs to be dissolved in water to give 50.0 cm^3 of a solution with a concentration of 2.00 mol dm^{-3}?

Volume of solution in dm^3 = 50 ÷ 1000 = 0.05 dm^3
Number of moles NaOH = 2.00 mol dm^{-3} × 0.0500 dm^3 = 0.100
M_r of NaOH = 23.0 + 16.0 + 1.0 = 40.0
Mass = number of moles × M_r = 0.100 × 40.0 = **4.00 g**

1 dm^3 = 1000 cm^3
So to convert from cm^3 to dm^3 you need to divide by 1000.

The Mole

Ideal Gas equation — $pV = nRT$

The **ideal gas equation** lets you find the **number of moles** in a certain volume of gas. You just need to know the temperature and pressure that the gas is at.

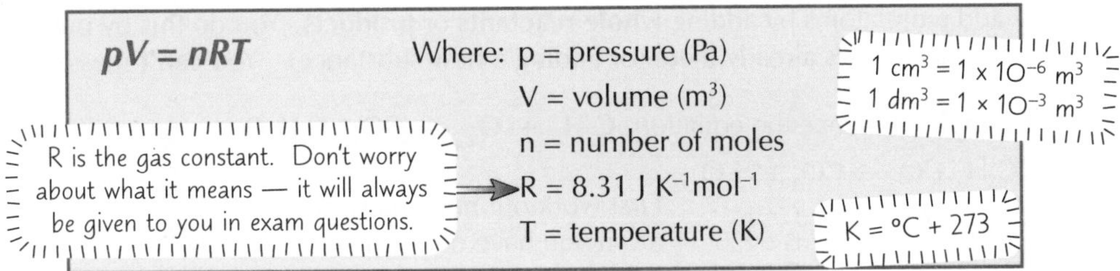

pV = nRT
Where: p = pressure (Pa)
V = volume (m³)
n = number of moles
R = 8.31 J K⁻¹mol⁻¹
T = temperature (K)
1 cm³ = 1 × 10⁻⁶ m³
1 dm³ = 1 × 10⁻³ m³
R is the gas constant. Don't worry about what it means — it will always be given to you in exam questions.
K = °C + 273

Example:

At a temperature of 60.0 °C and a pressure of 250 kPa, a gas occupied a volume of 1100 cm^3 and had a mass of 1.60 g. Find its relative molecular mass. The gas constant is 8.31 J $K^{-1}mol^{-1}$.

Use the ideal gas equation to find the number of moles of gas present.
$p = 250 \times 1000 = 250 \times 10^3$ Pa, $V = 1100 \times (1 \times 10^{-6}) = 1.10 \times 10^{-3}$ m^3,
$R = 8.31$ J $K^{-1}mol^{-1}$, $T = 60.0 + 273 = 333$ K

Start off by putting everything into the right units.

$$n = \frac{pV}{RT} = \left(\frac{(250 \times 10^3) \times (1.10 \times 10^{-3})}{8.31 \times 333}\right) = 0.0994 \text{ moles}$$

M_r of gas = mass ÷ number of moles = 1.60 g ÷ 0.0994 = **16.1** (3 s.f.)

Warm-Up Questions

PRACTICE QUESTIONS

Q1 How many molecules are there in one mole of ethane molecules?*

Q2 How many atoms are in there 0.500 moles of carbon?*

Q3 A student dissolves 0.100 moles of NaCl in 0.500 dm^3 of water. Find the concentration of the solution.*

Q4 Write down the ideal gas equation.

*Answers on page 115.

Exam Questions

Q1 How many moles of calcium sulfate are there in 34.05 g of $CaSO_4$? [1 mark]

Q2 Calculate the mass of 0.360 moles of ethanoic acid (CH_3COOH). [1 mark]

Q3 How many moles of nitric acid are there in 50.0 cm^3 of 0.250 mol dm^{-3} of HNO_3? [1 mark]

Q4 What mass of H_2SO_4 is needed to produce 60.0 cm^3 of 0.250 mol dm^{-3} solution? [2 marks]

Q5 Calculate the concentration, in mol dm^{-3}, of 3.65 g of HCl dissolved in 100 cm^3 of water. [2 marks]

Q6 What volume, in m^3, will be occupied by 88.0 g of propane gas (C_3H_8) at 25.0 °C and 100 kPa? Give your answer to 3 significant figures. The gas constant is R = 8.31 J K^{-1} mol^{-1}. [3 marks]

Q7 At 301 K, a 35.2 g sample of CO_2 has a volume of 20.0 dm^3. What pressure is the gas at (to 3 significant figures)?

A 10 000 kPa B 100 kPa C 200 kPa D 10.0 kPa [1 mark]

Molasses — 6.02×10^{23} donkeys...

You need this stuff for loads of the calculation questions you might get, so learn it inside out. Before you start plugging numbers into formulas, make sure they're in the right units. If they're not, you need to know how to convert them or you'll be tossing marks out the window. Learn all the definitions and formulas, then have a bash at the questions.

Equations and Calculations

Balancing equations might cause you a few palpitations — as soon as you make one bit right, the rest goes pear-shaped.

Balanced Equations have **Equal Numbers** of each Atom on **Both Sides**

1) Balanced equations have the **same number** of each atom on **both** sides. They're... well... you know... balanced.
2) You can only add more atoms by adding **whole reactants** or **products**. You do this by putting a number **in front** of a substance that's already there (or adding a new substance). You **can't** mess with formulas — ever.

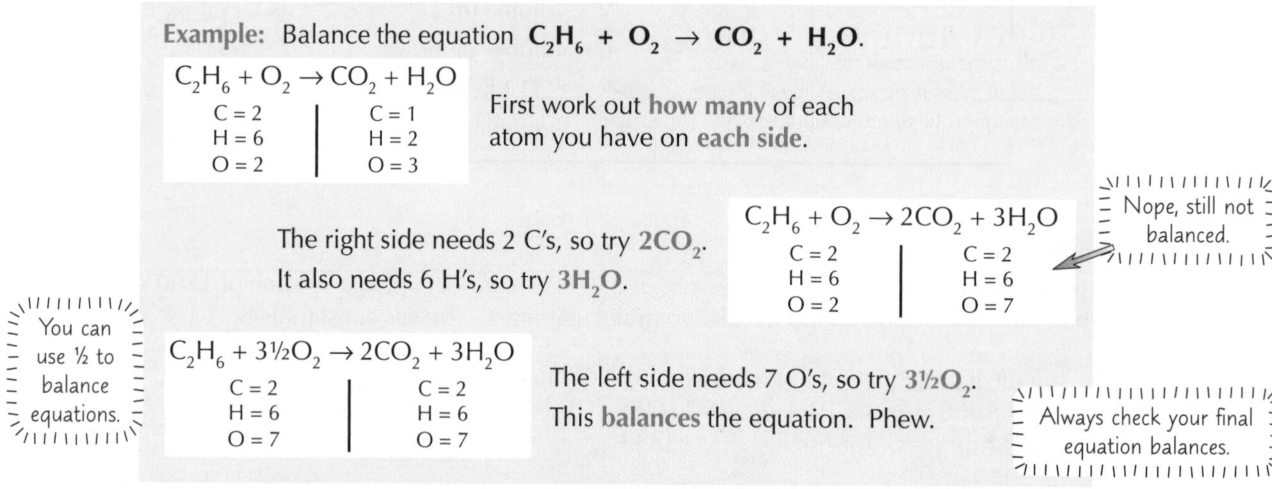

Example: Balance the equation $C_2H_6 + O_2 \rightarrow CO_2 + H_2O$.

$C_2H_6 + O_2 \rightarrow CO_2 + H_2O$

Left	Right
C = 2	C = 1
H = 6	H = 2
O = 2	O = 3

First work out **how many** of each atom you have on **each side**.

The right side needs 2 C's, so try $2CO_2$. It also needs 6 H's, so try $3H_2O$.

$C_2H_6 + O_2 \rightarrow 2CO_2 + 3H_2O$

Left	Right
C = 2	C = 2
H = 6	H = 6
O = 2	O = 7

Nope, still not balanced.

You can use ½ to balance equations.

$C_2H_6 + 3½O_2 \rightarrow 2CO_2 + 3H_2O$

Left	Right
C = 2	C = 2
H = 6	H = 6
O = 7	O = 7

The left side needs 7 O's, so try $3½O_2$. This **balances** the equation. Phew.

Always check your final equation balances.

Ionic Equations Only Show the **Reacting Particles**

1) You can also write an **ionic equation** for any reaction involving **ions** that happens **in solution**.
2) In an ionic equation, only the **reacting particles** (and the **products** they form) are included.

Example: Here is the **full balanced equation** for the reaction of **nitric acid** with **sodium hydroxide**:

$$HNO_3 + NaOH \rightarrow NaNO_3 + H_2O$$

The **ionic** substances in this equation will **dissolve**, breaking up into ions in solution. You can rewrite the equation to show all the **ions** that are in the reaction mixture:

$$H^+ + NO_3^- + Na^+ + OH^- \rightarrow Na^+ + NO_3^- + H_2O$$

Leave anything that isn't an ion in solution (like the H_2O) as it is.

To get from this to the ionic equation, just cross out any ions that appear on **both sides** of the equation — in this case, that's the sodium ions (Na^+) and the nitrate ions (NO_3^-).

An ion that's present in the reaction mixture, but doesn't get involved in the reaction is called a spectator ion.

So the **ionic equation** for this reaction is:

$$H^+ + OH^- \rightarrow H_2O$$

3) When you've written an ionic equation, check that the **charges** are **balanced**, as well as the atoms — if the charges don't balance, the equation isn't right.

In the example above, the **net charge** on the left hand side is +1 + −1 = **0** and the net charge on the right hand side is **0** — so the charges balance.

State Symbols Give a bit More Information about the Substances

State symbols are put after each reactant or product in an equation. They tell you what **state of matter** things are in.

s = solid
l = liquid
g = gas
aq = aqueous (solution in water)

To show you what I mean, here's an example —

$$CaCO_{3\,(s)} + 2HCl_{(aq)} \rightarrow CaCl_{2\,(aq)} + H_2O_{(l)} + CO_{2\,(g)}$$

solid — aqueous — aqueous — liquid — gas

Equations and Calculations

Balanced Equations can be used to Work out Masses

This is handy for working out how much **reactant** you need to make a certain **mass of product** (or **vice versa**).

Example: Calculate the mass of iron oxide produced if 27.9 g of iron is burnt in air.

$$4Fe + 3O_2 \rightarrow 2Fe_2O_3$$

M_r of Fe = 55.8, so the number of moles in 27.9 g of Fe = $\frac{\text{mass}}{M_r} = \frac{27.9}{55.8}$ = 0.500 moles

From the equation: 4 moles of Fe gives 2 moles of Fe_2O_3, so 0.500 moles of Fe would give 0.250 moles of Fe_2O_3.

M_r of Fe_2O_3 = (2 × 55.8) + (3 × 16.0) = 159.6

Mass of Fe_2O_3 produced = moles × M_r = 0.250 × 159.6 = **39.9 g**.

Once you know the number of moles and the M_r of Fe_2O_3, it's easy to work out the mass.

That's not all... Balanced Equations can be used to Work Out Gas Volumes

It's pretty handy to be able to use the ideal gas equation to work out **how much gas** a reaction will produce, so that you can use **large enough apparatus**. Or else there might be a rather large bang.

Example: What volume of gas, in dm^3, is produced when 15.0 g of sodium reacts with excess water at a temperature of 25.0 °C and a pressure of 100 kPa? The gas constant is 8.31 J K^{-1} mol^{-1}.

$$2Na_{(s)} + 2H_2O_{(l)} \rightarrow 2NaOH_{(aq)} + H_{2\,(g)}$$

'Excess water' just means that you know all of the sodium will react.

M_r of Na = 23.0, so number of moles in 15.0 g of Na = $\frac{15.0}{23.0}$ = 0.652 moles

From the equation, 2 moles of Na produces 1 mole of H_2,
so 0.652 moles of Na must produce $\frac{0.652}{2}$ = 0.326 moles of H_2.

Volume of H_2 = $\frac{nRT}{p} = \frac{0.326 \times 8.31 \times 298}{100 \times 10^3}$ = 0.00807 m^3 = **8.07 dm^3** (3 s.f.)

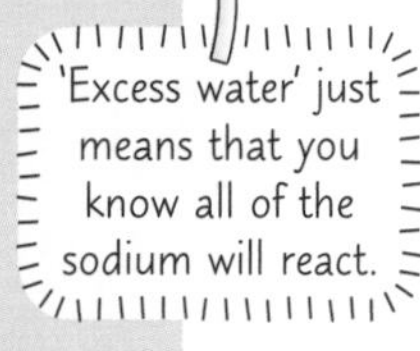

Warm-Up Questions

Q1 What is the difference between a full equation and an ionic equation?

Q2 Chlorine (Cl_2) reacts with potassium bromide (KBr) in solution to give potassium chloride (KCl) and bromine (Br_2).
a) Write a full balanced equation for this reaction.* b) Write an ionic equation for this reaction.*

Q3 What is the state symbol for a solution of sodium chloride dissolved in water?

*Answers on page 116.

Exam Questions

Q1 Calculate the mass of ethene required to produce 258 g of chloroethane, C_2H_5Cl.

$$C_2H_4 + HCl \rightarrow C_2H_5Cl$$ [3 marks]

Q2 15.0 g of calcium carbonate is heated strongly so that it fully decomposes. $CaCO_{3\,(s)} \rightarrow CaO_{(s)} + CO_{2\,(g)}$

a) Calculate the mass of calcium oxide produced. [3 marks]

b) Calculate the volume of gas produced in m^3 at 25.0 °C and 100 kPa. The gas constant is 8.31 J K^{-1} mol^{-1}. [3 marks]

Q3 Balance this equation: $KI + Pb(NO_3)_2 \rightarrow PbI_2 + KNO_3$ [1 mark]

Don't get in a state about equations...

Balancing equations is a really, really important skill in Chemistry, so make sure you can do it. You will ONLY be able to calculate reacting masses and gas volumes if you've got a balanced equation to work from. I've said it once, and I'll say it again — practise, practise, practise... it's the only road to salvation. (By the way, exactly where is salvation anyway?)

Titrations

Titrations are used to find out the concentration of acid or alkali solutions. You'll probably get to do a titration or two (lucky you) and you'll definitely need to know all the ins and outs of how to do them for your exams. So read on...

A **Standard Solution** Has a **Known** Concentration

Standard solutions can also be called volumetric solutions.

Before you do a titration, you might have to make up a **standard solution** to use.
A **standard solution** is any solution that you **know** the **exact concentration** of. Making a standard solution involves dissolving a **known amount** of **solid** in a known amount of **water** to create a known concentration.

Example: Make 250 cm^3 of a 2.00 mol dm^{-3} solution of sodium hydroxide.

1) First work out how many **moles** of sodium hydroxide you need using the formula: **moles = concentration × volume**
$= 2.00 \text{ mol dm}^{-3} \times 0.250 \text{ dm}^3 = 0.500 \text{ moles}$

Remember, the volume needs to be in dm^3 for this bit.

2) Now work out how many **grams** of sodium hydroxide you need using the formula: **mass = moles × M_r**
$= 0.500 \times 40.0 = 20.0 \text{ g}$

M_r of NaOH: $23.0 + 16.0 + 1.0 = 40.0$

3) Place a weighing boat on a **digital balance** and weigh out this mass of solid. Tip it into a beaker. Now **re-weigh** the boat (which may still contain traces of the solid). Subtract the mass of the boat from the mass of the boat and solid together to find the **precise mass** of solid used.

4) Add **distilled water** to the beaker and **stir** until all the sodium hydroxide has **dissolved**.

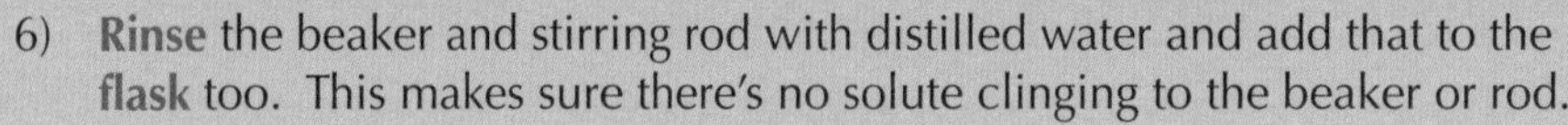

5) Tip the solution into a **volumetric flask** — make sure it's the right size for the volume that you're making (250 cm^3 in this case). Use a **funnel** to make sure it all goes in.

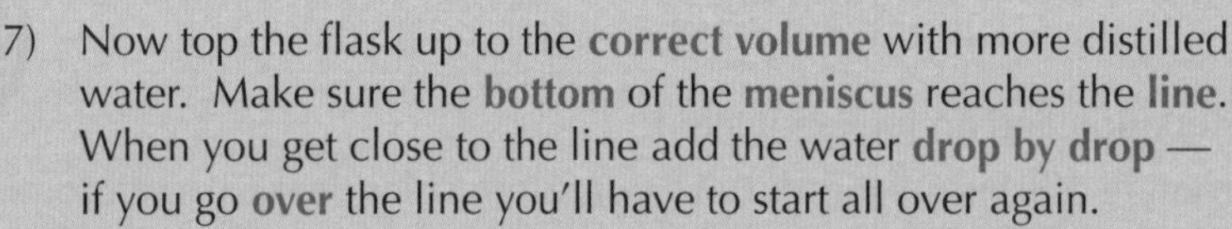

6) **Rinse** the beaker and stirring rod with distilled water and add that to the **flask** too. This makes sure there's no solute clinging to the beaker or rod.

7) Now top the flask up to the **correct volume** with more distilled water. Make sure the **bottom** of the **meniscus** reaches the **line**. When you get close to the line add the water **drop by drop** — if you go **over** the line you'll have to start all over again.

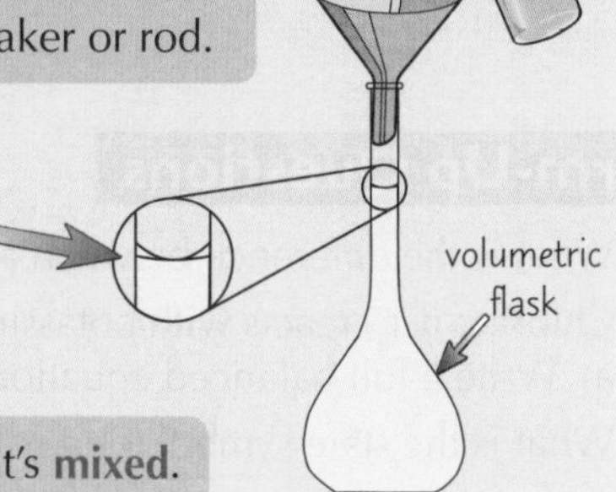

8) **Stopper** the flask and turn it upside down a few times to make sure it's **mixed**.

Titrations let you work out the **Concentration** of an **Acid** or **Alkali**

1) A **titration** allows you to find out **exactly** how much acid is needed to **neutralise** a measured quantity of alkali (or the other way round).
2) You can use this data to work out the **concentration** of the alkali.
3) Start off by using a **pipette** to measure out a set volume of the solution that you want to know the concentration of. Put it in a flask.
4) Add a few drops of an appropriate **indicator** (see next page) to the flask.
5) Then fill a **burette** (see next page) with a **standard solution** of the acid — remember, that means you know its exact concentration.
6) Use a **funnel** to carefully pour the acid into the burette. Always do this **below eye level** to avoid any acid splashing on to your face or eyes. (You should wear **safety glasses** too.)
7) Now you're ready to **titrate**...

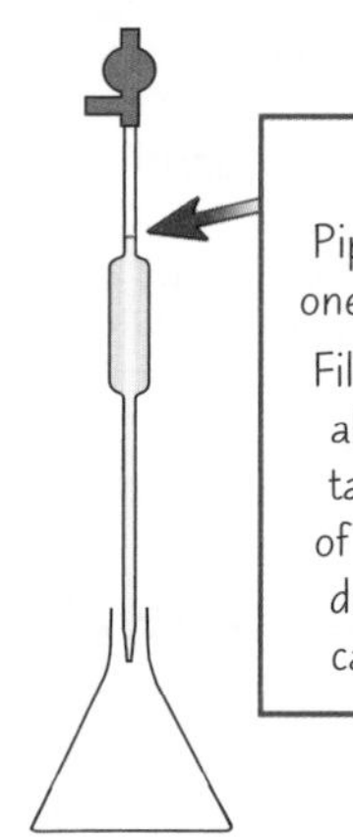

Pipette
Pipettes measure only one volume of solution.
Fill the pipette to just above the line, then take the pipette out of the solution. Then drop the level down carefully to the line.

Titrations

Titrations need to be done **Really Accurately**

PRACTICAL SKILLS

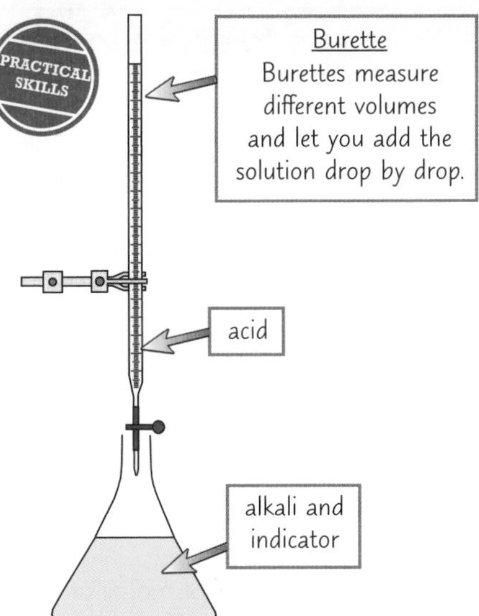

Burette
Burettes measure different volumes and let you add the solution drop by drop.
acid
alkali and indicator

1) First do a **rough titration** to get an idea where the **end point** (the exact point where the alkali is **neutralised** and the indicator changes colour) is. Add the **acid** to the alkali using a **burette**, giving the flask a regular **swirl**.
2) Now do an **accurate** titration. Take an initial reading to see exactly how much acid is in the burette. Then run the acid in to within 2 cm^3 of the end point. When you get to this stage, add it **dropwise** — if you don't notice exactly when the colour changes you'll **overshoot** and your result won't be accurate.
3) Work out the **amount** of acid used to **neutralise** the alkali. This is just the final reading minus the initial reading. This volume is known as the **titre**.
4) **Repeat** the titration a few times, until you have at least three results that are **concordant** (very similar).
5) Use the results from each repeat to calculate the **mean** volume of acid used. Remember to leave out any **anomalous results** when calculating your mean — they can distort your answer.

There's more stuff about how to record and handle the data you get from experiments like this in the Practical Skills section. Have a look if you want to know more about means, anomalous results, precision and experimental error.

Choppy seas made it difficult for Captain Cod to read the burette accurately.

Indicators Show you when the Reaction's **Just Finished**

PRACTICAL SKILLS

In titrations, indicators that change colour quickly over a **very small pH range** are used so you know **exactly** when the reaction has ended.

The main two indicators for **acid/alkali reactions** are:

1) **methyl orange** — this is **red** in acid and **yellow** in alkali.
2) **phenolphthalein** — this is **colourless** in acid and **pink** in alkali.

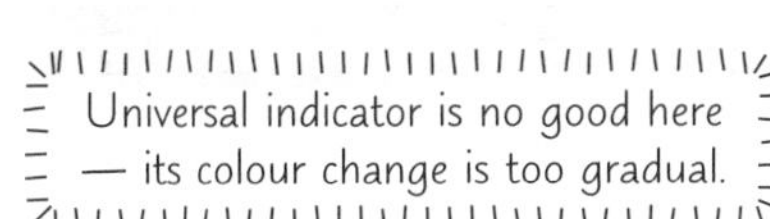

Universal indicator is no good here — its colour change is too gradual.

It's a good idea to stand your flask on a white tile — it'll make it easier to see exactly when the end point is.

You can Calculate **Concentrations** from Titrations

The next step is to use the **mean volume** from your titrations to find the **concentration** of the solution in the flask.

Example: In a titration experiment, 25.0 cm^3 of 0.500 mol dm^{-3} HCl neutralised 35.0 cm^3 of NaOH solution. Calculate the concentration of the sodium hydroxide solution in mol dm^{-3}.

First write a **balanced equation** and decide **what you know** and what you **need to know**:

HCl +	$NaOH \rightarrow NaCl + H_2O$
25.0 cm^3	**35.0 cm^3**
0.500 mol dm^{-3}	**?**

Now work out how many **moles of HCl** you have:

$$\text{Number of moles HCl} = \text{concentration} \times \text{volume } (dm^3) = 0.500 \times \frac{25.0}{1000} = 0.0125 \text{ moles}$$

This is the formula from page 14.

From the equation, you know 1 mole of HCl neutralises 1 mole of NaOH.
So 0.0125 moles of HCl must neutralise **0.0125** moles of NaOH.

Now it's a doddle to work out the **concentration of NaOH**:

$$\text{Concentration of NaOH} = \text{moles} \div \text{volume } (dm^3) = 0.0125 \div \frac{35.0}{1000} = \mathbf{0.357 \text{ mol } dm^{-3}}$$

Titrations

You use a Pretty Similar Method to Calculate Volumes for Reactions

Example: 20.4 cm^3 of a 0.500 mol dm^{-3} solution of sodium carbonate reacts with 1.50 mol dm^{-3} nitric acid. Calculate the volume of nitric acid required to neutralise the sodium carbonate.

Like before, first write a balanced equation for the reaction and decide what you know and what you want to know:

Na_2CO_3	$+ 2HNO_3$	$\rightarrow 2NaNO_3 + H_2O + CO_2$
20.4 cm^3	?	
0.500 mol dm^{-3}	1.50 mol dm^{-3}	

Now work out how many moles of Na_2CO_3 you've got:

$$\text{Number of moles of } Na_2CO_3 = \text{concentration} \times \text{volume } (dm^3) = 0.500 \times \frac{20.4}{1000} = 0.0102 \text{ moles.}$$

1 mole of Na_2CO_3 neutralises 2 moles of HNO_3,
so 0.0102 moles of Na_2CO_3 neutralises 0.0204 moles of HNO_3.

Now you know the number of moles of HNO_3 and the concentration, you can work out the volume:

$$\text{Volume of } HNO_3 = \frac{\text{number of moles}}{\text{concentration}} = \frac{0.0204}{1.50} = 0.0136 \text{ dm}^3$$

That's 0.0136 × 1000 = 13.6 cm^3.

Warm-Up Questions

Q1 What is a standard solution? Describe how to make one.

Q2 When you're doing a titration, why do you add the acid dropwise when you're getting near the end point?

Q3 Write down the formula for calculating number of moles from the concentration and volume of a solution. Rearrange it so that you could use it to calculate concentration. Then do the same for volume.

Exam Questions

PRACTICE QUESTIONS

Q1 Calculate the concentration in mol dm^{-3} of a solution of ethanoic acid (CH_3COOH) if 25.4 cm^3 of it is neutralised by 14.6 cm^3 of 0.500 mol dm^{-3} sodium hydroxide solution.
The equation for this reaction is: $CH_3COOH + NaOH \rightarrow CH_3COONa + H_2O$. [3 marks]

Q2 You are supplied with 0.750 g of calcium carbonate and a solution of 0.250 mol dm^{-3} sulfuric acid.
What volume of acid will be needed to neutralise the calcium carbonate?
The equation for this reaction is: $CaCO_3 + H_2SO_4 \rightarrow CaSO_4 + H_2O + CO_2$. [4 marks]

Q3 50.0 cm^3 of nitric acid was titrated with 0.400 mol dm^{-3} sodium hydroxide solution.
The equation for this reaction is: $HNO_3 + NaOH \rightarrow NaNO_3 + H_2O$.
The results of the titration are shown in the table on the right.

a) Identify any anomalous results, explaining your reasoning. [1 mark]

b) Calculate the mean titre, ignoring anomalous results. [1 mark]

c) Calculate the concentration of the nitric acid. [3 marks]

Titration	Volume NaOH (cm^3)
1	45.00
2	45.10
3	42.90
4	44.90

Burettes and pipettes — big glass things, just waiting to be dropped...

Titrations are fiddly. But you do get to use big, impressive-looking equipment and feel like you're doing something important. Then there are the results to do calculations with. The best way to start is always to write out the balanced equation and put what you know about each substance underneath it. Then think about what you're trying to find out.

Formulas, Yield and Atom Economy

Here's another topic that's piled high with numbers — it's all just glorified maths really.

Empirical and Molecular Formulas are Ratios

You have to know what's what with empirical and molecular formulas, so here goes...

1) The **empirical formula** gives just the simplest whole number ratio of atoms of each element in a compound.
2) The **molecular formula** gives the **actual** numbers of atoms of each element in a compound.
3) The **molecular formula** is made up of a whole **number** of empirical units.

Example: A molecule with $M_r = 166.0$ has the empirical formula $C_4H_3O_2$. Find its molecular formula.

First find the **empirical mass** (that's just the total mass of all the atoms in the empirical formula):

$$(4 \times 12.0) + (3 \times 1.0) + (2 \times 16.0) = 48.0 + 3.0 + 32.0 = 83.0$$

Now compare the empirical mass with the **molecular mass**: $M_r = 166$, so there are $\frac{166.0}{83.0} = 2$ empirical units in the molecule.

The molecular formula must be the **empirical formula × 2**, so the molecular formula is $C_8H_6O_4$.

Empirical Formulas can be Calculated from Percentage Composition

You can work out the empirical formula of a compound from the **percentages** of the different elements it contains.

Example: A compound is found to have percentage composition 56.5% potassium, 8.70% carbon and 34.8% oxygen by mass. Find its empirical formula.

In **100 g** of the compound there would be:

Use $n = \frac{\text{mass}}{M_r}$

$\frac{56.5}{39.1} = 1.445$ moles of K $\frac{8.70}{12.0} = 0.725$ moles of C $\frac{34.8}{16.0} = 2.175$ moles of O

Divide each number of moles by the **smallest** of these **numbers** — in this case it's 0.725.

K: $\frac{1.445}{0.725} = 2.00$ C: $\frac{0.725}{0.725} = 1.00$ O: $\frac{2.175}{0.725} = 3.01$

The ratio of K : C : O is 2 : 1 : 3. So the empirical formula's got to be K_2CO_3.

Empirical Formulas can be Calculated from Experiments

You need to be able to work out empirical formulas using **masses** from **experimental results** too.

Example: When a hydrocarbon is burnt in excess oxygen, 4.40 g of carbon dioxide and 1.80 g of water are made. What is the empirical formula of the hydrocarbon?

First work out how many moles of the products you have.

No. of moles of $CO_2 = \frac{\text{mass}}{M_r} = \frac{4.40}{12.0 + (16.0 \times 2)} = \frac{4.40}{44.0} = 0.100$ moles

1 mole of CO_2 contains 1 mole of carbon atoms, so the original hydrocarbon must have contained **0.100 moles** of **carbon atoms.**

No. of moles of $H_2O = \frac{\text{mass}}{M_r} = \frac{1.80}{(2 \times 1.0) + 16.0} = \frac{1.80}{18.0} = 0.100$ moles

1 mole of H_2O contains 2 moles of hydrogen atoms, so the original hydrocarbon must have contained **0.200 moles** of **hydrogen atoms.**

This works because the only place the carbon in the carbon dioxide and the hydrogen in the water could have come from is the hydrocarbon.

Ratio C : H = 0.100 : 0.200. Now divide both numbers by the smallest — here it's 0.100.

Ratio **C : H = 1 : 2**. So the empirical formula must be CH_2.

Formulas, Yield and Atom Economy

Percentage Yield Is Never 100%

1) The **theoretical yield** is the **mass of product** that **should** be formed in a chemical reaction. It assumes **no** chemicals are '**lost**' in the process. You can use the **masses of reactants** and a **balanced equation** to calculate the theoretical yield for a reaction.

Example: 1.40 g of iron filings reacts with ammonia and sulfuric acid to make hydrated ammonium iron(II) sulfate.

$$Fe_{(s)} + 2NH_{3\,(aq)} + 2H_2SO_{4\,(aq)} + 6H_2O_{(l)} \rightarrow (NH_4)_2Fe(SO_4)_2.6H_2O_{(s)} + H_{2\,(g)}$$

Calculate the theoretical yield of the reaction.

You started with 1.40 g of iron filings and iron has a relative atomic mass of 55.8, so:

Number of moles of iron (A_r = 55.8) reacted = $\frac{\text{mass}}{M_r} = \frac{1.40}{55.8} = 0.0251$

From the equation, **moles of iron : moles of hydrated ammonium iron(II) sulfate** is **1 : 1**, so 0.0251 moles of hydrated ammonium iron(II) sulfate should form.

M_r of $(NH_4)_2Fe(SO_4)_2.6H_2O_{(s)}$ = 392.0
Theoretical yield = moles × M_r = 0.0251 × 392.0 = **9.84 g**

2) For any reaction, the **actual** mass of product (the **actual yield**) will always be **less** than the theoretical yield. There are many reasons for this. For example, sometimes not all the 'starting' chemicals react fully. And some chemicals are always 'lost', e.g. some solution gets left on filter paper, or is lost during transfers between containers.
3) Once you know the **theoretical yield** and the **actual yield**, you can use them to work out the **percentage yield**.

$$\text{Percentage Yield} = \frac{\text{Actual Yield}}{\text{Theoretical Yield}} \times 100$$

4) So, in the ammonium iron(II) sulfate example above, the theoretical yield was 9.84 g. Say you weighed the hydrated ammonium iron(II) sulfate crystals that you had produced and found the actual yield was **5.22 g**. Now you can just pop these numbers into the formula to find the percentage yield:

Percentage yield = (5.22 ÷ 9.84) × 100 = **53.0%**

Here's another example of calculating the percentage yield:

Example: 0.475 g of CH_3Br reacts with excess NaOH in the following reaction:

$$CH_3Br + NaOH \rightarrow CH_3OH + NaBr$$

0.153 g of CH_3OH is produced. What is the percentage yield?

Find the number of moles of $\mathbf{CH_3Br}$ that you started off with:

Number of moles of CH_3Br = $\frac{\text{mass}}{M_r} = \frac{0.475}{(12.0 + (3 \times 1.0) + 79.9)} = \frac{0.475}{94.9} = 0.00501$ mol

From the equation, **moles of $\mathbf{CH_3Br}$: $\mathbf{CH_3OH}$** is **1 : 1**, so 0.00501 moles of CH_3OH should form.

M_r of CH_3OH = 32.0
Theoretical yield = 0.00501 × 32.0 = **0.160 g.**

Now put these numbers into the percentage yield formula:

Percentage yield = $\frac{\text{Actual Yield}}{\text{Theoretical Yield}} \times 100 = \frac{0.153\text{ g}}{0.160\text{ g}} \times 100 =$ **95.6%**

Formulas, Yield and Atom Economy

Atom Economy is a Measure of the Efficiency of a Reaction

1) **Percentage yield** tells you how wasteful a **process** is — it's based on how much of the product is **lost** during the process (see previous page).
2) But percentage yield doesn't measure how wasteful the **reaction** itself is. A reaction with a 100% yield could still be wasteful if a lot of the atoms from the **reactants** wind up in **by-products** rather than the **desired product**.
3) **Atom economy** is a measure of the proportion of reactant **atoms** that become part of the desired product (rather than by-products) in the **balanced** chemical equation. It's calculated using this formula:

$$\%\text{ atom economy} = \frac{\text{molecular mass of desired product}}{\text{sum of molecular masses of all reactants}} \times 100$$

Example: Ethanol (C_2H_5OH) can be produced by fermenting glucose ($C_6H_{12}O_6$):

$$C_6H_{12}O_6 \rightarrow 2C_2H_5OH + 2CO_2$$

Calculate the atom economy for this reaction.

Always make sure you're using a balanced equation.

$$\%\text{ atom economy} = \frac{\text{molecular mass of desired product}}{\text{sum of molecular masses of all reactants}} \times 100$$

Remember to use the number of moles from the balanced equation.

$$= \frac{2 \times ((2 \times 12.0) + (5 \times 1.0) + (16 + 1.0))}{(6 \times 12.0) + (12 \times 1.0) + (6 \times 16.0)} \times 100 = \frac{92.0}{180.0} \times 100 = 51.1\%$$

4) Wherever possible, companies in the chemical industry try to use processes with **high atom economies**.
5) Processes with high atom economies are better for the **environment** because they produce less **waste**. Any waste that's made needs to be **disposed of safely** so the less that's made, the better.
6) They make more efficient use of **raw materials**, so they're more **sustainable** (they use up natural resources more slowly).
7) They're also **less expensive**. A company using a process with a high atom economy will spend less on separating the desired product from the waste products and also less on treating waste.

Warm-Up Questions

PRACTICE QUESTIONS

Q1 Define 'empirical formula'.

Q2 What is the difference between a molecular formula and an empirical formula?

Q3 Write down the formula for calculating percentage yield.

Q4 Write down the formula for calculating atom economy.

Q5 Explain why it is important for chemical companies to develop processes that have high atom economies

Exam Questions

Q1 Hydrocarbon X has a relative molecular mass of 78.0. It is found to have 92.3% carbon and 7.70% hydrogen by mass. Find the empirical and molecular formulae of X. [4 marks]

Q2 Phosphorus trichloride (PCl_3) can react with chlorine to give phosphorus pentachloride (PCl_5). This is the equation for this reaction: $PCl_3 + Cl_2 \rightarrow PCl_5$

a) If 0.275 g of PCl_3 ($M_r = 137.5$) reacts with chlorine, what is the theoretical yield of PCl_5? [3 marks]

b) When this reaction is performed 0.198 g of PCl_5 is collected. Calculate the percentage yield. [1 mark]

c) State the atom economy of this reaction. Explain your answer. [2 marks]

The Empirical Strikes Back...

This is the kind of topic where it isn't enough to just learn the facts — you have to know how to do the calculations too. That takes practice — so make sure you understand all the examples on these pages, then test yourself on the questions.

Ionic Bonding

Every atom's aim in life is to have a full outer shell of electrons. Once they've managed this, they're happy.

Compounds are **Atoms** of Different Elements **Bonded** Together

1) When different elements join or bond together, you get a **compound**.
2) There are two main types of bonding in compounds — **ionic** and **covalent**. You need to make sure you've got them **both** totally sussed.

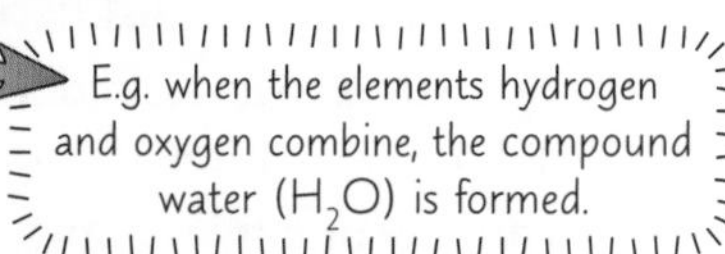

E.g. when the elements hydrogen and oxygen combine, the compound water (H_2O) is formed.

Ionic Bonding is when **Ions** are Held Together by **Electrostatic Attraction**

1) Ions are formed when one or more electrons are **transferred** from one atom to another.
2) The simplest ions are single atoms which have either lost or gained electrons so that they've got a **full outer shell**. Here are some examples of ions:

A sodium atom (Na) **loses** 1 electron to form a sodium ion (Na^+)	$Na \rightarrow Na^+ + e^-$
A magnesium atom (Mg) **loses** 2 electrons to form a magnesium ion (Mg^{2+})	$Mg \rightarrow Mg^{2+} + 2e^-$
A chlorine atom (Cl) **gains** 1 electron to form a chloride ion (Cl^-)	$Cl + e^- \rightarrow Cl^-$
An oxygen atom (O) **gains** 2 electrons to form an oxide ion (O^{2-})	$O + 2e^- \rightarrow O^{2-}$

3) You **don't** have to remember what ion **each element** forms — for many of them you just look at the Periodic Table. Elements in the same **group** all have the same number of **outer electrons**. So they have to **lose or gain** the same number to get the full outer shell that they're aiming for. And this means that they form ions with the **same charges**.
4) **Electrostatic attraction** holds positive and negative ions together — it's **very** strong. When atoms are held together like this, it's called **ionic bonding**.

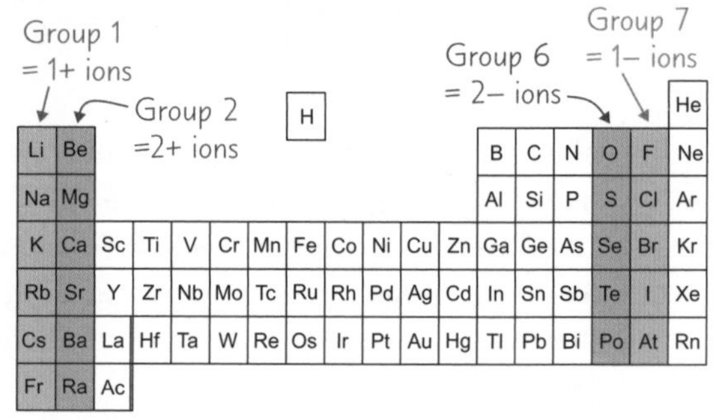

Not all **Ions** are Made From **Single Atoms**

There are lots of ions that are made up of **groups** of atoms with an **overall charge**. These are called **compound ions**. You need to remember the formulas of these ones:

Sulfate	**Hydroxide**	**Nitrate**	**Carbonate**	**Ammonium**
SO_4^{2-}	OH^-	NO_3^-	CO_3^{2-}	NH_4^+

Look at **Charges** to Work Out the **Formula** of an **Ionic Compound**

1) Ionic compounds are made up of a **positively charged** part and a **negatively charged** part.
2) The overall charge of any compound is **zero**. So all the negative charges in the compound must **balance** all the positive charges.
3) You can use the charges on the individual ions present to work out the **formula** of an ionic compound:

Sodium nitrate contains **Na^+ (1+)** and **NO_3^- (1–)** ions. The charges are balanced with one of each ion, so the formula of sodium nitrate is **$NaNO_3$**.

Magnesium chloride contains **Mg^{2+} (2+)** and **Cl^- (1–)** ions.
Because a chloride ion only has a **1–** charge we will need **two** of them to balance out the **2+** charge of a magnesium ion. This gives the formula **$MgCl_2$**.

Ionic Bonding

Sodium Chloride has a **Giant Ionic Lattice** Structure

1) Ionic crystals are giant lattices of ions. A **lattice** is just a **regular structure**.
2) The structure's called '**giant**' because it's made up of the same basic unit repeated over and over again.
3) In **sodium chloride**, the Na^+ and Cl^- ions are packed together. The sodium chloride lattice is **cube** shaped — different ionic compounds have different shaped structures, but they're all still giant lattices.

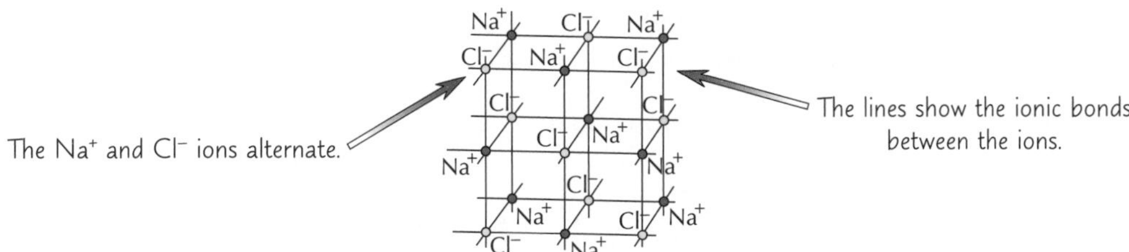
The Na^+ and Cl^- ions alternate.
The lines show the ionic bonds between the ions.
Na^+
Cl^-

The structure of ionic compounds determines their **physical properties**...

Ionic Structure Explains the **Behaviour** of Ionic Compounds

1) **Ionic compounds conduct electricity when they're molten or dissolved — but not when they're solid.**
   The ions in a liquid are free to move (and they carry a charge).
   In a solid the ions are fixed in position by strong ionic bonds.
2) **Ionic compounds have high melting points.**
   Giant ionic lattices are held together by strong electrostatic forces. It takes loads of energy to overcome these forces, so melting points are very high (for example, 801 °C for sodium chloride).
3) **Ionic compounds tend to dissolve in water.**
   Water molecules are polar — part of the molecule has a small negative charge and other bits have small positive charges (see page 30). These charged parts pull ions away from the lattice, causing it to dissolve.

Warm-Up Questions

PRACTICE
QUESTIONS

Q1 What's a compound?

Q2 What type of force holds ionic substances together?

Q3 Sulfur is in group 6 of the periodic table. What will the charge on a sulfide ion be?

Q4 Do ionic compounds tend to dissolve in water? Why?

Exam Questions

Q1 a) Draw a labelled diagram to show the structure of sodium chloride.
Your diagram should show at least eight ions. [3 marks]

b) What is the name of this type of structure? [1 mark]

c) Would you expect sodium chloride to have a high or a low melting point?
Explain your answer. [3 marks]

Q2 What is the formula of the ionic compound magnesium carbonate? [1 mark]

Q3 Solid lead(II) bromide does not conduct electricity, but molten lead(II) bromide does.
Explain this with reference to ionic bonding. [3 marks]

Atom 1 says, "I think I lost an electron." Atom 2 replies, "are you positive?"...

Make sure that you can explain why ionic compounds do what they do. Their properties are down to the fact that ionic crystals are made up of oppositely charged ions attracted to each other. Ionic bonding ONLY happens between a metal and a non-metal. If you've got two non-metals or two metals, they'll do different sorts of bonding — keep reading...

Covalent Bonding

And now for covalent bonding — this is when atoms share electrons with one another so they've all got full outer shells.

Molecules are Groups of Atoms Bonded Together

1) Molecules form when **two or more** atoms bond together — it doesn't matter if the atoms are the **same** or **different**. Chlorine gas (Cl_2), carbon monoxide (CO), water (H_2O) and ethanol (C_2H_5OH) are all molecules.
2) Molecules are held together by strong **covalent bonds**.
3) A single covalent bond contains a **shared pair** of electrons.

Covalent bonding happens between non-metals.

In covalent bonding, two atoms **share** electrons, so they've **both** got **full outer shells** of electrons. Both the positive nuclei are attracted **electrostatically** to the shared electrons.

E.g. two iodine atoms bond covalently to form a molecule of iodine (I_2).

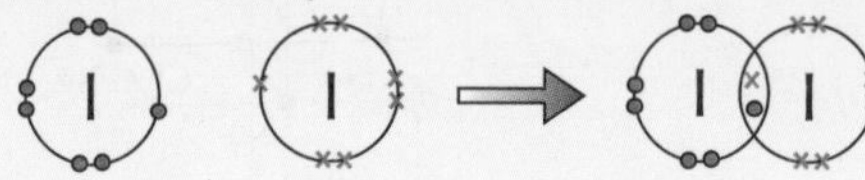

These diagrams don't show all the electrons, just the ones in the outer shells.

4) Here are a few more examples:

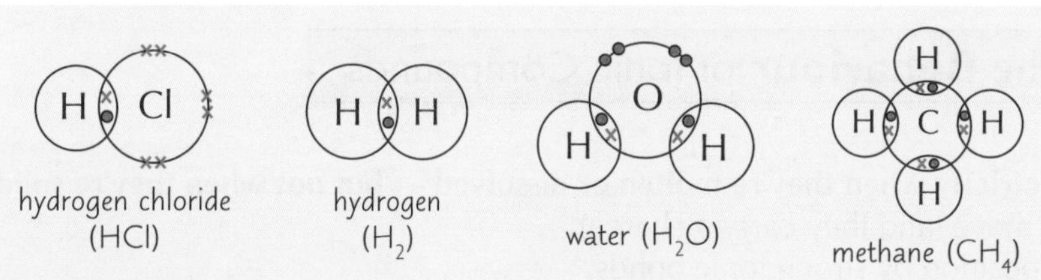

You can also show covalent bonds by drawing lines to represent each bond. E.g. methane is often drawn like this:

methane

```
   H
   |
H—C—H
   |
   H
```

5) The **typical properties** of simple covalent molecules are covered on page 34.

Some Molecules have Double or Triple Bonds

1) Atoms don't just form single bonds — **double** or even **triple covalent bonds** can be formed between atoms too.
2) These multiple bonds contain **multiple shared pairs** of electrons.

Double bond: O C O — carbon dioxide (CO_2)

Triple bond: N N — nitrogen (N_2)

Multiple covalent bonds can be shown using multiple lines, e.g. you can draw N_2 like this: N≡N.

There are Giant Covalent Structures Too

1) **Giant covalent** structures have a huge network of **covalently** bonded atoms. (They're sometimes called **macromolecular structures**.)
2) **Carbon** atoms can form this type of structure because they can each form **four** strong, covalent bonds. There are two types of giant covalent carbon structure you need to know about — **graphite** and **diamond**.

Graphite — Sheets of Hexagons with Delocalised Electrons

The carbon atoms are arranged in sheets of flat hexagons covalently bonded with three bonds each. The fourth outer electron of each carbon atom is delocalised.

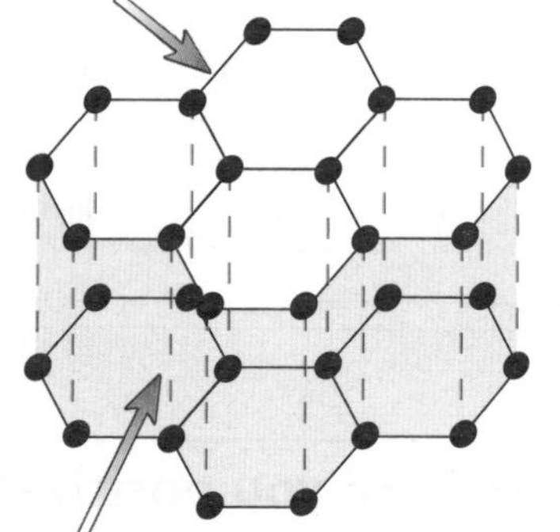

The sheets of hexagons are bonded together by weak van der Waals forces (see page 31).

The **structure** of graphite explains its **properties**:

1) The weak bonds **between** the layers in graphite are easily broken, so the sheets can slide over each other — graphite feels **slippery** and is used as a **dry lubricant** and in **pencils**.
2) The '**delocalised**' electrons in graphite aren't attached to any particular carbon atoms and are **free to move** along the sheets carrying a **charge**. So graphite is an **electrical conductor**.
3) The layers are quite **far apart** compared to the length of the covalent bonds, so graphite has a **low density** and is used to make **strong, lightweight** sports equipment.
4) Because of the **strong covalent bonds** in the hexagon sheets, graphite has a **very high melting point** (it sublimes at over 3900 K).
5) Graphite is **insoluble** in any solvent. The covalent bonds in the sheets are **too strong** to break.

'Sublime' means to change straight from a solid to a gas

Covalent Bonding

Diamond is the Hardest Known Substance

Diamond is also made up of **carbon atoms**. Each carbon atom is **covalently bonded** to **four** other carbon atoms. The atoms arrange themselves in a **tetrahedral** shape.

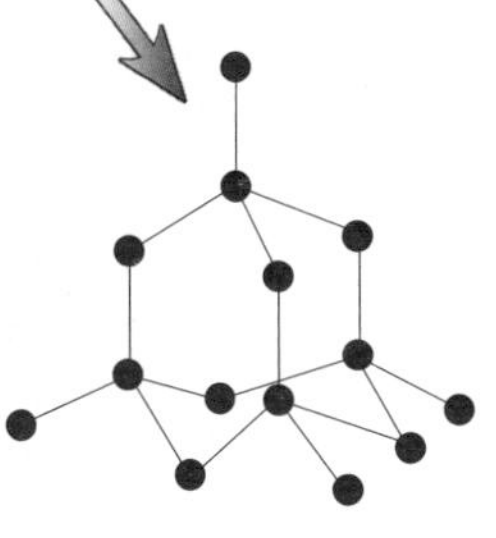

Diamond

Because of its **strong covalent** bonds:

1) Diamond has a **very high melting point** — it also sublimes at over 3900 K.
2) Diamond is extremely **hard** — it's used in diamond-tipped drills and saws.
3) **Vibrations** travel easily through the stiff lattice, so it's a **good thermal conductor**.
4) It **can't conduct** electricity — all the outer electrons are held in localised bonds.
5) Like graphite, diamond won't dissolve in **any** solvent.
6) You can 'cut' diamond to form **gemstones**. Its structure makes it **refract light** a lot, which is why it sparkles.

Dative Covalent Bonding is where Both Electrons come from One Atom

The **ammonium ion** (NH_4^+) is a classic example of dative covalent (or coordinate) bonding. It forms when the nitrogen atom in an ammonia molecule **donates a pair of electrons** to a proton (H^+):

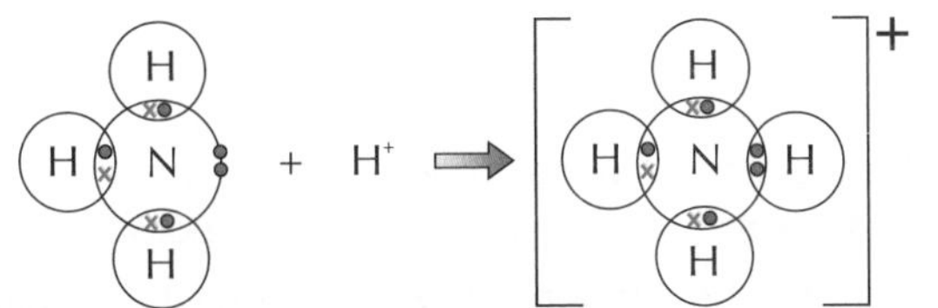

or

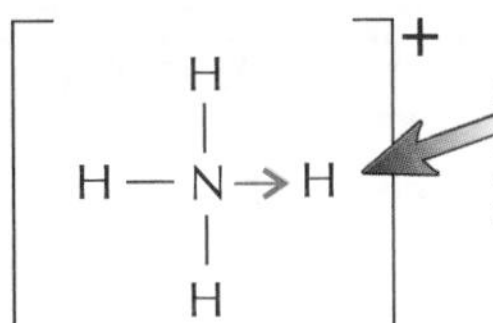

Dative covalent bonding is shown in diagrams by an arrow, pointing away from the 'donor' atom.

Warm-Up Questions

Q1 Describe how atoms are held together in covalent molecules.

Q2 Draw a diagram to show the arrangement of the outer electrons in a molecule of iodine, I_2.

Q3 How are the sheets of carbon atoms in graphite held together?

Q4 In diamond, how many other carbons is each carbon atom bonded to?

Exam Questions

Q1 Ethene, C_2H_4, is an covalently bonded organic compound.
It contains four carbon-hydrogen single bonds and one carbon-carbon double bond.

a) What is a covalent bond? [1 mark]

b) Explain how a single covalent bond differs from a double covalent bond. [1 mark]

Q2 a) What type of bond is formed when an ammonia molecule (NH_3) reacts with a hydrogen ion (H^+)? [1 mark]

b) Explain how this type of bonding occurs. [1 mark]

Q3 Carbon can be found as diamond and as graphite.

a) What type of structure do diamond and graphite display? [1 mark]

b) Draw diagrams to illustrate the structures of diamond and graphite. [2 marks]

c) Compare and explain the electrical conductivities of diamond and graphite in terms of their structure and bonding. [4 marks]

Carbon is a girl's best friend...

OK, so first things first: make sure you've got the hang of what covalent bonding is. You need to know the structures of graphite and diamond too, and why the differences in their structures gives them such different properties. Pretty amazing isn't it — they're both just carbon, but one's crumbly and grey and the other's hard and shiny. And expensive...

Shapes of Molecules

Chemistry would be heaps more simple if all molecules were flat. But they're not.

Molecular Shape depends on Electron Pairs around the Central Atom

Molecules and ions come in loads of **different shapes**.
Their shape depends on the **number of pairs** of electrons in the outer shell of the central atom.

For example, in **ammonia** the outermost shell of the **nitrogen atom** contains **four** pairs of electrons.

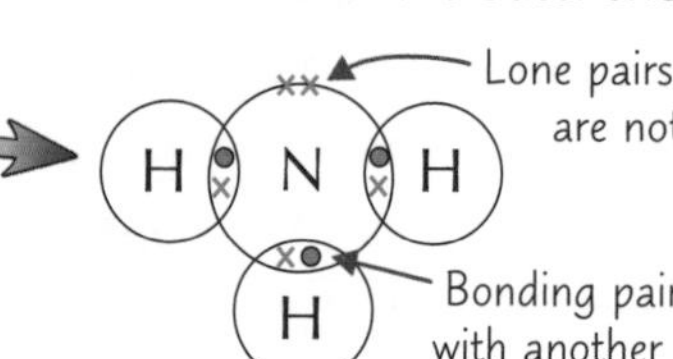

H
N
H
H
Lone pairs of electrons are not shared.
Bonding pairs of electrons are shared with another atom in a covalent bond.

A lone pear

Electron Pairs exist as Charge Clouds

Bonding pairs and lone pairs of electrons exist as **charge clouds**.
A charge cloud is an area where you have a really **big chance** of finding an electron pair. The electrons don't stay still — they **whizz around** inside the charge cloud.

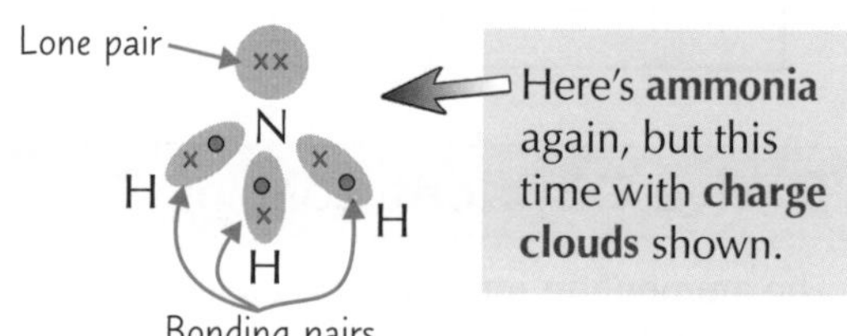

Here's **ammonia** again, but this time with **charge clouds** shown.

Electron Charge Clouds Repel Each Other

1) Electrons are all **negatively charged**, so the charge clouds will **repel** each other as much as they can. So the **pairs of electrons** in the outer shell of an atom will sit as **far apart** from each other as they possibly can.
2) This sounds straightforward, but the **shape** of the charge cloud affects **how much** it repels other charge clouds. Lone-pair charge clouds repel **more** than bonding-pair charge clouds.
3) So, the **greatest** angles are between **lone pairs** of electrons, and bond angles between bonding pairs are often **reduced** because they are pushed together by lone-pair repulsion.

Lone-pair/lone-pair angles are the biggest.	**Lone-pair/bonding-pair angles are the second biggest.**	**Bonding-pair/bonding-pair angles are the smallest.**

The central atoms in these molecules all have **four pairs** of electrons in their outer shells, but they're all **different shapes**:

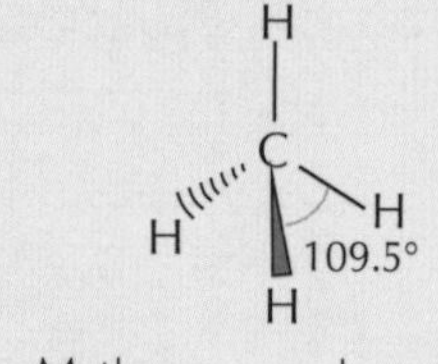

Methane — no lone pairs

The lone pair repels the bonding pairs

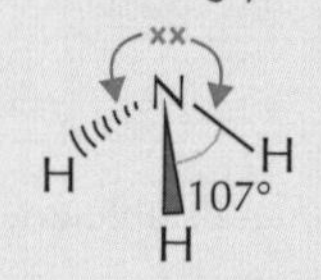

Ammonia — 1 lone pair

2 lone pairs reduce the bond angle even more

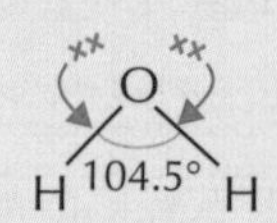

Water — 2 lone pairs

Wedges show bonds that are sticking out of the page towards you. Broken lines show bonds that go into the page.

4) This is sometimes known by the long-winded name '**Valence-Shell Electron-Pair Repulsion Theory**'.

Use the Number of Electron Pairs to Predict the Shape of a Molecule

To predict the shape of a molecule, you'll need to know how many **bonding** and **lone electron pairs** there are on the central atom of the molecule. Here's how:

1) First work out which one is the **central atom** (that's the one all the other atoms are bonded to).
2) Use the periodic table to work out the **number of electrons** in the **outer shell** of the central atom.
3) **Add one** to this number for every atom that the central atom is **bonded** to.
4) **Divide by 2** to find the number of electron pairs on the central atom.
5) **Compare** the number of **electron pairs** to the number of **bonds** to find the number of lone pairs and the number of bonding pairs on the cental atom.

Now you can use this information to work out the shape of the molecule...

If you're dealing with an ion, you need to take its charge into account too. After step 3, add 1 for each negative charge on the ion (or subtract 1 for each positive charge).

Shapes of Molecules

Molecules With Different Numbers of **Electron Pairs Have Different Shapes**

Here are the **shapes** that molecules with different numbers of electron pairs will take (and some handy examples):

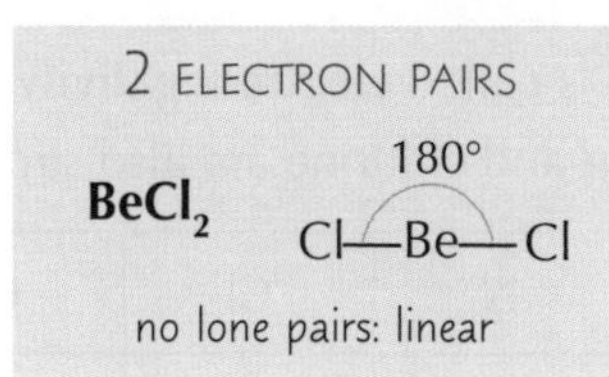

2 ELECTRON PAIRS
BeCl2
180°
Cl—Be—Cl
no lone pairs: linear

3 ELECTRON PAIRS

BF_3

F F B F 120°

no lone pairs: trigonal planar

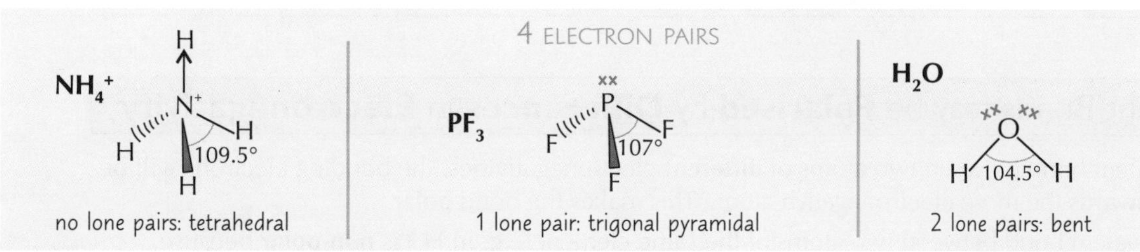

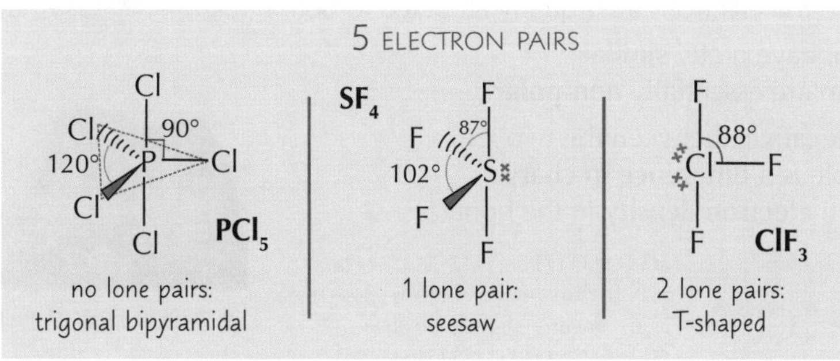

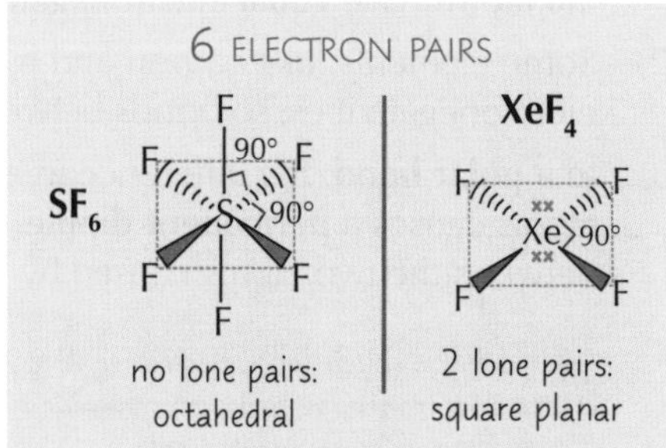

Molecules with 5 electron pairs and 1 lone pair are pretty rare — they have a shape like SF_6, but with the bottom F replaced by the lone pair.

Example: Predicting the Shape of the Molecule **H_2S**

1) The central atom is **sulfur**.
2) Sulfur is in Group 6, so it has **6 electrons** in its outer shell to start with.
3) The sulfur atom is bonded to 2 hydrogen atoms, so it has (6 + 2) = **8 electrons** in its outer shell in H_2S.
4) The number of electron pairs on the central sulfur atom is 8 ÷ 2 = **4 pairs**.
5) The sulfur atom has **4 electron pairs** and has made **2 bonds** — so it has **2 bonding pairs** and **2 lone pairs**.

This means that H_2S will have a **bent** shape (like water).

S

H H

Warm-Up Questions

Q1 What is a lone pair of electrons?

Q2 Write down the order of the strength of repulsion between different kinds of electron pair.

Q3 Draw an example of a tetrahedral molecule.

Exam Question

Q1 Nitrogen and boron can form the chlorides NCl_3 and BCl_3.

a) Draw the shape of NCl_3. Show the approximate value of the bond angles name the shape. [3 marks]

b) Draw the shape of BCl_3. Show the approximate value of the bond angles name the shape. [3 marks]

c) Explain why the shapes of NCl_3 and BCl_3 are different. [3 marks]

These molecules ain't square...

Don't panic if you get asked to predict the shape of a molecule that you don't know — it'll be just like one you do know (e.g. PH_3 is like NH_3). So learn the shapes on this page — and make sure you remember the bond angles too.

Polarisation and Intermolecular Forces

Intermolecular forces hold molecules together. They're pretty important, cos we'd all be gassy clouds without them. Some of these intermolecular forces are down to polarisation. So you best make sure you know about that first...

Some Atoms **Attract** Bonding Electrons More than Other Atoms

1) An atom's ability to attract the electron pair in a covalent bond is called **electronegativity**.
2) **Fluorine** is the most electronegative element. Oxygen, nitrogen and chlorine are also strongly electronegative.

Element	H	C	N	Cl	O	F
Electronegativity (Pauling Scale)	2.2	2.5	3.0	3.0	3.4	4.0

Covalent Bonds may be **Polarised** by **Differences** in **Electronegativity**

In a covalent bond between two atoms of **different** electronegativities, the bonding electrons will be **pulled towards** the more electronegative atom. This makes the bond **polar**.

1) A covalent bond between two atoms of the same element (e.g. in H_2) is **non-polar** because the atoms have **equal** electronegativities, so the electrons are equally attracted to both nuclei.

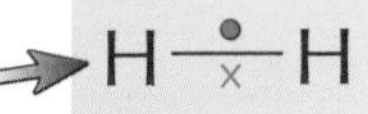

2) Some elements, like carbon and hydrogen, have pretty **similar** electronegativities, so bonds between them are essentially **non-polar**.
3) In a **polar bond**, the difference in electronegativity between the two atoms causes a **permanent dipole**. A dipole is a **difference in charge** between the two atoms caused by a shift in **electron density** in the bond.

Permanent polar bonding

Chlorine is much more electronegative than hydrogen, so hydrogen chloride has a permanent dipole.

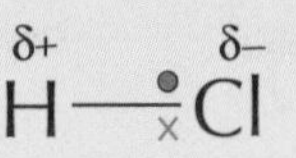
δ+ δ–
H—Cl

'δ' (delta) means 'slightly', so 'δ+' means 'slightly positive'.

4) The greater the **difference** in electronegativity between the atoms, the **more polar** the bond.

Whole Molecules can be **Polar** Too

1) If you have a molecule that contains polar bonds, you can end up with an uneven distribution of charge across the whole molecule. When this happens, the molecule is **polar**.
2) Not all molecules that contain polar bonds are polar though. If the polar bonds are arranged **symmetrically** in the molecule, then the charges **cancel out** and there is no permanent dipole

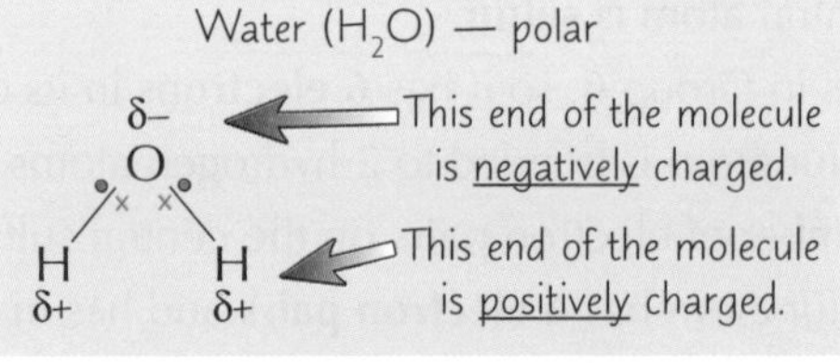
Water (H_2O) — polar
This end of the molecule is negatively charged.
This end of the molecule is positively charged.
δ–
O
H H
δ+ δ+

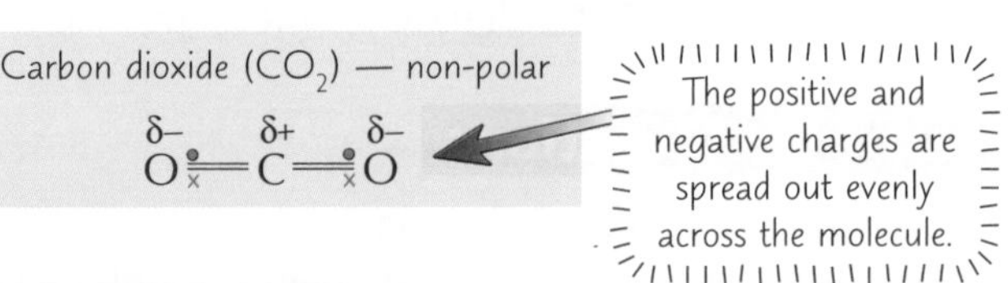
Carbon dioxide (CO_2) — non-polar
δ– δ+ δ–
O=C=O
The positive and negative charges are spread out evenly across the molecule.

Polar Molecules have **Permanent Dipole-Dipole** Forces

In a substance made up of molecules that have **permanent dipoles**, there will be **weak electrostatic forces** of attraction **between** the δ+ and δ– charges on neighbouring molecules.

E.g. hydrogen chloride gas has polar molecules:

δ+ δ– δ+ δ– δ+ δ–
H—Cl······H—Cl······H—Cl

The δ– chlorine is attracted to the δ+ hydrogen on the next molecule.

If you put a **charged rod** next to a jet of a polar liquid, like water, the liquid will **move** towards the rod. It's because **polar liquids** contain molecules with **permanent dipoles**. It doesn't matter if the rod is **positively** or **negatively** charged. The polar molecules in the liquid can **turn around** so the oppositely charged end is attracted towards the rod.

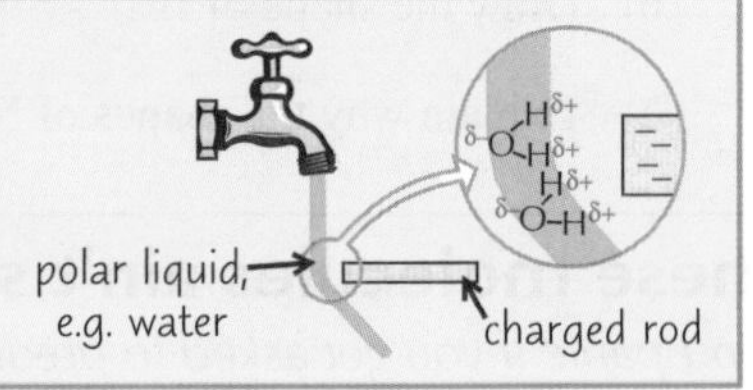
polar liquid, e.g. water
charged rod

Polarisation and Intermolecular Forces

Intermolecular Forces are **Very Weak**

Intermolecular forces are forces **between** molecules. They're much **weaker** than covalent, ionic or metallic bonds. There are three types you need to know about:

1) **Induced dipole-dipole** or **van der Waals** forces.
2) **Permanent dipole-dipole forces** (these are the ones caused by polar molecules — see previous page).
3) **Hydrogen bonding.**

Intermolecular forces are important because they affect the **physical properties** of a compound.

Van der Waals Forces are Found Between **All** Atoms and Molecules

Van der Waals forces cause **all** atoms and molecules to be **attracted** to each other.

1) **Electrons** in charge clouds are always **moving** really quickly. At any moment, the electrons in an atom are likely to be more to one side than the other. At this moment, the atom would have a **temporary dipole**.
2) This dipole can cause **another** temporary dipole in the opposite direction on a neighbouring atom. The two dipoles are then **attracted** to each other.
3) The second dipole can cause yet another dipole in a **third atom**. It's kind of like a domino effect.
4) Because the electrons are constantly moving, the dipoles are being **created** and **destroyed** all the time. Even though the dipoles keep changing, the **overall effect** is for the atoms to be **attracted** to each another.

Van der Waals Forces Can Hold Molecules in a **Lattice**

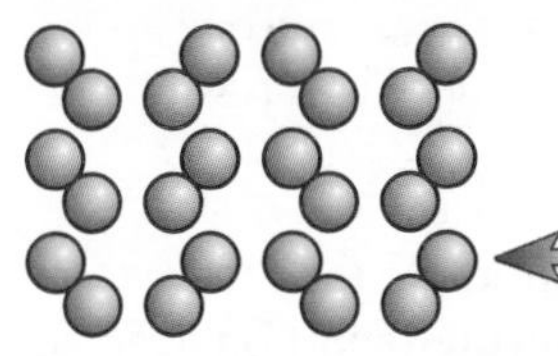

Iodine (I_2) is a **solid** at room temperature. It's the **Van der Waals forces** between the iodine molecules that are responsible for holding them together in a **lattice**:

1) Iodine atoms are held together in pairs by **strong** covalent bonds to form I_2 molecules.
2) But the molecules are then held together in a **molecular lattice** arrangement by **weak** van der Waals attractions.

Stronger **Van der Waals Forces** mean **Higher Boiling Points**

1) Not all van der Waals forces are the same strength — larger molecules have **larger electron clouds**, meaning **stronger** van der Waals forces.
2) The **shape** of molecules also affects the strength of Van der Waals forces. Long, straight molecules can lie closer together than branched ones — the **closer** together two molecules get, the **stronger** the forces between them are.
3) When you **boil** a liquid, you need to **overcome** the intermolecular forces, so that the particles can **escape** from the liquid surface. It stands to reason that you need **more energy** to overcome **stronger** intermolecular forces, so liquids with stronger van der Waals forces will have **higher boiling points**.

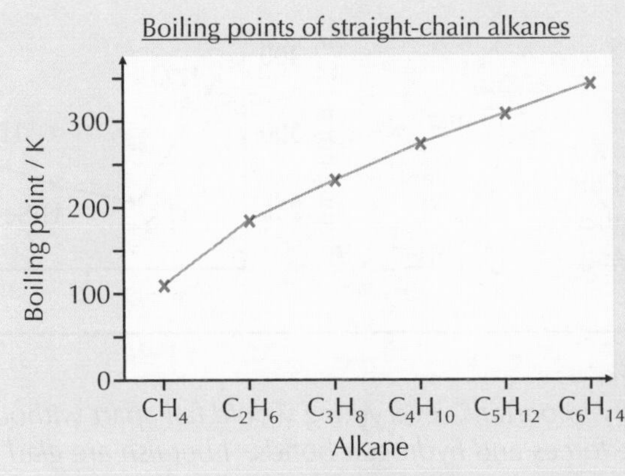

As the alkane chains get **longer**, the **number of electrons** in the molecules increases.

This means the van der Waals forces are **stronger**, and so the boiling points **increase**.

Van der Waals forces affect other physical properties too, such as melting point and viscosity.

Polarisation and Intermolecular Forces

Hydrogen Bonding is the Strongest Intermolecular Force

1) Hydrogen bonding **only** happens when **hydrogen** is covalently bonded to **fluorine**, **nitrogen** or **oxygen**.
2) Fluorine, nitrogen and oxygen are very **electronegative**, so they draw bonding electrons away from the hydrogen atom. The bond is so **polarised**, and hydrogen has such a **high charge density** (because it's so small), that the hydrogen atoms form weak bonds with **lone pairs of electrons** on the fluorine, nitrogen or oxygen atoms of **other molecules**.
3) Molecules which have hydrogen bonding usually contain **-OH** or **-NH** groups. **Water** and **ammonia** both have hydrogen bonding.

Water:

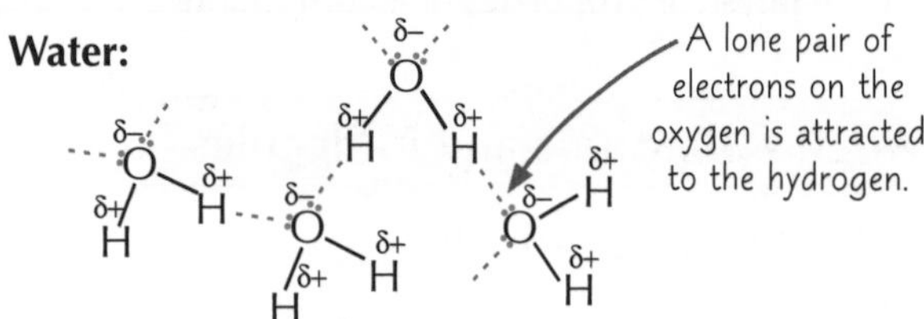

Ammonia:

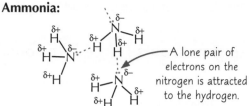

A lone pair of electrons on the nitrogen is attracted to the hydrogen.

4) Hydrogen bonding has a **huge effect** on the properties of substances:

Substances with hydrogen bonds have **higher boiling** and **melting points** than other similar molecules because of the **extra energy** needed to break the hydrogen bonds.

This is the case with **water** and also **hydrogen fluoride**, which has a **much higher boiling point** than other hydrogen halides:

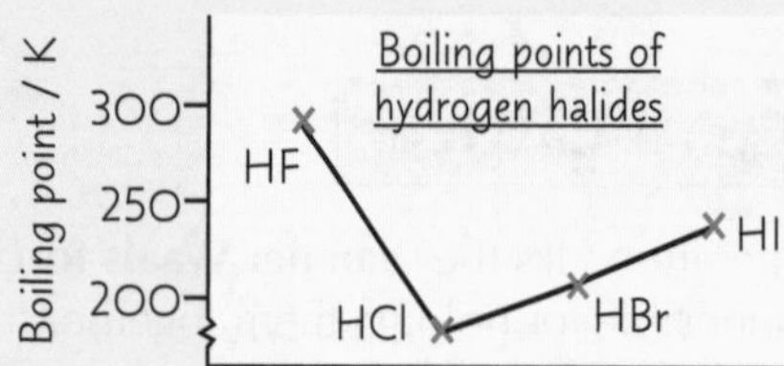

As liquid water cools to form **ice**, the molecules make **more hydrogen bonds** and arrange themselves into a regular **lattice** structure:

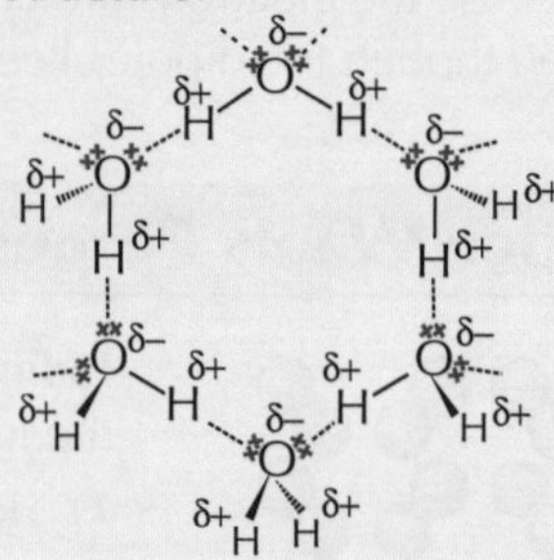

In this regular structure the H_2O molecules are **further apart** on average than the molecules in liquid water — so ice is **less dense** than liquid water.

Warm-Up Questions

Q1 Define the term electronegativity.

Q2 What is a dipole?

Q3 Write down the three types of intermolecular force.

Exam Questions

Q1 Predict whether octene (C_8H_{16}) or decene ($C_{10}H_{20}$) will have a higher boiling point. Explain your answer. [3 marks]

Q2 a) State whether the C–Cl covalent bond is polar. Explain your answer. [1 mark]

b) The molecule CCl_4 has a tetrahedral shape. Will CCl_4 be polar? Explain your answer. [2 marks]

Q3 a) Draw a labelled diagram to show the intermolecular forces that exist between two molecules of water. Include all lone pairs and partial charges in your diagram. [3 marks]

b) The graph on the right shows the boiling points of some of the group 6 hydrides. Explain why water's boiling point is higher than expected in comparison to the other Group 6 hydrides. [3 marks]

Boiling point / K: 400, 300, 200; H_2O, H_2S, H_2Se, H_2Te

Van der Waal — a German hit for Oasis...

Intermolecular forces are a bit wimpy and weak, but they're really important. Everything would fall apart without them. Learn the three types — van der Waals, permanent dipole-dipole forces and hydrogen bonds. I bet fish are glad that water forms hydrogen bonds. If it didn't, their water would boil. (And they wouldn't have evolved in the first place.)

Metallic Bonding and Properties of Materials

A bit of a mish-mash of a topic now to finish off the section — starting with a bit about bonding in metals.

Metals have Giant Structures

Metal elements exist as **giant metallic lattice structures**.

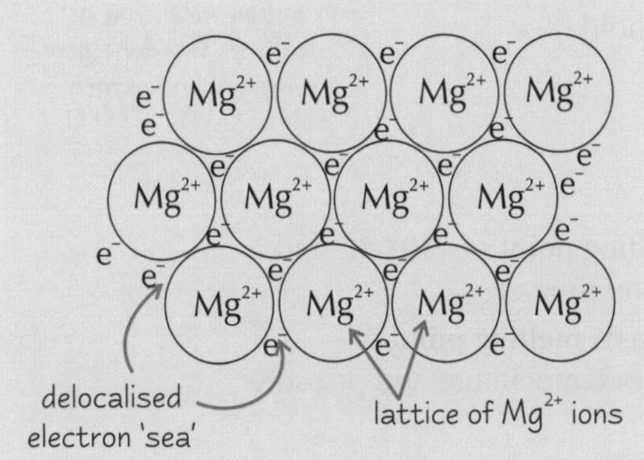

1) The outermost shell of electrons of a metal atom is **delocalised** — the electrons are free to move about the metal. This leaves a **positive metal ion**, e.g. Na^+, Mg^{2+}, Al^{3+}.
2) The positive metal ions are **attracted** to the delocalised negative electrons. They form a lattice of closely packed positive ions in a **sea** of delocalised electrons — this is **metallic bonding**.

Metallic Bonding Explains the **Properties** of Metals

1) Metals have **high melting points** because of the strong **electrostatic attraction** between the positive metal ions and the delocalised sea of electrons.
2) The **number of delocalised electrons per atom** affects the melting point. The **more** there are, the **stronger** the bonding will be and the **higher** the melting point. For example, $\mathbf{Mg^{2+}}$ has **two** delocalised electrons per atom, so it's got a **higher melting point** than Na^+, which only has **one**.
3) The delocalised electrons can pass **kinetic energy** to each other, making metals **good thermal conductors**.
4) Metals are **good electrical conductors** because the **delocalised electrons** can move and carry a **current**.
5) Metals are **insoluble** (except in **liquid metals**), because of the **strength** of the metallic bonds.

Right, well that's all you need to know about metals. So, a change of topic now — it's the properties of materials...

The **Physical Properties** of Solids, Liquids and Gases Depend on **Particles**

1) A typical **solid** has its particles very **close** together. This gives it a high density and makes it **incompressible**. The particles **vibrate** about a **fixed point** and can't move about freely.
2) A typical **liquid** has a similar density to a solid and is virtually **incompressible**. The particles move about **freely** and **randomly** within the liquid, allowing it to flow.
3) In **gases**, the particles have **loads more** energy and are much **further apart**. So the density is generally pretty low and it's **very compressible**. The particles move about **freely**, with not a lot of attraction between them, so they'll quickly **diffuse** to fill a container.
4) In order to **change** from a solid to a liquid or a liquid to a gas, you need to **break** the forces that are holding the particles together. To do this you need to give the particles more **energy,** e.g. by **heating** them.

Taylor's demonstration of how the particles in a liquid behave had got a bit out of hand.

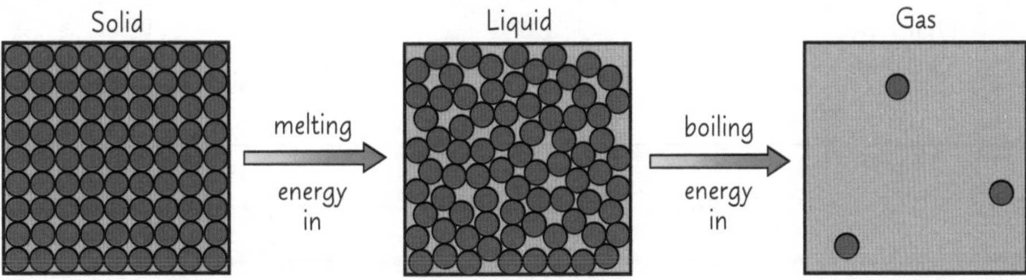

Metallic Bonding and Properties of Materials

Covalent Bonds **Don't** Break during **Melting** and **Boiling***

**Except for giant covalent substances, like diamond.*

This is something that confuses loads of people — prepare to be enlightened...

1) To **melt** or **boil** a simple covalent compound you only have to overcome the **intermolecular forces** that hold the molecules together.
2) You **don't** need to break the much stronger covalent bonds that hold the atoms together in the molecules.
3) That's why simple covalent compounds have relatively **low melting** and **boiling points**. For example:

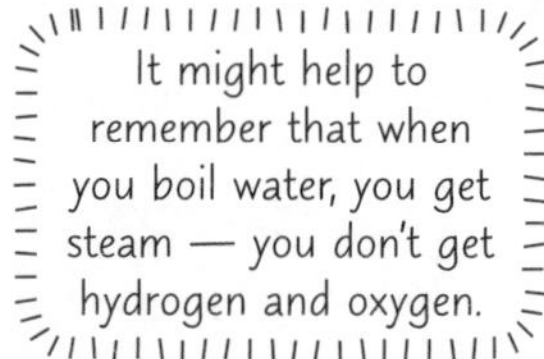

It might help to remember that when you boil water, you get steam — you don't get hydrogen and oxygen.

- **Chlorine**, Cl_2, is a **simple covalent** substance. It has a **melting point** of **–101 °C** and a **boiling point** of **–34 °C** — it's a **gas** at room temperature and pressure.
- **Pentane**, C_5H_{12}, is also a **simple covalent** compound. It has a **melting point** of **–130 °C** and a **boiling point** of **36 °C** — it's a **liquid** at room temperature and pressure.

- By contrast, **diamond**, is a **giant covalent** substance, so you **do** have to break the covalent bonds between atoms to turn it into a liquid or a gas. It never really melts, but **sublimes** at over **3600 °C**.

The Physical Properties of a **Solid** Depend on the **Nature** of its Particles

Here are a just a few examples of the ways in which the particles that make up a substance affect it properties:

1) The **melting** and **boiling points** of a substance are determined by the strength of the **attraction** between its particles.
2) A substance will only **conduct electricity** if it contains **charged particles** that are **free to move**.
3) How **soluble** a substance is in **water** depends on the **type** of particles that it contains. Water is a **polar solvent**, so substances that are **polar** or **charged** will dissolve in it well, whereas **non-polar** or **uncharged** substances won't.

Learn the **Properties** of the Main Substance Types

Make sure you know this stuff like the back of your hand:

Bonding	Examples	Melting and boiling points	Typical state at room temperature and pressure	Does solid conduct electricity?	Does liquid conduct electricity?	Is it soluble in water?
Ionic	NaCl $MgCl_2$	High	Solid	No (ions are held in place)	Yes (ions are free to move)	Yes
Simple covalent (molecular)	CO_2 I_2 H_2O	Low (involves breaking intermolecular forces but <u>not</u> covalent bonds)	May be solid (like I_2) but usually liquid or gas.	No	No	Depends on how polarised the molecule is
Giant covalent (macromolecular)	Diamond Graphite SiO_2	High	Solid	No (except graphite)	— (sublimes rather than melting)	No
Metallic	Fe Mg Al	High	Solid	Yes (delocalised electrons)	Yes (delocalised electrons)	No

Metallic Bonding and Properties of Materials

You Can Use the **Properties** of a Material to **Predict its Structure**

You need to be able to predict the type of structure from a list of its properties.
Here's a quick example.

Example: Substance X has a melting point of 1045 K. When solid, it is an insulator, but once melted it conducts electricity. Identify the type of structure present in substance X.

1) Substance X **doesn't** conduct electricity when it's **solid**, but **does** conduct electricity once **melted**. So it looks like it's **ionic** — that would fit with the fact that it has a **high melting point** too.
2) You can also tell that it definitely **isn't simple covalent** because it has a **high melting point**, it definitely **isn't metallic** because it **doesn't** conduct electricity when it's **solid**, and it definitely **isn't giant covalent** because it **does** conduct electricity when **melted**.

So substance X must be **ionic**.

Warm-Up Questions

Q1 Describe the structure of a giant metallic lattice.

Q2 Explain why metals have high melting points.

Q3 Describe how the particles are arranged in a typical solid, a typical liquid and a typical gas.

Q4 In which state will the particles of a substance have the least energy — solid, liquid or gas?

Q5 If a substance has a low melting point, what type of structure is it most likely to have?

Q6 Out of the four main types of structure (ionic, simple covalent, giant covalent and metallic), which will conduct electricity when they are liquids?

Exam Questions

Q1 a) Illustrate the structure of magnesium metal using a labelled diagram. [2 marks]

b) Explain why metals are good conductors of electricity. [1 mark]

Q2 The table below describes the properties of four compounds, A, B, C and D.

Substance	Melting point	Electrical conductivity of solid	Electrical conductivity of liquid	Solubility in water
A	high	poor	good	soluble
B	low	poor	poor	insoluble
C	high	good	good	insoluble
D	very high	poor	— (compound sublimes rather than melting)	insoluble

Identify the type of structure present in each substance. [4 marks]

Q3 Explain why iodine, I_2, has a much lower boiling point than graphite. [4 marks]

I never used to like Chemistry, but after this I feel we've truly bonded...

You need to learn the info in the table on page 34. With a quick glance in my crystal ball, I can almost guarantee you'll need a bit of it in your exam... let me look closer and tell you which bit.... hmm.... No, it's clouded over. You'll have to learn the lot. Sorry. Tell you what — close the book and see how much of the table you can scribble out from memory.

Enthalpy Changes

If you just can't get enough of physical chemistry, there's more. If you can get enough — there's still more. Sorry...

Chemical Reactions Usually Have **Enthalpy Changes**

When a chemical reaction happens, there is usually a **change in energy**.
The souped-up chemistry term for this is **enthalpy change**:

> **Enthalpy change**, ΔH (delta H), is the heat energy transferred in a reaction at **constant pressure**. The units of ΔH are **kJ mol^{-1}**.

You might see the symbol $^\ominus$ by an enthalpy change (like this: $\Delta H^\ominus$). It's telling you that the substances were in their **standard states** and the measurement was made under **standard conditions**. Standard conditions are **100 kPa pressure** and a stated temperature (e.g. ΔH_{298}). In this book, all standard enthalpy changes are measured at 298 K (25 °C).

Reactions can be either **Exothermic** or **Endothermic**

> **Exothermic** reactions **give out** energy. ΔH is **negative**.

In exothermic reactions, the temperature usually goes up.

Oxidation reactions are usually exothermic. Here are two examples:

- The **combustion** of a fuel like methane:
  $CH_{4(g)} + 2O_{2(g)} \rightarrow CO_{2(g)} + 2H_2O_{(l)}$ $\Delta_c H^\ominus = -890$ kJ mol^{-1} **exothermic**
- The oxidation of **carbohydrates**, such as glucose, $C_6H_{12}O_6$, in respiration.

> **Endothermic** reactions **absorb** energy. ΔH is **positive**.

In endothermic reactions, the temperature usually falls.

- The **thermal decomposition** of calcium carbonate is endothermic.
  $CaCO_{3(s)} \rightarrow CaO_{(s)} + CO_{2(g)}$ $\Delta_c H^\ominus = +178$ kJ mol^{-1} **endothermic**
- The main reactions of **photosynthesis** are also endothermic — sunlight supplies the energy.

Reactions are all about **Breaking** and **Making** Bonds

Horace definitely didn't have the energy to break any bonds.

When reactions happen, **reactant bonds** are **broken** and **product bonds** are **formed**.

1) You **need energy** to break bonds, so bond breaking is **endothermic** (ΔH is **positive**). **Stronger** bonds take **more** energy to break.
2) Energy is **released** when bonds are formed, so bond making is **exothermic** (ΔH is **negative**). **Stronger** bonds release **more** energy when they form.
3) The **enthalpy change** for a reaction is the **overall effect** of these two changes. If you need **more** energy to **break** bonds than is released when bonds are made, ΔH is **positive**. If it's less, ΔH is **negative**.

Mean Bond Enthalpies are **not Exact**

You can look mean bond enthalpies up in data books.

1) **Bond enthalpy** is the energy **required** to **break bonds**.
2) You'd think that every time you broke the **same type of bond** it would require the **same amount of energy**, but annoyingly that's not true — the energy needed to break a bond depends on the environment it's in.
3) In calculations, you use **mean bond enthalpy** — that's the **average energy** needed to break a certain type of bond, over a range of compounds.

> For example, **water** (H_2O) has **two O–H bonds**.
> For the **first** bond, $H\text{–}OH_{(g)}$: E(H–OH) = +492 kJ mol^{-1}
> For the **second** bond, $H\text{–}O_{(g)}$: E(H–O) = +428 kJ mol^{-1}
> **Mean** bond enthalpy = (492 + 428) ÷ 2 = **+460 kJ mol^{-1}**.

The data book says the bond enthalpy for O–H is +463 kJ mol^{-1}. It's a bit different because it's the average for a bigger range of molecules (not just water). For example, it includes the O–H bonds in alcohols and carboxylic acids too.

4) Breaking bonds is **always endothermic**, so mean bond enthalpies are **always positive**.

Enthalpy Changes

Enthalpy Changes Can Be Calculated using **Mean Bond Enthalpies**

In any chemical reaction, energy is **absorbed** to **break bonds** and **given out** during **bond formation**. The difference between the energy absorbed to break bonds and released in making bonds is the overall **enthalpy change of reaction**:

Enthalpy change of reaction = total energy absorbed – total energy released

Example: Calculate the overall enthalpy change for this reaction: $N_{2(g)} + 3H_{2(g)} \rightarrow 2NH_{3(g)}$
Use the mean bond enthalpy values in the table below.

Bond	Mean Bond Enthalpy
N≡N	945 kJ mol^{-1}
H–H	436 kJ mol^{-1}
N–H	391 kJ mol^{-1}

Bonds broken: 1 N≡N bond broken = 1 × 945 = 945 kJ mol^{-1}
3 H–H bonds broken = 3 × 436 = 1308 kJ mol^{-1}

Total Energy Absorbed = 945 + 1308 = **2253 kJ mol^{-1}**

Bonds formed: 6 N–H bonds formed = 6 × 391 = 2346 kJ mol^{-1}

Total Energy Released = **2346 kJ mol^{-1}**

Enthalpy change of reaction = total energy absorbed – total energy released = 2253 – 2346 = **–93 kJ mol^{-1}**

Because they use **average** values, enthalpy changes calculated using mean bond enthalpies **aren't exact** — they are slightly less accurate than enthalpy change value calculated using **Hess's Law** (see page 40).

There are **Different Types** of ΔH

1) **Standard enthalpy of formation**, $\Delta_f H^\ominus$, is the enthalpy change when **1 mole** of a **compound** is formed from its **elements** in their standard states under standard conditions, e.g. $2C_{(s)} + 3H_{2(g)} + \frac{1}{2}O_{2(g)} \rightarrow C_2H_5OH_{(l)}$.
2) **Standard enthalpy of combustion**, $\Delta_c H^\ominus$, is the enthalpy change when **1 mole** of a substance is completely **burned in oxygen** under standard conditions, e.g. $C_2H_{4(g)} + 3O_{2(g)} \rightarrow 2CO_{2(g)} + 2H_2O_{(l)}$.

Warm-Up Questions

Q1 Explain the terms 'exothermic reaction' and 'endothermic reaction'.

Q2 Define 'mean bond enthalpy'.

Q3 Define 'standard enthalpy of formation' and 'standard enthalpy of combustion'.

Exam Questions

Q1 The table on the right shows some mean bond enthalpy values.

Bond	C–H	C=O	O=O	O–H
Mean bond enthalpy (kJ mol^{-1})	435	805	498	464

The complete combustion of methane can be represented by this equation: $CH_{4(g)} + 2O_{2(g)} \rightarrow CO_{2(g)} + 2H_2O_{(l)}$

a) Use the table of mean bond enthalpies to calculate the enthalpy change for this reaction. [3 marks]

b) Is the reaction endothermic or exothermic? Explain your answer. [1 mark]

Q2 Methanol, CH_3OH, when blended with petrol, can be used as a fuel. $\Delta_c H^\ominus [CH_3OH] = -726$ kJ mol^{-1}

a) Write an equation, including state symbols, for the standard enthalpy of combustion of methanol. [1 mark]

b) Write an equation, including state symbols, for the standard enthalpy of formation of methanol. [1 mark]

Q3 Petroleum gas is a fuel that contains propane, C_3H_8.
Explain why the following equation does not represent a standard enthalpy of combustion:

$$2C_3H_{8(g)} + 10O_{2(g)} \rightarrow 6CO_{2(g)} + 8H_2O_{(g)} \qquad \Delta H = -4113 \text{ kJ mol}^{-1}$$

[1 mark]

No Mr bond, I expect you to break endothermically...

So, there you go, breaking bonds needs energy, but making bonds gives out energy. To be honest, all this energy stuff has tired me out. No escaping it though, so just keep ploughing on, brave chemistry warrior. It's worth learning those sneaky ΔH definitions at the end too — I can't help but think that they'll be cropping up again later in the section...

Calorimetry

You can find some enthalpy changes by doing an experiment and then a calculation...

You can find **Enthalpy Changes** using **Calorimetry**

1) You use **calorimetry** to find out how much heat is given out by a reaction by measuring a **temperature change**.
2) To find the enthalpy of **combustion** of a **flammable liquid**, you burn it inside some apparatus like this (called a **calorimeter**):
3) As the fuel burns, it heats the water. You can work out the **heat energy** that has been **absorbed** by the water if you know the **mass of the water**, the **temperature change** (ΔT), and the **specific heat capacity of water** (= 4.18 J g^{-1} K^{-1}) — see the next page for the details of how to do this.
4) Ideally, all the heat given out by the fuel as it burns would be **absorbed** by the water — allowing you to work out the enthalpy change of combustion exactly.
5) But in **any** calorimetry experiment, you **always** lose heat **to the surroundings** (however well your calorimeter is **insulated**). This makes it hard to get an **accurate result**.
6) Also, when you burn a fuel, some of the combustion may be **incomplete** (meaning **less energy** is given out). Flammable liquids are often quite **volatile** too, so you may lose some fuel to evaporation.

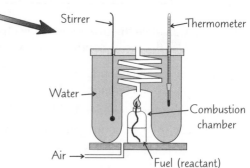

You Can Use a **Graph** to Find an **Accurate Temperature Change**

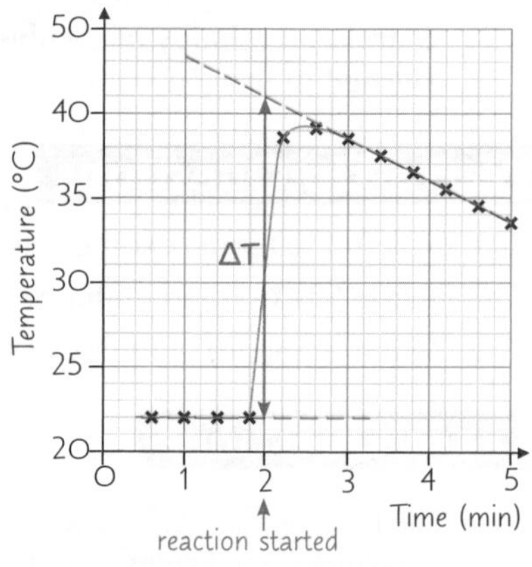

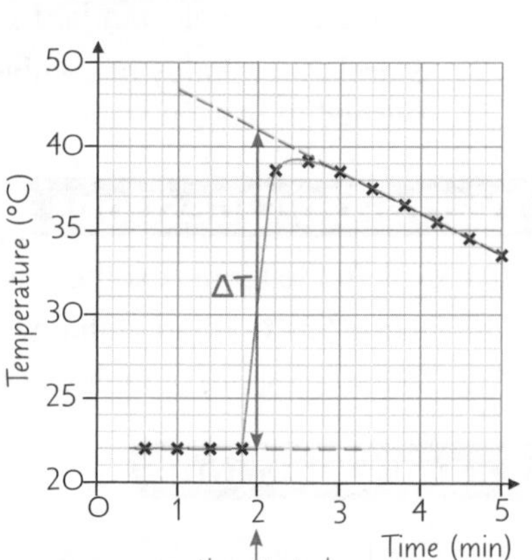

1) The most obvious way of finding the **temperature change** in a calorimetry experiment is to subtract the **starting temperature** from the **highest temperature** you recorded. But that **won't** give you a very **accurate** value (because of the heat lost to the surroundings).
2) You can use a **graph** of your results to find an **accurate value**.
3) During the experiment, record the temperature at regular intervals, beginning a couple of minutes **before** you start the reaction.
4) Plot a **graph** of your results. Draw two **lines of best fit**: one through the points **before** the reaction started and one through the points **after** it started.
5) Extend both lines so they **both** pass the time when the reaction started.
6) The **distance between the two lines** at the time the reaction started (before any heat was lost) is the accurate temperature change (**ΔT**) for the reaction.

You can also use **Calorimetry** to **Measure Enthalpy Changes** in **Solution**

1) Calorimetry can also be used to calculate the enthalpy change for reactions that happen **in solution** too, such as **neutralisation**, **dissolution** (**dissolving**) or **displacement**. For example:

   1) To find the enthalpy change for a **neutralisation reaction**, add a **known volume** of acid to an **insulated container** (e.g. a polystyrene cup) and measure the **temperature**.
   2) Then add a **known volume** of alkali and record the **temperature** of the mixture at regular intervals over a period of time. (Stir the solution to make sure it's evenly heated.)
   3) Find the **temperature change** for the experiment using the graph method. Use it to calculate the **enthalpy change** of the reaction (using the formula on the next page).

   Or a known mass if one of the reactants is a solid.

2) You'll need to know the **mass** of the solutions that you've used in order to calculate the enthalpy change of the reaction. You can assume that all solutions have the **same density as water**. Since 1 cm^3 of water has a mass of 1 g, if you have e.g. 50 cm^3 of solution you can assume that it has a mass of 50 g.

   If you've mixed two solutions, you'll need to include the masses of both.

3) If you're trying to find the energy change **per mole** of reactant, you might need the formula **moles = concentration (mol dm^{-3}) × volume (dm^3)** to find the number of moles of a substance in a solution.

Calorimetry

Calculate **Enthalpy Changes** Using the **Equation** $q = mc\Delta T$

Here's the snazzy formula that you need to calculate an **enthalpy change** from a **calorimetry experiment**:

$$q = mc\Delta T$$

where, q = heat lost or gained (in joules). This is the same as the enthalpy change if the pressure is constant.

m = mass of water (or other solution) in the calorimeter (in grams)

c = specific heat capacity of water (4.18 J $g^{-1}K^{-1}$)

ΔT = the change in temperature (in Kelvin) of the water or solution

The specific heat capacity of water is the amount of heat energy it takes to raise the temperature of 1 g of water by 1 K.

You do need to learn the **units** for everything in this formula. (But it's worth knowing that though the official unit for ΔT is **K**, the value is actually the same in **°C** — so if ΔT = 5 °C, then ΔT = 5 K.)

Example: In a laboratory experiment, 1.16 g of an organic liquid fuel were completely burned in oxygen. The heat formed during this combustion raised the temperature of 100 g of water from 295 K to 358 K. Calculate the standard enthalpy of combustion, $\Delta_c H^\ominus$, of the fuel. Its M_r is 58.0.

1) First off, you need to calculate the **amount of heat** given out by the fuel using the formula $q = mc\Delta T$:
   $q = 100 \times 4.18 \times (358 - 295) = 26\,334$ J

   Remember — m is the mass of the water, <u>not</u> the mass of fuel.

2) Standard enthalpies of combustion are always given in units of **kJ mol^{-1}**.
   So the next thing to do is to change the **units of q** from **joules** to **kilojoules**: (26 334 J ÷ 1000) = 26.334 kJ

3) The standard enthalpy of combustion is the energy produced by burning **1 mole** of fuel. So next you need to find out **how many moles** of fuel produced this much energy, using the old 'number of moles = mass ÷ M_r' formula.
   number of moles of fuel = $\frac{1.16}{58.0} = 0.0200$

4) So the heat produced by 1 mole of fuel ($\Delta_c H^\ominus$) = $\frac{-26.334}{0.0200}$ = –1316.7 kJ mol^{-1}
   = **–1320 kJ mol^{-1}** (3 s.f.).

You need to add a minus sign here because the reaction's exothermic — you know this because it raised the temperature of the water.

Warm-Up Questions

Q1 Briefly describe an experiment that you could do to find the standard enthalpy change of a combustion reaction.

Q2 Briefly describe an experiment that you could do to find the enthalpy change of a neutralisation reaction.

Q3 Give the formula that you would use to calculate heat change from the results of a calorimetry experiment.

Exam Questions

Q1 The initial temperature of 25.0 cm^3 of 1.00 mol dm^{-3} hydrochloric acid in a polystyrene cup was measured as 19.0 °C. This acid was exactly neutralised by 25 cm^3 of 1.00 mol dm^{-3} sodium hydroxide solution. The maximum temperature of the resulting solution was measured as 25.5 °C.

Calculate the molar enthalpy of neutralisation for the hydrochloric acid. You may assume the neutral solution formed has a specific heat capacity of 4.18 J K^{-1} g^{-1}. [5 marks]

Q2 A 50.0 cm^3 sample of 0.200 M copper(II) sulfate solution was measured out into a polystyrene beaker. A temperature increase of 2.60 K was recorded when excess zinc powder was stirred in.
The equation for this reaction is: $Zn_{(s)} + CuSO_{4(aq)} \rightarrow Cu_{(s)} + ZnSO_{4(aq)}$

Calculate the enthalpy change when 1 mole of zinc reacts. Assume the specific heat capacity of the solution is 4.18 J $g^{-1}K^{-1}$. Ignore the increase in volume of the solution due to the zinc. [4 marks]

Having trouble with calorimetry? I can enthalpise...

These calculations look a bit nasty, but really they just come down to learning the formula off by heart and getting some practice at using it. Remember to learn all of the units that go with the formula — I know there's a lot of them, but they're really important. There's no point coming out with the answer 8.1 if you don't know what you've got 8.1 of...

Hess's Law

Sometimes you can't work out an enthalpy change by measuring a single temperature change. But there's still a way. You can work it out from the enthalpies of formation or combustion without the need for messy experiments.

Hess's Law — the Total Enthalpy Change is Independent of the Route Taken

Hess's Law says that:

> The **total enthalpy change** of a reaction is **independent** of the **route** taken.

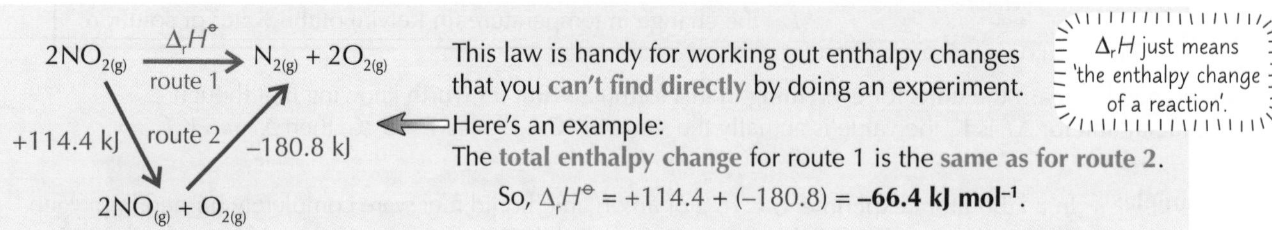

This law is handy for working out enthalpy changes that you **can't find directly** by doing an experiment.

Here's an example:

The **total enthalpy change** for route 1 is the **same as for route 2**.

So, $\Delta_r H^\circ = +114.4 + (-180.8) = \mathbf{-66.4\ kJ\ mol^{-1}}$.

$\Delta_r H$ just means 'the enthalpy change of a reaction'.

Enthalpy Changes Can be Worked Out From **Enthalpies of Formation**

1) **Enthalpy changes of formation** are useful for calculating enthalpy changes you can't find directly.
2) To do this, you'll need to know $\Delta_f H^\circ$ for **all** the reactants and products that are **compounds**. (Don't panic though — you'll be given the information you need in exam questions.)
3) The value of $\Delta_f H^\circ$ for all **elements** is zero — the element's being 'formed' from the element, so there's no change.

Here's how to calculate $\Delta_r H^\circ$ for this reaction: $SO_{2(g)} + 2H_2S_{(g)} \rightarrow 3S_{(s)} + 2H_2O_{(l)}$

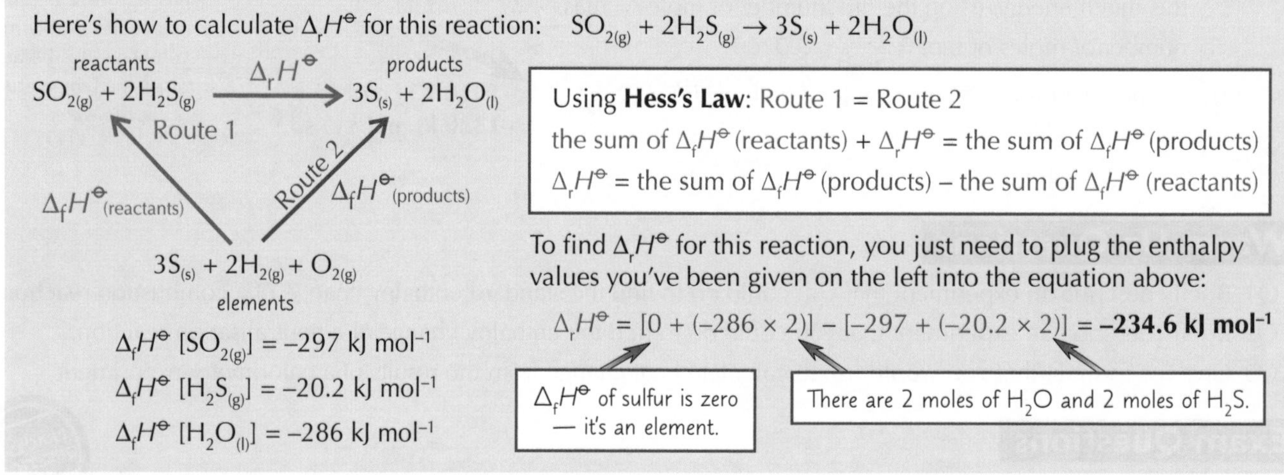

$\Delta_f H^\circ [SO_{2(g)}] = -297\ kJ\ mol^{-1}$

$\Delta_f H^\circ [H_2S_{(g)}] = -20.2\ kJ\ mol^{-1}$

$\Delta_f H^\circ [H_2O_{(l)}] = -286\ kJ\ mol^{-1}$

Using **Hess's Law**: Route 1 = Route 2

the sum of $\Delta_f H^\circ$ (reactants) + $\Delta_r H^\circ$ = the sum of $\Delta_f H^\circ$ (products)

$\Delta_r H^\circ$ = the sum of $\Delta_f H^\circ$ (products) – the sum of $\Delta_f H^\circ$ (reactants)

To find $\Delta_r H^\circ$ for this reaction, you just need to plug the enthalpy values you've been given on the left into the equation above:

$\Delta_r H^\circ = [0 + (-286 \times 2)] - [-297 + (-20.2 \times 2)] = \mathbf{-234.6\ kJ\ mol^{-1}}$

$\Delta_f H^\circ$ of sulfur is zero — it's an element.

There are 2 moles of H_2O and 2 moles of H_2S.

It **always** works, no matter how complicated the reaction:

Here's how to calculate $\Delta_r H^\circ$ for this reaction: $2NH_4NO_{3(s)} + C_{(s)} \rightarrow 2N_{2(g)} + CO_{2(g)} + 4H_2O_{(l)}$

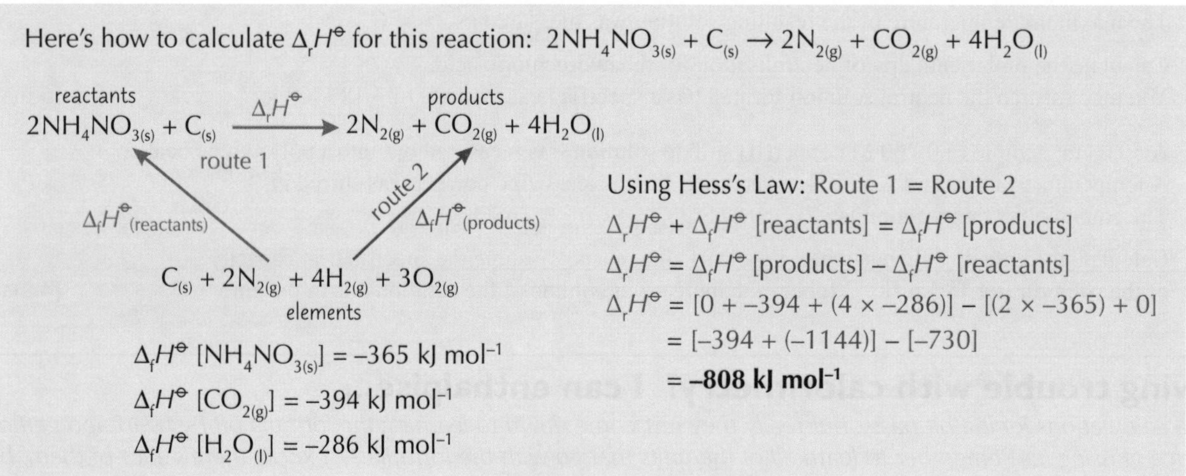

$\Delta_f H^\circ [NH_4NO_{3(s)}] = -365\ kJ\ mol^{-1}$

$\Delta_f H^\circ [CO_{2(g)}] = -394\ kJ\ mol^{-1}$

$\Delta_f H^\circ [H_2O_{(l)}] = -286\ kJ\ mol^{-1}$

Using Hess's Law: Route 1 = Route 2

$\Delta_r H^\circ + \Delta_f H^\circ$ [reactants] = $\Delta_f H^\circ$ [products]

$\Delta_r H^\circ = \Delta_f H^\circ$ [products] – $\Delta_f H^\circ$ [reactants]

$\Delta_r H^\circ = [0 + -394 + (4 \times -286)] - [(2 \times -365) + 0]$

$= [-394 + (-1144)] - [-730]$

$= \mathbf{-808\ kJ\ mol^{-1}}$

Hess's Law

Enthalpy Changes Can be Worked Out From **Enthalpies of Combustion**

You can use a similar method to find an enthalpy change from **enthalpy changes of combustion.**

Here's how to use enthalpy changes of combustion to calculate $\Delta_f H^\ominus$ of **ethanol** (C_2H_5OH):

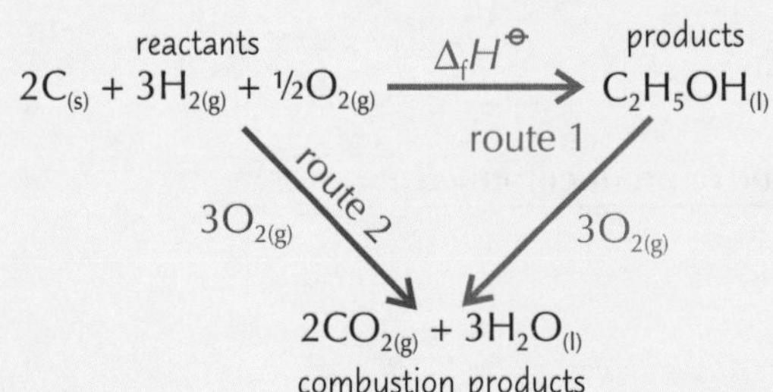

Using Hess's Law: Route 1 = Route 2

$\Delta_f H^\ominus [C_2H_5OH] + \Delta_c H^\ominus [C_2H_5OH] = 2\Delta_c H^\ominus [C] + 3\Delta_c H^\ominus [H_2]$

$\Delta_f H^\ominus [C_2H_5OH] + (-1367) = (2 \times -394) + (3 \times -286)$

$\Delta_f H^\ominus [C_2H_5OH] = -788 + -858 - (-1367)$

$= \mathbf{-279\ kJ\ mol^{-1}}$

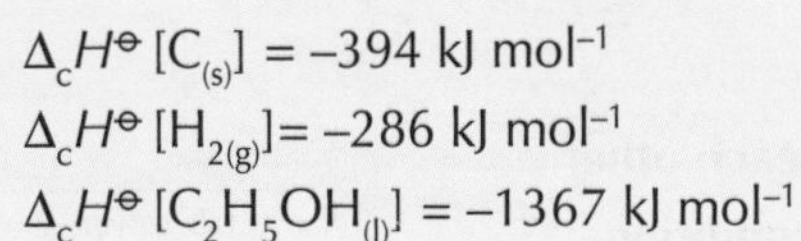

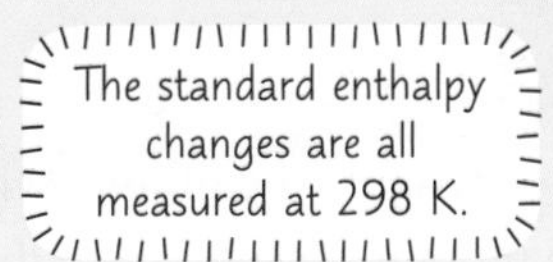

The Loch Hess Monster: Brilliant at chemistry but very, very shy.

If you ever need to go along an arrow **backwards** in a Hess's Law diagram, you **subtract** the enthalpy change that goes with that arrow. For example, you could find the $\Delta_f H^\ominus$ for ethanol using these routes instead: This time, route 1 is just $\Delta_f H^\ominus [C_2H_5OH]$, while route 2 involves going **forwards** along the step 1 blue arrow and **backwards** along the step 2 blue arrow.

$\Delta_f H^\ominus [C_2H_5OH] = 2\Delta_c H^\ominus [C] + 3\Delta_c H^\ominus [H_2] - \Delta_c H^\ominus [C_2H_5OH]$

$= (2 \times -394) + (3 \times -286) - (-1367) = \mathbf{-279\ kJ\ mol^{-1}}$

$2C_{(s)} + 3H_{2(g)} + \frac{1}{2}O_{2(g)} \xrightarrow{\Delta_f H^\ominus} C_2H_5OH_{(l)}$ (route 1)

route 2: step ① ($3O_{2(g)}$), step ② ($3O_{2(g)}$) → $2CO_{2(g)} + 3H_2O_{(l)}$

$\Delta_c H^\ominus [C_{(s)}] = -394\ kJ\ mol^{-1}$

$\Delta_c H^\ominus [H_{2(g)}] = -286\ kJ\ mol^{-1}$

$\Delta_c H^\ominus [C_2H_5OH_{(l)}] = -1367\ kJ\ mol^{-1}$

Warm-Up Questions

Q1 What does Hess's Law state?

Q2 State the value of the standard enthalpy change of formation of any element.

Q3 Use the diagram on the right to find the enthalpy change of formation of methane*.

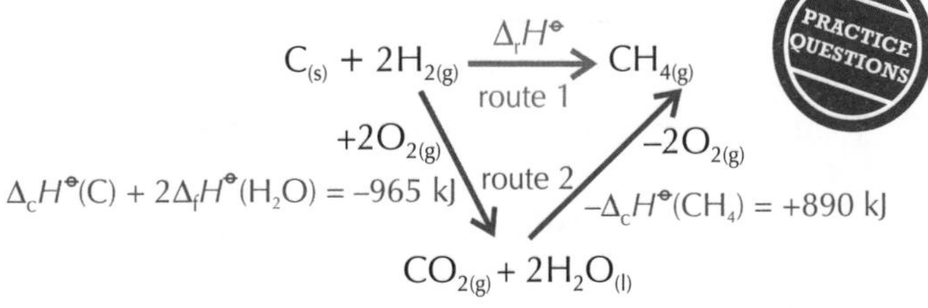

PRACTICE QUESTIONS

*Answer on page 118.

Exam Questions

Q1 Using the facts that (at 298 K) the standard enthalpy change of formation of $Al_2O_{3(s)}$ is $-1676\ kJ\ mol^{-1}$ and the standard enthalpy change of formation of $MgO_{(s)}$ is $-602\ kJ\ mol^{-1}$, calculate the enthalpy change of the following reaction.

$$Al_2O_{3(s)} + 3Mg_{(s)} \rightarrow 2Al_{(s)} + 3MgO_{(s)}$$

[2 marks]

Q2 Calculate the enthalpy change for the hydrogenation of ethene at 298 K: $C_2H_{4(g)} + H_{2(g)} \rightarrow C_2H_{6(g)}$

Use the following standard enthalpies of combustion in your calculations:

$\Delta_c H^\ominus (C_2H_4) = -1400\ kJ\ mol^{-1}$ $\Delta_c H^\ominus (C_2H_6) = -1560\ kJ\ mol^{-1}$ $\Delta_c H^\ominus (H_2) = -286\ kJ\ mol^{-1}$ [2 marks]

The law is an ass — not in this case though...obviously...

To get your head around those Hess diagrams, you're going to have to do more than skim them. You need to be able to use this stuff for any reaction they give you. It'll also help if you know the definitions for those standard enthalpy thingumabobs on page 37. If you didn't bother learning them, have a quick flick back and remind yourself about them.

Reaction Rates

The rate of a reaction is just how quickly it happens. Lots of things can make it go faster or slower.

Reaction Rate is the Amount of Stuff Reacting Divided by Time

1) **Reaction rate** is defined as the **change** in **concentration** (or **amount**) of a reactant or product over **time**.
2) A simple formula for finding the rate of a chemical reaction is:

$$\text{rate of reaction} = \frac{\text{amount of reactant used or product formed}}{\text{time}}$$

Particles Must Collide to React

1) Particles in liquids and gases are **always moving** and **colliding** with **each other**.
2) They **don't** react every time they collide though — only when the **conditions** are right. A reaction **won't** take place between two particles **unless**:

> - They collide in the **right direction** — they need to be **facing** each other in the right way.
> - They collide with at least a certain **minimum** amount of kinetic (movement) **energy**.

3) This stuff's called **collision theory**.

Particles Must have Enough Energy for a Reaction to Happen

> The **minimum amount of kinetic energy** that particles need to react is called the **activation energy**.

The particles must have at least this much energy to **break their bonds** and start the reaction. To make this a bit clearer, here's an **enthalpy profile diagram**:

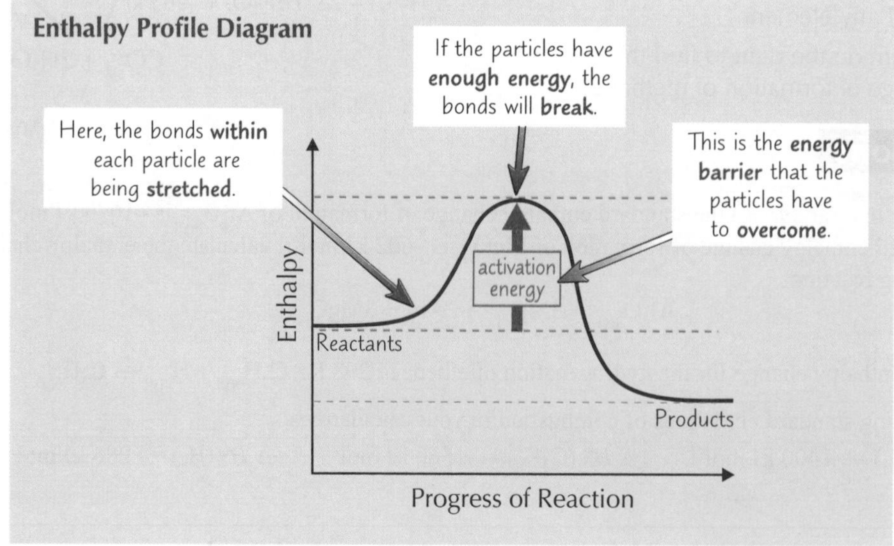

Reactions with **low activation energies** often happen **pretty easily**. But reactions with **high activation energies** don't. You need to give the particles extra energy by **heating** them.

Reaction Rates

Molecules in a Gas Don't all have the Same Amount of Energy

1) Imagine looking down on Oxford Street when it's teeming with people. You'll see some people ambling along **slowly**, some hurrying **quickly**, but most of them will be walking with a **moderate speed**.
2) It's the same with the **molecules** in a **gas**. Some **don't have much kinetic energy** and move **slowly**. Others have **loads** of **kinetic energy** and **whizz** along. But most molecules are somewhere **in between**.
3) If you plot a **graph** of the **numbers of molecules** in a **gas** with different **kinetic energies** you get a **Maxwell-Boltzmann distribution**. They look like this:

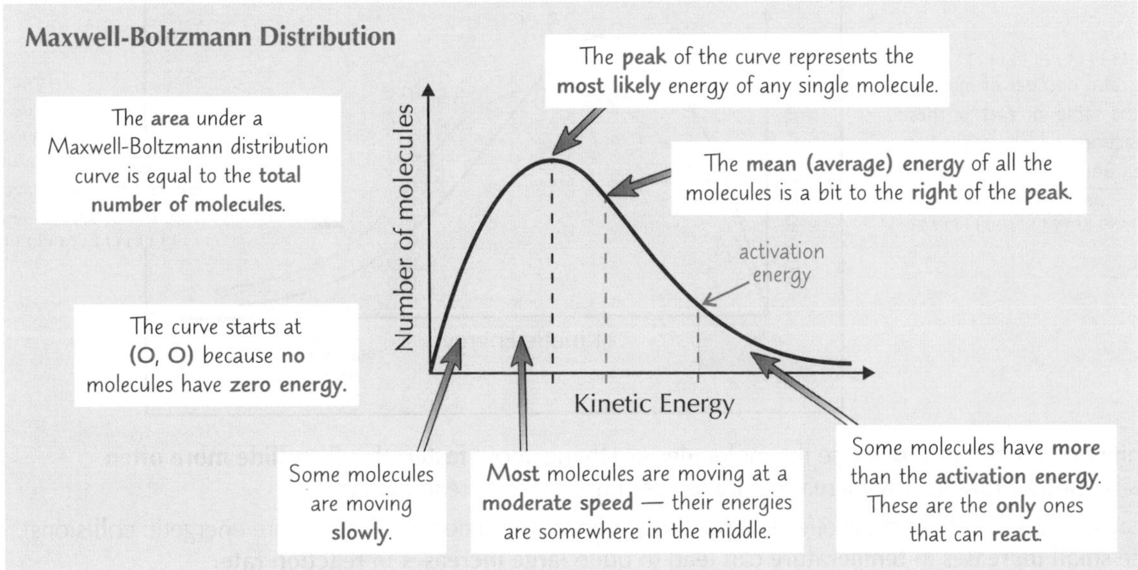
Maxwell-Boltzmann Distribution
The area under a Maxwell-Boltzmann distribution curve is equal to the total number of molecules.
The peak of the curve represents the most likely energy of any single molecule.
The mean (average) energy of all the molecules is a bit to the right of the peak.
activation energy
Number of molecules
Kinetic Energy
The curve starts at (0, 0) because no molecules have zero energy.
Some molecules are moving slowly.
Most molecules are moving at a moderate speed — their energies are somewhere in the middle.
Some molecules have more than the activation energy. These are the only ones that can react.

Warm-Up Questions

Q1 Explain what is meant by the term reaction rate.

Q2 Define the term 'activation energy'.

Q3 What does the area under a Maxwell-Boltzmann distribution curve represent?

PRACTICE QUESTIONS

Exam Questions

Q1 Nitrogen oxide (NO) and ozone (O_3) react to produce nitrogen dioxide (NO_2) and oxygen (O_2). Collisions between the two molecules do not always lead to a reaction, even if the molecules are orientated correctly. Explain why this is. [1 mark]

Q2 The Maxwell-Boltzmann distribution curve on the right shows the distribution of molecular energies in a sample of a gas at 25 °C.

a) Label the *y*-axis. [1 mark]

b) Shade the area of the curve representing molecules with energy greater than the activation energy. [1 mark]

c) Draw a cross on the *x*-axis to mark the position of the most likely energy of a molecule of the gas. [1 mark]

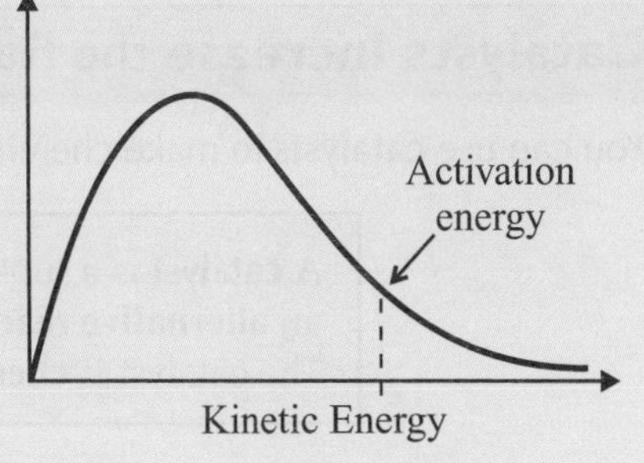
Activation energy
Kinetic Energy

Chemical reactions and waking up — both require activation energy...

Collision theory and activation energy make a lot of sense when you think about them. Particles have to both meet in the first place and have enough energy to react. Make sure you've got the hang of what Maxwell-Boltzmann distributions look like, and where to find the mean and most likely energy — they're easy marks if this topic crops up in the exam...

More on Reaction Rates

Knowing about reaction rates is all well and good, but how do you get a reaction to speed up or slow down? Read on...

Increasing the **Temperature** makes Reactions **Faster**

1) If you increase the **temperature** of a reaction, the particles will on average have more **kinetic energy** and will move **faster**.
2) So, a **greater proportion** of molecules will have at least the **activation energy** and be able to **react**. This changes the **shape** of the **Maxwell-Boltzmann distribution curve** — it pushes it over to the **right**.

The total number of molecules is the same for each of these reactions, which means the area under both curves must be the same too.

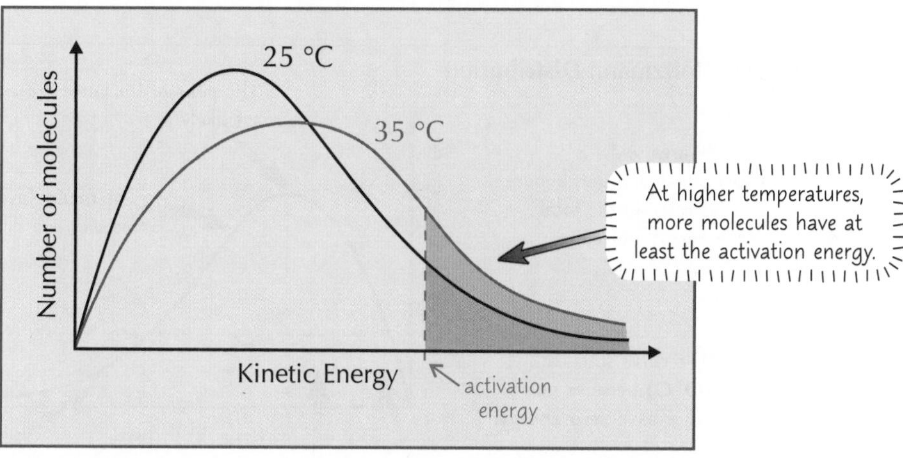

3) At higher temperatures, because the molecules are flying about **faster**, they'll **collide more often**. This is **another reason** why increasing the temperature makes a reaction faster.
4) Because you get **both** of these effects happening at once (more collisions and more energetic collisions), quite **small increases** in **temperature** can lead to quite **large increases** in **reaction rate**.

Increasing Concentration also **Increases** the **Rate** of **Reaction**

1) If you increase the **concentration** of reactants in a **solution**, the particles will on average be **closer together**.
2) If they're closer, they'll **collide more often**. If collisions occur **more frequently**, they'll have **more chances** to react. This is why increasing **concentration** increases **reaction rate**.

Increasing Pressure Increases the **Rate of Reaction** Too

1) If a reaction involves gases, increasing the **pressure** works in just the same way as increasing concentration.
2) Raising the pressure pushes all of the gas particles **closer** together, making them **more likely** to collide. So **collisions** take place **more frequently** and the reaction rate **increases**.

Catalysts Increase the **Rate** of **Reactions** Too

You can use **catalysts** to make chemical reactions happen **faster**. Learn this definition:

> A **catalyst** is a substance that increases the **rate** of a reaction by providing an **alternative reaction pathway** with a **lower activation energy**. The catalyst is **chemically unchanged** at the end of the reaction.

There's more about this on the next page. I can't wait...

1) Catalysts are **great**. They **don't** get used up in reactions, so you only need a **tiny bit** of catalyst to catalyse a **huge** amount of stuff. They **do** take part in reactions, but they're **remade** at the end.
2) Catalysts are **very fussy** about which reactions they catalyse. They often **only** work on a single reaction.
3) Because catalysts allow you to make the same amount of product **faster** (and often at a **lower temperature** too), they **save heaps of money** in industrial processes.

More on Reaction Rates

Maxwell-Boltzmann Distributions Show Why **Catalysts** Work

If you look at an **energy profile** together with a **Maxwell-Boltzmann distribution**, you can see **why** catalysts work.

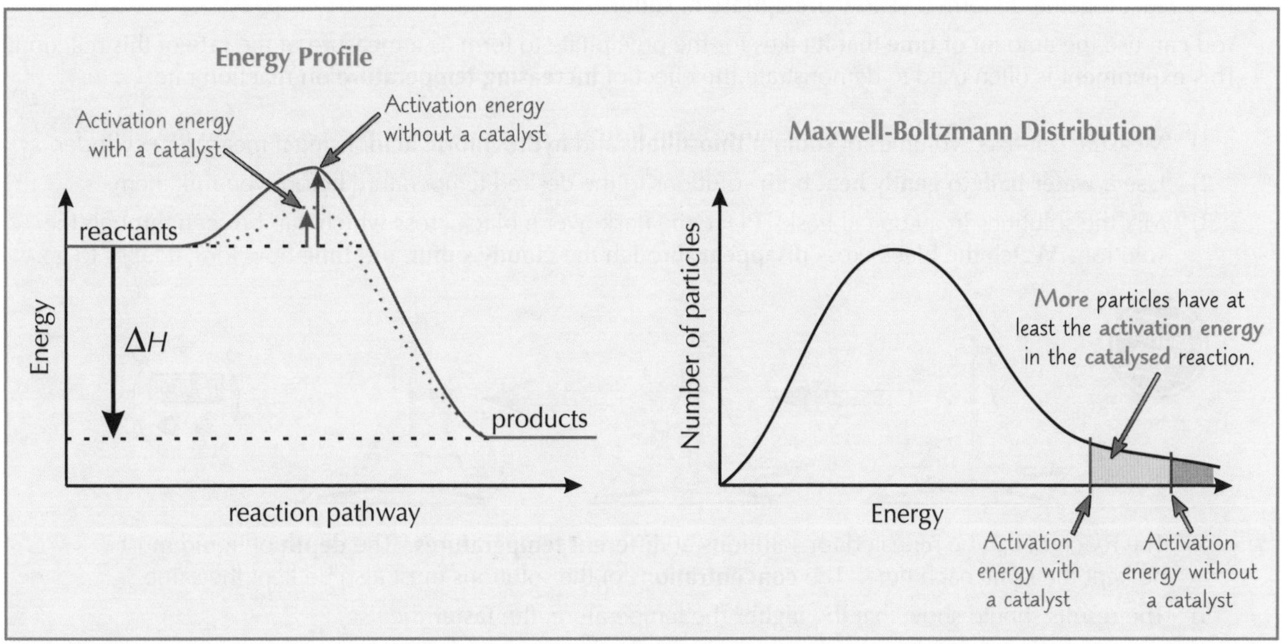

The catalyst **lowers the activation energy**, meaning there's **more particles** with **enough energy** to react when they collide. It does this by allowing the reaction to go **via a different route**. So, in a certain amount of time, **more particles react**.

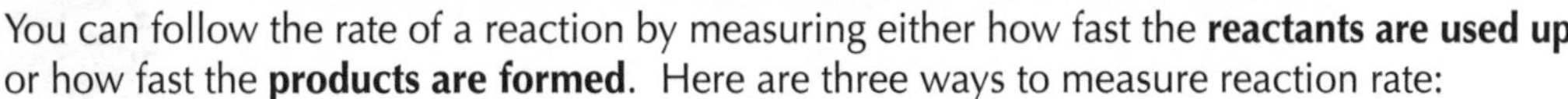

There are **Different** Ways to **Measure** Reaction Rates

You can follow the rate of a reaction by measuring either how fast the **reactants are used up** or how fast the **products are formed**. Here are three ways to measure reaction rate:

Timing how long a precipitate takes to form.

1) You can use this method when the product is a **precipitate** which clouds a solution.
2) You watch a **mark** through the solution and time how long it takes to be **obscured**.
3) If the **same observer** uses the **same mark** each time, you can compare the rates of reaction, because (roughly) the same amount of precipitate will have been **formed** when the mark becomes obscured.
4) But this method is **subjective** — different people might not agree on the exact moment the mark disappears.

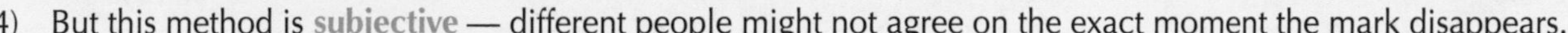

Measuring a decrease in mass.

1) When one or more of the products is a **gas**, you can measure the rate of formation using a **mass balance**.
2) As gas is given off, the mass of the reaction mixture decreases.
3) This method is **accurate** and easy to do. But it does release gas into the atmosphere, so it's usually done in a **fume cupboard**.

Measuring the volume of gas given off.

1) This involves using a **gas syringe** to measure the **volume** of gas being produced.
2) You can only use this method when one or more of the products is a **gas**.
3) Gas syringes usually give volumes to the nearest 0.1 cm^3, so this method is **accurate**.

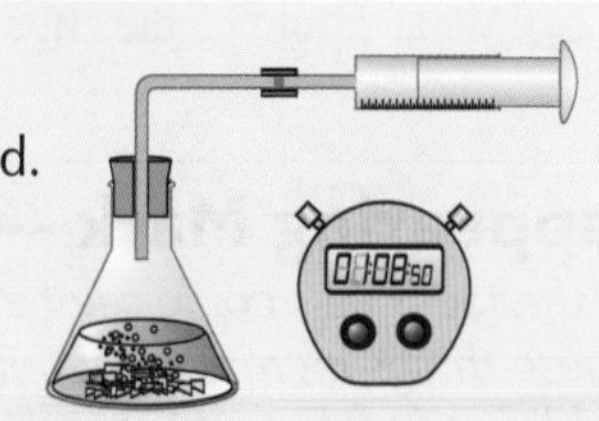

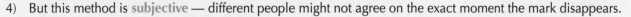

More on Reaction Rates

Example: The Reaction Between **Sodium Thiosulfate** and **Hydrochloric Acid**

Sodium thiosulfate and hydrochloric acid are both **clear, colourless solutions.**
They react together to form a **yellow precipitate** of **sulfur**.

You can use the amount of **time** that it takes for the precipitate to form as a measure of the **rate** of this reaction. This experiment is often used to demonstrate the effect of **increasing temperature** on reaction rate:

1) Measure out fixed volumes of **sodium thiosulfate** and **hydrochloric acid**, using a measuring cylinder.
2) Use a **water bath** to **gently heat** both solutions to the desired temperature before you mix them.
3) Mix the solutions in a conical flask. Place the flask over a black cross which can be seen through the solution. Watch the black cross **disappear** through the **cloudy sulfur** and **time** how long it takes to go.

PRACTICAL SKILLS

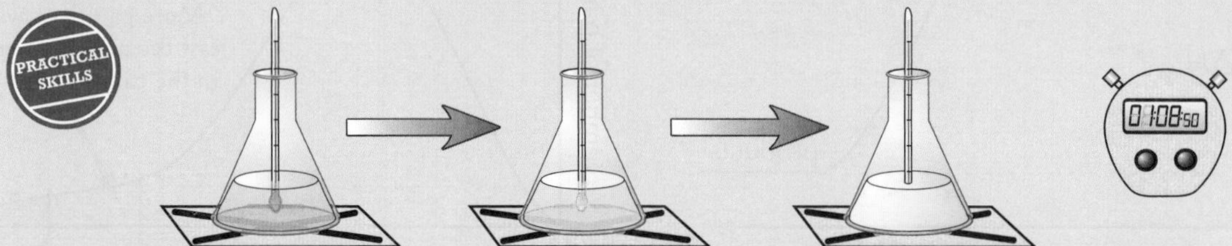

4) The reaction can be repeated for solutions at **different temperatures**. The **depth** of liquid must be kept the same each time. The **concentrations** of the solutions must also be kept the same.
5) The results should show that the **higher** the temperature, the **faster** the reaction rate and therefore the **less time** it takes for the mark to **disappear**.

Warm-Up Questions

Q1 Sketch Maxwell-Boltzmann distribution curves for the molecules in a gas at two different temperatures.

Q2 Explain why increasing the concentration of solutions increases reaction rate.

Q3 Explain what a catalyst is.

Q4 Describe a way to measure the rate of a reaction where the product is a gas.

PRACTICE QUESTIONS

Exam Question

Q1 The decomposition of hydrogen peroxide, H_2O_2, into water and oxygen is catalysed by manganese(IV) oxide, MnO_2. The Maxwell-Boltzmann distribution for the H_2O_2 molecules at 25 °C is shown below.

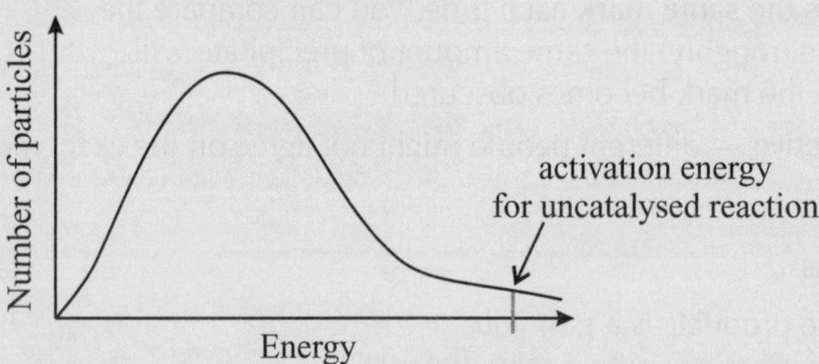

a) Draw a line on the *x*-axis to mark the approximate position of the activation energy for the catalysed process. [1 mark]

b) Explain how manganese(IV) oxide acts as a catalyst. [1 mark]

c) What would be the effect of raising the temperature on the rate of this reaction? Explain this effect. [4 marks]

Disappearing Mark — the worst magician I've ever seen...

...and the fact that I could see him was the problem to be honest. Talk about an anticlimax. Anyhow, you need to know that these things increase reaction rate: increasing temperature, increasing concentration, increasing pressure (for gases) and adding a catalyst. You need to know how they all do it too, so if you can't remember, now's the time to look back.

Reversible Reactions

There's a lot of to-ing and fro-ing on these pages. Mind your head doesn't start spinning.

Reversible Reactions Can Reach **Dynamic Equilibrium**

1) Lots of chemical reactions are **reversible** — they go **both ways**.
2) To show a reaction's reversible, you stick in a $\rightleftharpoons$. Here's an example:

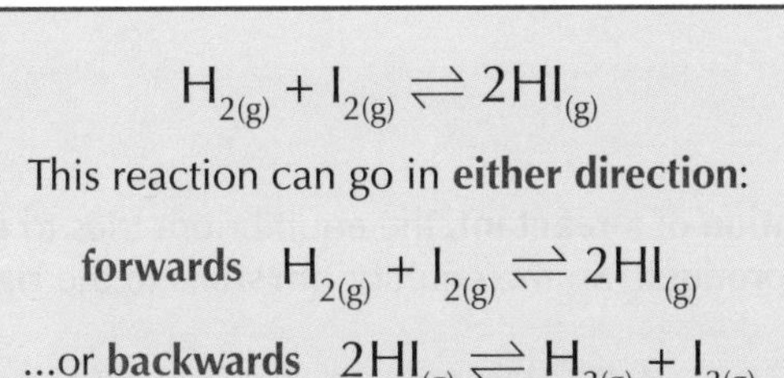

$$H_{2(g)} + I_{2(g)} \rightleftharpoons 2HI_{(g)}$$

This reaction can go in **either direction**:

forwards $H_{2(g)} + I_{2(g)} \rightleftharpoons 2HI_{(g)}$

...or **backwards** $2HI_{(g)} \rightleftharpoons H_{2(g)} + I_{2(g)}$

3) As the **reactants** get used up, the **forward** reaction **slows down** — and as more **product** is formed, the **reverse** reaction **speeds up**.
4) After a while, the forward reaction will be going at exactly the **same rate** as the backward reaction so the amounts of reactants and products **won't be changing** any more — it'll seem like **nothing's happening**.
5) This is called **dynamic equilibrium**. At equilibrium, the **concentrations** of **reactants** and **products** stay **constant**.
6) A **dynamic equilibrium** can only happen in a **closed system**. This just means nothing can get in or out.

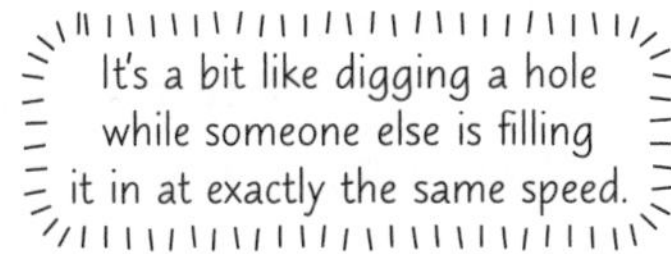

It's a bit like digging a hole while someone else is filling it in at exactly the same speed.

Le Chatelier's Principle Predicts what will Happen if **Conditions are Changed**

If you **change** the **concentration**, **pressure** or **temperature** of a reversible reaction, you're going to **alter** the **position of equilibrium**. This just means you'll end up with **different amounts** of reactants and products at equilibrium.

If the position of equilibrium moves to the **left**, you'll get more **reactants**.

$$H_{2(g)} + I_{2(g)} \rightleftharpoons 2HI_{(g)}$$

lots of H_2 and I_2 — not much HI

If the position of equilibrium moves to the **right**, you'll get more **products**.

$$H_{2(g)} + I_{2(g)} \rightleftharpoons 2HI_{(g)}$$

not much H_2 and I_2 — lots of HI

Mr and Mrs Le Chatelier celebrate another successful year in the principle business.

Le Chatelier's principle tells you how the **position of equilibrium** will change if a **condition changes**:

If a reaction at **equilibrium** is subjected to a change in **concentration**, **pressure** or **temperature**, the position of equilibrium will move to **counteract** the change.

So, basically, if you **raise the temperature**, the position of equilibrium will shift to try to **cool things down**.
And, if you **raise the pressure or concentration**, the position of equilibrium will shift to try to **reduce it again**.

Reversible Reactions

Here's Some **Handy Rules** for Using **Le Chatelier's Principle**

1) You can use Le Chatelier's principle to work out what effect changing the **concentration**, **pressure** or **temperature** will have on the **position of equilibrium**.
2) This only applies to **homogeneous equilibria** — that means reactions where every species is in the **same physical state** (e.g. all liquid or all gas).

CONCENTRATION

1) If you **increase** the **concentration** of a **reactant**, the equilibrium tries to **get rid** of the extra reactant. It does this by making **more product**. So the equilibrium shifts to the **right**.

$2SO_{2(g)} + O_{2(g)} \rightleftharpoons 2SO_{3(g)}$ — If you increase the concentration of SO_2 or O_2, the speed of the forward reaction will increase (to use up the extra reactant), moving the equilibrium to the right.

2) If you **increase** the **concentration** of the **product** (SO_3), the equilibrium tries to remove the extra product. This makes the **reverse reaction** go faster. So the equilibrium shifts to the **left**.
3) **Decreasing** the concentrations has the **opposite effect**.

PRESSURE (Changing this only affects **equilibria involving gases**.)

1) **Increasing** the pressure shifts the equilibrium to the side with **fewer** gas molecules. This **reduces** the pressure.

$2SO_{2(g)} + O_{2(g)} \rightleftharpoons 2SO_{3(g)}$ — There are 3 moles of gas on the left, but only 2 on the right. So, an increase in pressure shifts the equilibrium to the right.

2) **Decreasing** the pressure shifts the equilibrium to the side with **more** gas molecules. This **raises** the pressure again.

TEMPERATURE

1) **Increasing** the temperature means **adding heat**. The equilibrium shifts in the **endothermic (positive ΔH) direction** to absorb this heat.

$2SO_{2(g)} + O_{2(g)} \rightleftharpoons 2SO_{3(g)} \quad \Delta H = -197 \text{ kJ mol}^{-1}$ — This reaction's exothermic in the forward direction. If you increase the temperature, the equilibrium shifts to the left to absorb the extra heat.

2) **Decreasing** the temperature means **removing heat**. The equilibrium shifts in the **exothermic (negative ΔH) direction** to produce more heat, in order to counteract the drop in temperature.
3) If the forward reaction's **endothermic**, the reverse reaction will be **exothermic**, and vice versa.

Catalysts **Don't Affect** The Position of Equilibrium

Catalysts have **NO EFFECT** on the **position of equilibrium**.
They **can't** increase **yield** — but they **do** mean equilibrium is reached **faster**.

Reversible Reactions

In Industry the **Reaction Conditions** Chosen are a **Compromise**

Companies have to think about how much it **costs** to run a reaction and how much money they can make from it. This means they have a few factors to think about when they're choosing the best conditions for a reaction.

For example, **ethanol** can be produced via a reversible exothermic reaction between **ethene** and **steam**:

$$C_2H_{4(g)} + H_2O_{(g)} \rightleftharpoons C_2H_5OH_{(g)} \qquad \Delta H = -46 \text{ kJ mol}^{-1}$$

This reaction is carried out at pressures of **60-70 atmospheres** and a temperature of **300 °C**, with a catalyst of **phosphoric acid**.

1) Because this is an **exothermic reaction**, **lower** temperatures favour the forward reaction. This means that at lower temperatures **more** ethene and steam is converted to ethanol — you get a better **yield**.
2) But **lower temperatures** mean a **slower rate of reaction**. There's **no point** getting a **very high yield** of ethanol if it takes you 10 years. So 300 °C is a **compromise** between a **reasonable yield** and a **faster reaction**.
3) **High pressure** shifts the equilibrium to the side with **fewer molecules**, which favours the **forward reaction** here. **High pressure** increases the **rate** of this reaction too. So a pressure of **60-70 atmospheres** is used.
4) Cranking up the pressure even higher than that might sound like a great idea. But **very high pressures** are **really expensive** to produce. You need really strong **pipes** and **containers** to withstand high pressures.
5) So the **60-70 atmospheres** is a **compromise** — it gives a **reasonable yield** for the lowest possible **cost**.

Warm-Up Questions

Q1 Explain what the terms 'reversible reaction' and 'dynamic equilibrium' mean.

Q2 If an equilibrium moves to the right, do you get more products or reactants?

Q3 A reaction at equilibrium is endothermic in the forward direction.
What happens to the position of equilibrium as the temperature is increased?

Q4 What effect do catalysts have on equilibrium position?

Exam Questions

Q1 Nitrogen and oxygen gases were reacted together in a closed flask and allowed to reach equilibrium, with the gas nitrogen monoxide formed: $N_{2(g)} + O_{2(g)} \rightleftharpoons 2NO_{(g)}$ $\Delta H = +181 \text{ kJ mol}^{-1}$

a) State Le Chatelier's principle. [1 mark]

b) Explain how the following changes would affect the position of equilibrium of the above reaction:

i) Pressure is increased. [2 marks]

ii) Temperature is reduced. [2 marks]

iii) The concentration of nitrogen monoxide is reduced. [2 marks]

c) State the effect that a catalyst would have on the composition of the equilibrium mixture. [1 mark]

Q2 Ethanol can be manufactured from ethene and steam: $C_2H_{4(g)} + H_2O_{(g)} \rightleftharpoons C_2H_5OH_{(g)}$ $\Delta H = -46 \text{ kJ mol}^{-1}$
Typical conditions are 300 °C and 60-70 atmospheres.

a) Explain why, for this reaction, decreasing the temperature would increase the yield of ethanol. [3 marks]

b) i) What effect would increasing pressure have on the yield of ethanol? [2 marks]

ii) Suggest why a pressure higher than the one quoted is not often used. [1 mark]

Reverse psychology — don't bother learning this rubbish...

Make sure that you know what happens to a reaction at equilibrium if you change the conditions. A quick reminder about pressure — remember that if there are the same number of molecules of gas on each side of the equation, then you can raise the pressure as high as you like and it won't make a blind bit of difference to the position of equilibrium.

The Equilibrium Constant

You don't just need to know what dynamic equilibrium means. It's nice to be able to describe what's going on but you know scientists — they do insist on using mathsy stuff. Here come the numbers...

K_c is the **Equilibrium Constant**

[X] = the concentration of species X in mol dm^{-3}.

If you know the **molar concentration** of each substance at equilibrium, you can work out the **equilibrium constant, K_c**.
The equilibrium constant can be written as an expression, like this:

$$aA + bB \rightleftharpoons dD + eE, \quad K_c = \frac{[D]^d[E]^e}{[A]^a[B]^b}$$

You can just bung the **equilibrium concentrations** into your expression to work out the **value** for K_c.
The **units** are a bit trickier though — they **vary**, so you have to work them out after each calculation.

Example: Hydrogen gas and iodine gas are mixed in a closed flask. Hydrogen iodide is formed.

$$H_{2(g)} + I_{2(g)} \rightleftharpoons 2HI_{(g)}$$

Calculate the equilibrium constant for the reaction at 640 K. The equilibrium concentrations are:
[HI] = 0.80 mol dm^{-3}, [H_2] = 0.10 mol dm^{-3}, and [I_2] = 0.10 mol dm^{-3}.

Just stick the concentrations into the **expression** for K_c: $K_c = \frac{[HI]^2}{[H_2][I_2]} = \frac{0.80^2}{0.10 \times 0.10} = 64$

To work out the **units** of K_c put the units in the expression instead of the numbers:

Units of $K_c = \frac{(\text{mol dm}^{-3})^2}{(\text{mol dm}^{-3})(\text{mol dm}^{-3})}$ — the concentration units cancel, so there are **no units** for K_c.

So K_c is just **64**.

You Might Need to **Work Out** the **Equilibrium Concentrations**

You might have to figure out some of the **equilibrium concentrations** before you can find K_c:

Example: 0.20 moles of phosphorus(V) chloride decomposes at 600 K in a vessel of 5.00 dm^3.
The equilibrium mixture is found to contain 0.080 moles of chlorine.
Write the expression for K_c and calculate its value, including units.

$$PCl_{5(g)} \rightleftharpoons PCl_{3(g)} + Cl_{2(g)}$$

First find out how many moles of PCl_5 and PCl_3 there are at equilibrium:

The **equation** tells you that when **1 mole of PCl_5** decomposes, **1 mole of PCl_3** and **1 mole of Cl_2** are formed.
So if 0.080 moles of chlorine are produced at equilibrium, then there will be **0.080 moles** of PCl_3 as well.
0.080 moles of PCl_5 must have decomposed, so there will be **0.12 moles** left (0.20 – 0.080).

Divide each number of moles by the volume of the flask to give the molar concentrations:

[PCl_3] = [Cl_2] = 0.080 ÷ 5.00 = **0.016 mol dm^{-3}** [PCl_5] = 0.12 ÷ 5.00 = **0.024 mol dm^{-3}**

Put the concentrations in the expression for K_c and calculate it: $K_c = \frac{[PCl_3][Cl_2]}{[PCl_5]} = \frac{0.016 \times 0.016}{0.024} = 0.011$

Now find the units of K_c: Units of $K_c = \frac{(\text{mol dm}^{-3})(\text{mol dm}^{-3})}{(\text{mol dm}^{-3})}$ = **mol dm^{-3}** So K_c = **0.011 mol dm^{-3}**

The Equilibrium Constant

K_c can be used to Find **Concentrations** in an **Equilibrium Mixture**

Example: When ethanoic acid was allowed to reach equilibrium with ethanol at 25 °C, it was found that the equilibrium mixture contained 2.0 mol dm⁻³ ethanoic acid and 3.5 mol dm⁻³ ethanol. The K_c of the equilibrium is 4.0 at 25 °C. What are the concentrations of the other components?

$$CH_3COOH_{(l)} + C_2H_5OH_{(l)} \rightleftharpoons CH_3COOC_2H_{5(l)} + H_2O_{(l)}$$

Put all the values you know in the K_c expression: $K_c = \frac{[CH_3COOC_2H_5][H_2O]}{[CH_3COOH][C_2H_5OH]} \Rightarrow 4.0 = \frac{[CH_3COOC_2H_5][H_2O]}{2.0 \times 3.5}$

Rearranging this gives: $[CH_3COOC_2H_5][H_2O] = 4.0 \times 2.0 \times 3.5 = 28$

From the equation you know that $[CH_3COOC_2H_5] = [H_2O]$, so: $[CH_3COOC_2H_5] = [H_2O] = \sqrt{28} = 5.3 \text{ mol dm}^{-3}$

The concentration of $CH_3COOC_2H_5$ and H_2O is **5.3 mol dm⁻³**

Temperature Changes Alter K_c

Remember: if the temperature rises, the equilibrium shifts in the endothermic (+ve ΔH) direction to absorb the heat. If the temperature falls, the equilibrium shifts in the exothermic (–ve ΔH) direction to replace the heat.

1) The value of K_c is only **valid** for one particular **temperature**.
2) If you change the temperature of the system, you will also change the **equilibrium concentrations** of the products and reactants, so **K_c will change**.
3) If the temperature change means there's **more product** at equilibrium, **K_c will rise.** If it means there's **less product** at equilibrium, **K_c will decrease.** For example:

The reaction on the right is exothermic in the forward direction. If you **increase** the temperature, you favour the **endothermic** reaction. This means that **less product** is formed.

Exothermic ⟶

$$N_{2(g)} + 3H_{2(g)} \rightleftharpoons 2NH_{3(g)} \quad \Delta H = -46.2 \text{ kJ mol}^{-1}$$

⟵ Endothermic

$$K_c = \frac{[NH_3]^2}{[N_2][H_2]^3}$$

$[NH_3]^2$ ⟵ The concentration of NH_3 will be reduced.
$[N_2][H_2]^3$ ⟵ The concentrations of N_2 and H_2 will increase.

As the temperature **increases**, $[NH_3]$ will **decrease** and $[N_2]$ and $[H_2]$ will **increase**, so K_c will **decrease**.

4) Changing the **concentration** of a reactant or product, will **not affect** the value of K_c.
5) **Catalysts** don't affect K_c either — they'll speed up the reaction in both directions by the same amount, so they just help the system to reach equilibrium **faster**.

Warm-Up Question

Q1 If a reversible reaction has an exothermic forward reaction, how will increasing the temperature affect K_c?

Exam Questions

Q1 A sample of pure hydrogen iodide is placed in a sealed flask, and heated to 443 °C.
The following equilibrium is established: $2HI_{(g)} \rightleftharpoons H_{2(g)} + I_{2(g)}$ ($K_c = 0.0200$)
At equilibrium, $[I_2] = 0.770$ mol dm⁻³. Find the equilibrium concentration of HI. [4 marks]

Q2 Nitrogen dioxide dissociates according to the equation $2NO_{2(g)} \rightleftharpoons 2NO_{(g)} + O_{2(g)}$

When 34.5 g of nitrogen dioxide were heated in a vessel of volume 9.80 dm³ at 500 °C, 7.04 g of oxygen were found in the equilibrium mixture.

a) Calculate: i) the number of moles of nitrogen dioxide originally. [1 mark]

ii) the number of moles of each gas in the equilibrium mixture. [3 marks]

b) Find the value of K_c at this temperature, and give its units. [4 marks].

I still don't like equilibrium positions — so nothing's changed there...

Working out K_c is easy as pie once you've got all the concentrations figured out. Make sure you practise writing down expressions for the equilibrium constant and doing all those mathsy bits — the questions here should help you with that.

Redox Reactions

This double page has more occurrences of "oxidation" than The Beatles "All You Need is Love" features the word "love".

If Electrons are Transferred, it's a **Redox Reaction**

1) A **loss** of electrons is called **oxidation**.
2) A **gain** in electrons is called **reduction**.
3) Reduction and oxidation happen **simultaneously** — hence the term "**redox**" reaction.
4) An **oxidising agent accepts** electrons and gets reduced.
5) A **reducing agent donates** electrons and gets oxidised.

Example: the formation of **sodium chloride** from sodium and chlorine is a **redox reaction**:

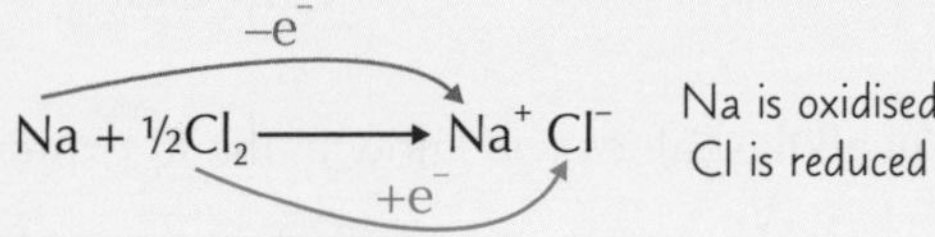

You Need to Know the **Rules for Assigning Oxidation States***

*Or 'oxidation numbers' if you prefer.

The oxidation state of an element tells you the **total number** of **electrons** it has **donated** or **accepted**. For example, in the redox reaction shown above, the sodium atom has **donated one electron**, so it has an oxidation state of **+1**. The chlorine atom has **accepted one electron**, so it has an oxidation state of **–1**.

There's a set of **rules** that you can use to work out the oxidation state of an atom when it's in a **compound**, in an **ion**, or just **on its own**. Take a deep breath, here we go...

1) Uncombined **elements**, like He and Ar, have an oxidation state of **0**.

2) Elements just bonded to **identical atoms**, like O_2 and H_2, also have an oxidation state of **0**.

3) The oxidation state of a simple **monatomic ion**, like Na^+, is the same as its **charge**.

In this case, that's +1.

4) In **compound ions**, the **overall oxidation state** is just the ion charge.

SO_4^{2-} — overall oxidation state = –2,
oxidation state of **O = –2** (total = 4 × –2 = –8),
so oxidation state of **S = –2 – (–8) = +6**

In a compound ion, the most electronegative element has a negative oxidation state. The other elements have more positive oxidation states.

5) The sum of the oxidation states for a **neutral compound** is 0.

Fe_2O_3 — overall oxidation state = 0
oxidation state of **O = –2** (total = 3 × –2 = –6),
so oxidation state of **Fe = (0 – (–6)) ÷ 2 = +3**

6) Combined **oxygen** is nearly always –2, except in peroxides, where it's –1,
(and in the fluorides OF_2, where it's +2, and O_2F_2, where it's +1 and O_2 where it's O).

In **H_2O**, oxidation state of **O = –2**, but in **H_2O_2**, oxidation state of **O = –1**.

7) Combined **hydrogen** is +1, except in metal hydrides where it is –1 (and H_2 where it's 0).

In **HF**, oxidation state of **H = +1**, but in **NaH**, oxidation state of **H = –1**.

Roman Numerals Show Oxidation States

Sometimes, oxidation states aren't clear from the formula of a compound.

If you see **Roman numerals** in a chemical name, it's an **oxidation number**.

E.g. iron has oxidation state **+2** in **iron(II) sulfate** ($FeSO_4$), but it has oxidation state **+3** in **iron(III) sulfate** ($Fe_2(SO_4)_3$).

Hands up if you like Roman numerals...

Redox Reactions

You can Write **Half-Equations** and Combine them into **Redox Equations**

1) **Ionic half-equations** show oxidation or reduction.
2) You show the **electrons** that are being lost or gained in a half-equation.
For example, this is the half-equation for the **oxidation of sodium**: $Na \rightarrow Na^+ + e^-$
3) You can **combine** half-equations for different oxidising or reducing agents together to make **full equations** for redox reactions.

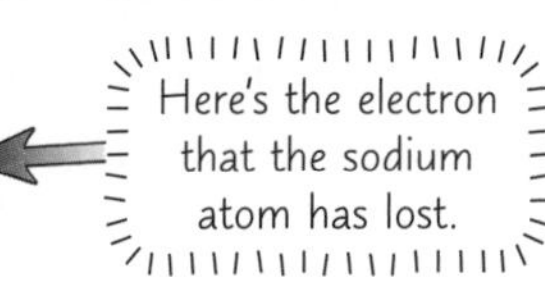

Here's the electron that the sodium atom has lost.

Magnesium burns in oxygen to form magnesium oxide.
Oxygen is reduced to O^{2-}:

$$O_2 + 4e^- \rightarrow 2O^{2-}$$

Make sure the atoms and charges balance.

Magnesium is oxidised to Mg^{2+}:

$$Mg \rightarrow Mg^{2+} + 2e^-$$

You need both equations to contain the same number of electrons. So double everything in the second equation.

$$2Mg \rightarrow 2Mg^{2+} + 4e^-$$

Combining the half-equations makes:

$$2Mg + O_2 \rightarrow 2MgO$$

The electrons aren't included in the full equation. You end up with four on each side — so they cancel.
$2Mg + O_2 + 4e^- \rightarrow 2MgO + 4e^-$

Aluminium reacts with **chlorine** to form **aluminium chloride**.
Aluminium is oxidised to Al^{3+}:

$$Al \rightarrow Al^{3+} + 3e^-$$

Make sure the atoms and charges balance.

Chlorine is reduced to Cl^-:

$$Cl_2 + 2e^- \rightarrow 2Cl^-$$

Now make sure the equations each contain the same number of electrons.

$$Al \rightarrow Al^{3+} + 3e^- \xrightarrow{\times 2} 2Al \rightarrow 2Al^{3+} + 6e^-$$
$$Cl_2 + 2e^- \rightarrow 2Cl^- \xrightarrow{\times 3} 3Cl_2 + 6e^- \rightarrow 6Cl^-$$

Combining the half-equations makes:

$$2Al + 3Cl_2 \rightarrow 2AlCl_3$$

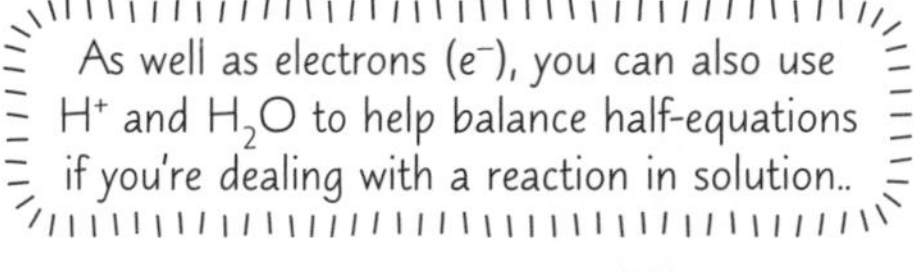

As well as electrons (e^-), you can also use H^+ and H_2O to help balance half-equations if you're dealing with a reaction in solution..

Warm-Up Questions

Q1 What is a reducing agent?
Q2 What is the oxidation state of hydrogen in H_2 gas?
Q3 What is the usual oxidation state of oxygen when it's in a compound?

Exam Questions

PRACTICE QUESTIONS

Q1 Lithium oxide forms when lithium is burned in air. Combustion is a redox reaction.
The equation for the combustion of lithium is: $4Li_{(s)} + O_{2(g)} \rightarrow 2Li_2O_{(s)}$

a) Define oxidation in terms of the movement of electrons. [1 mark]

b) What is the oxidation state of lithium in: i) Li ii) Li_2O [2 marks]

c) State which reactant is this reaction is reduced.
Write a half-equation for this reduction reaction. [2 marks]

Q2 The half-equation for chlorine acting as an oxidising agent is: $Cl_2 + 2e^- \rightarrow 2Cl^-$

a) Define the term oxidising agent in terms of electron movement. [1 mark]

b) Indium is a metal that can be oxidised by chlorine.
Write a balanced half-equation for the oxidation of indium metal to form In^{3+} ions. [1 marks]

c) Use your answer to b) and the equation above to form a balanced equation for the reaction of indium with chlorine by combining half-equations. [2 marks]

Oxidising agent SALE NOW ON — everything's reduced...

Half-equations look evil, with all those electrons flying about. But they're not too bad really. Just make sure you get lots of practice using them. (Oh, look, there are some handy questions up there).

And while we're on the redox page, I suppose you ought to learn the most famous memory aid thingy in the world...

OIL RIG
— **O**xidation **I**s **L**oss
— **R**eduction **I**s **G**ain
(of electrons)

Extra Exam Practice

That's Unit 1 Sections 1-5 all wrapped up. Time to put what you've learnt to the test. In your exams you could be asked questions on a variety of different topics. But for now, these questions are just based on the chemistry covered in the first five sections. So get stuck in and see what you know.

- Have a look at this example of how to answer a tricky exam question.
- Then check how much you've understood from Unit 1 Sections 1-5 by having a go at the questions on the next page.

There are also some synoptic questions covering the whole AS-level/Year 1 course on p.112-114. Have a go at those once you've mastered all the sections in this book.

1 30 cm^3 of 0.25 mol dm^{-3} silver nitrate solution was added to 0.30 g of zinc powder in a beaker. The products of the subsequent reaction were zinc nitrate and silver. During the reaction, the temperature changed from 18.0 °C to 23.1 °C.

Write a balanced equation for the reaction that takes place.
Calculate the enthalpy change per mole of zinc.
Assume the solution has a specific heat capacity of 4.18 J g^{-1} K^{-1}.

(7 marks)

In an extended calculation like this you should set out your working in a logical order so that the marker can follow it easily.

1

$Zn + 2AgNO_3 \rightarrow Zn(NO_3)_2 + 2Ag$

Make sure you know the charges on common ions to help you construct balanced chemical equations.

Change in temperature, ΔT = 23.1 − 18.0
= 5.1 °C

Heat gained in joules, $\boldsymbol{q = mc\Delta T}$
= 30 × 4.18 × 5.1
= 639.54 J

It's a good idea to state any equations you use.

Heat gained in kJ, q = **639.54 ÷ 1000**
= **0.63954** kJ

Enthalpy changes are measured in kJ per mole so convert heat energy gained to kJ.

Don't round any answers until the end. You can use your calculator memory to input long values.

Moles of $AgNO_3$ = volume × concentration
= (30 ÷ 1000) × 0.25
= 7.5 × 10^{-3} moles

Moles of Zn in beaker = mass ÷ M_r
= 0.30 ÷ 65.4
= 4.587... × 10^{-3} moles

To find the enthalpy change per mole of zinc, you need to work out how many moles of zinc took part in the reaction. So you have to calculate the amount of each reactant at the start of the reaction to see whether or not zinc was in excess.

From the balanced equation, 2 moles of $AgNO_3$ react with 1 mole of Zn.
So **moles of Zn reacting** = 7.5 × 10^{-3} ÷ 2
= 3.75 × 10^{-3} moles

Enthalpy change per mole of Zn, ΔH = q ÷ moles of zinc reacting
= 0.63954 ÷ (3.75 × 10^{-3})
= **−170.544** kJ mol^{-1}
= **−170** kJ mol^{-1}

The temperature increases, so this is an exothermic reaction and ΔH will be negative. You need to insert the minus sign into your answer.

Round your final answer to the lowest number of significant figures given in the question (in this case it's two).

You'd get 7 marks for the correct answer, but if you got the answer wrong, you'd get some marks for showing your working. There's 1 mark for giving a balanced equation, 1 mark for calculating the heat gained (q), 1 mark for calculating moles of silver nitrate, 1 mark for calculating moles of zinc in the beaker, 1 mark for calculating moles of zinc reacting and 1 mark for calculating ΔH.

Extra Exam Practice

2 Hydrogen can be produced by reacting methane gas and steam together at a high temperature.

$$CH_{4(g)} + H_2O_{(g)} \rightleftharpoons 3H_{2\,(g)} + CO_{(g)}$$

The Maxwell-Boltzmann curve in **Figure 1** shows the distribution of molecular kinetic energies in a sample of methane gas at 1000 K.

Figure 1

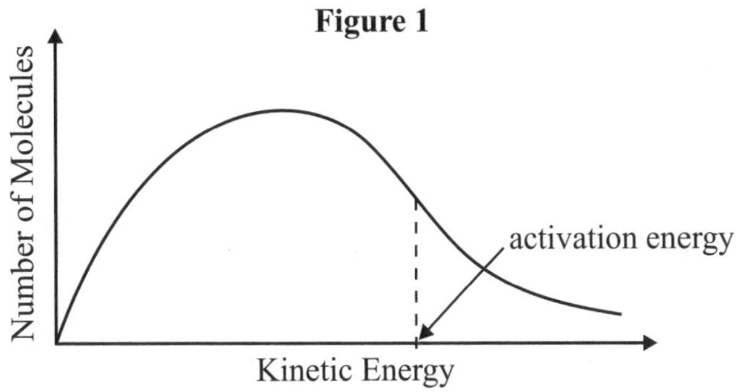

2.1 Sketch a curve on **Figure 1** to show the distribution of molecular energies of methane at 647 °C.
(2 marks)

2.2 Suggest why, at 1000 K, the curve does not touch the *x*-axis.
(1 mark)

2.3 A reaction between methane gas and excess steam takes place in a reaction vessel. 67.2 g of carbon monoxide is formed. The percentage yield for the reaction is 85.6%.

Calculate the mass of methane gas present in the vessel at the start of the reaction.
(4 marks)

3 Ammonia is produced in the Haber process according to the following equation:

$$N_2 + 3H_2 \rightleftharpoons 2NH_3$$

3.1 Ammonia is removed from the reaction mixture by cooling it.
Explain, in terms of intermolecular forces, why ammonia can be removed in this way.
(2 marks)

3.2 Ammonia reacts with oxygen in a combustion reaction to form water and a nitrogen-containing species where nitrogen has an oxidation state of +2.

Write an equation for calculating the enthalpy change of the reaction, given the enthalpies of formation for each product and reactant. Include a balanced reaction equation in your answer.
(3 marks)

3.3 The formula for calculating density is: density = $\frac{\text{mass}}{\text{volume}}$
The density of ammonia is 770 g m^{-3} at standard temperature and pressure (0 °C and 1.0×10^5 Pa).
Use this information to calculate the relative molecular mass of ammonia. R = 8.31 J K^{-1} mol^{-1}
(4 marks)

3.4 A sample of nitrogen was introduced into a TOF mass spectrometer in order to determine the relative molecular mass. Electrospray ionisation was used to ionise the sample.

Describe the process that occurs during this type of ionisation.
Suggest a value for the mass/charge ratio of the most abundant ion.
(2 marks)

Periodicity

Periodicity is one of those words you hear a lot in chemistry without ever really knowing what it means. Well it basically means trends that occur (in physical and chemical properties) as you move across the periods. E.g. metal to non-metal is a trend that occurs going left to right in each period... The trends repeat each period.

The **Periodic Table** arranges Elements by **Proton Number**

1) The periodic table is arranged into **periods** (rows) and **groups** (columns), by atomic (proton) number.
2) All the elements **within a period** have the same number of **electron shells** (if you don't worry about s and p sub-shells). E.g. the elements in Period 2 have 2 electron shells.
3) All the elements **within a group** have the **same number** of electrons in their **outer shell** — so they have **similar properties**.
4) The **group number** tells you the number of electrons in the outer shell, e.g. Group 1 elements have 1 electron in their outer shell, Group 4 elements have 4 electrons and so on. The **exception** is **Group 0**. Group 0 elements all have full outer shells — that's two electrons for Helium, and eight electrons for all the others.

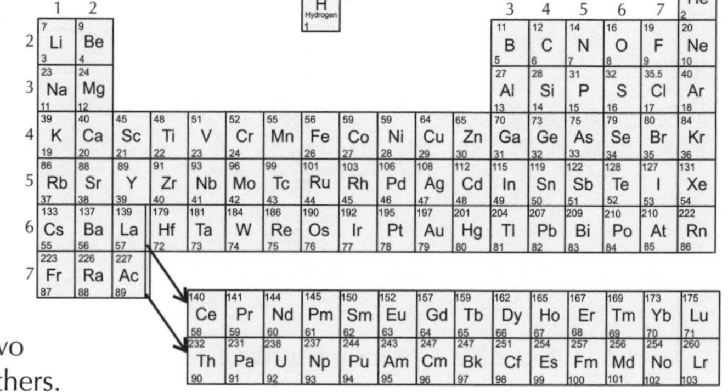

You can use the Periodic Table to work out **Electronic Configurations**

The periodic table can be split into an **s block**, **d block**, **p block** and **f block** like this: Doing this shows you which sub-shells all the electrons go into.

See page 8 if this sub-shell malarkey doesn't ring a bell.

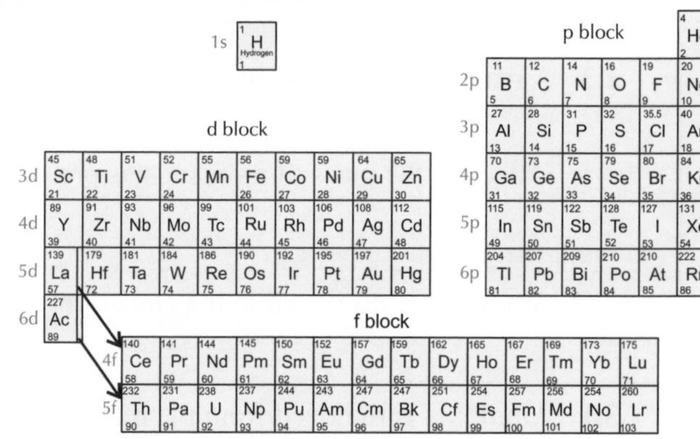

When you've got the periodic table **labelled** with the **shells** and **sub-shells** like the one on the right, it's pretty easy to read off the **electronic structure** of any element. Just start at the top and work your way across and down until you get to your element.

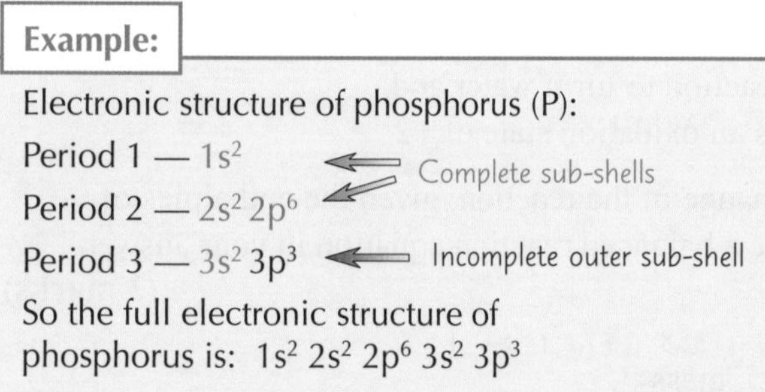
Example:

Electronic structure of phosphorus (P):

Period 1 — $1s^2$ ⟸ Complete sub-shells

Period 2 — $2s^2\ 2p^6$

Period 3 — $3s^2\ 3p^3$ ⟸ Incomplete outer sub-shell

So the full electronic structure of phosphorus is: $1s^2\ 2s^2\ 2p^6\ 3s^2\ 3p^3$

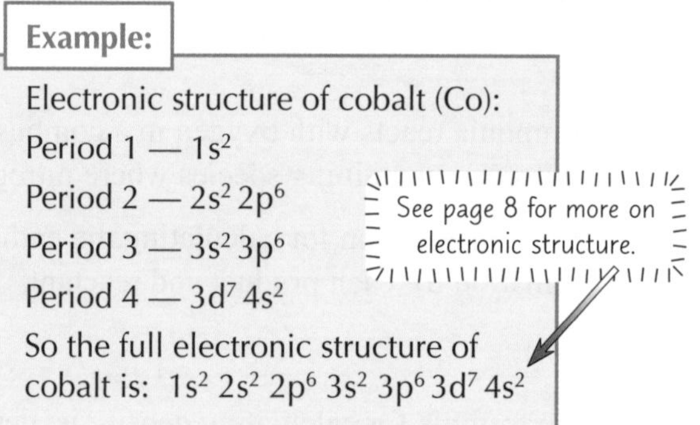
Example:

Electronic structure of cobalt (Co):

Period 1 — $1s^2$

Period 2 — $2s^2\ 2p^6$

Period 3 — $3s^2\ 3p^6$

Period 4 — $3d^7\ 4s^2$

So the full electronic structure of cobalt is: $1s^2\ 2s^2\ 2p^6\ 3s^2\ 3p^6\ 3d^7\ 4s^2$

See page 8 for more on electronic structure.

Atomic Radius **Decreases** across a Period

1) As the number of protons increases, the **positive charge** of the nucleus increases. This means electrons are **pulled closer** to the nucleus, making the atomic radius smaller.
2) The extra electrons that the elements gain across a period are added to the **outer energy level** so they don't really provide any extra shielding effect (shielding is mainly provided by the electrons in the inner shells).

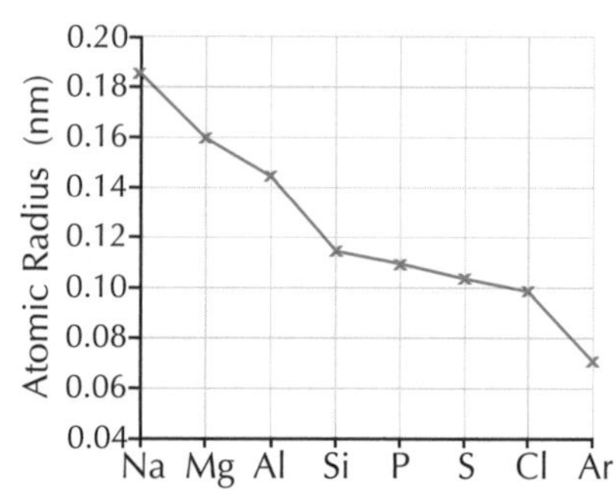

Periodicity

Melting Point is linked to **Bond Strength** and **Structure**

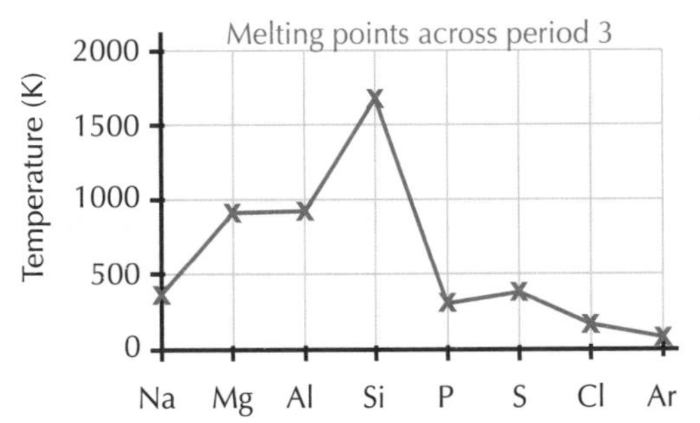

1) Melting points vary across a period as they depend on the **structure** of elements and the **bonding** within them. The graph on the left shows the melting points across **Period 3**.
2) Sodium, magnesium and aluminium are **metals**. Their melting and boiling points **increase** across the period because the **metal-metal bonds** get stronger. The bonds get stronger because the metal ions have an increasing positive charge, an increasing number of delocalised electrons and a decreasing radius.
3) Silicon is **macromolecular**, with a tetrahedral structure — **strong covalent bonds** link all its atoms together. **A lot** of energy is needed to break these bonds, so silicon has a **high** melting point.
4) Phosphorus (P_4), sulfur (S_8) and chlorine (Cl_2) are all **molecular substances**. Their melting points depend upon the strength of the **van der Waals forces** (see page 31) between the molecules. Van der Waals forces are weak and easily overcome so these elements have **low** melting points.
5) More atoms in a molecule mean stronger van der Waals forces. Sulfur is the **biggest molecule** (S_8), so it's got a higher melting point than phosphorus or chlorine.
6) Argon has a **very low** melting point because it exists as **individual atoms** (it's monatomic) resulting in **very weak** van der Waals forces.

Sam is looking hot in the latest periodic trends.

Ionisation Energy Generally **Increases** across a Period

This is because of the **increasing attraction** between the outer shell electrons and the nucleus, due to the number of **protons** increasing (there are a few blips in the trend however — check back to pages 12-13 for more details).

Warm-Up Questions

Q1 Which elements of Period 3 are found in the s block of the periodic table?

Q2 Write down the electronic configuration of sodium.

Q3 Which element in Period 3 has the largest atomic radius?

Q4 Which element in Period 3 has the highest melting point?

Exam Questions

Q1 Explain why the melting point of magnesium is higher than that of sodium. [3 marks]

Q2 This table shows the melting points for the Period 3 elements.

Element	Na	Mg	Al	Si	P	S	Cl	Ar
Melting point / K	371	923	933	1687	317	388	172	84

In terms of structure and bonding explain why:

a) silicon has a high melting point. [2 marks]

b) the melting point of sulfur is higher than phosphorus. [2 marks]

Q3 State and explain the trend in atomic radius across Period 3. [3 marks]

Periodic trends — isn't that just another name for retro chic...

OK, I'll admit it, when it comes to fashion, I'm behind the times. I refuse to stop wearing my favourite pair of neon legwarmers just because they're a tiny bit out of date. The thing is though, every now and then eighties stuff comes back into fashion for a while and suddenly I'm bang on trend. Mind you, that doesn't stop me looking totally ridiculous.

Group 2 — The Alkaline Earth Metals

Group 2, AKA the alkaline earth metals, are in the "s block" of the periodic table. There are four pages about these jolly fellas and their compounds, so we've got a lot to do — best get on...

Group 2 Elements **Lose Two Electrons** when they React

Element	Atom	Ion
Be	$1s^2 2s^2$	$1s^2$
Mg	$1s^2 2s^2 2p^6 3s^2$	$1s^2 2s^2 2p^6$
Ca	$1s^2 2s^2 2p^6 3s^2 3p^6 4s^2$	$1s^2 2s^2 2p^6 3s^2 3p^6$

Group 2 elements all have two electrons in their outer shell (s^2).

They lose their two outer electrons to form **2+ ions**. Their ions then have every atom's dream electronic structure — that of a **noble gas**.

Atomic Radius **Increases** Down the Group

As you go **down** a group in the periodic table, the **atomic radius** gets **larger**. This is because extra **electron shells** are added as you go down the group.

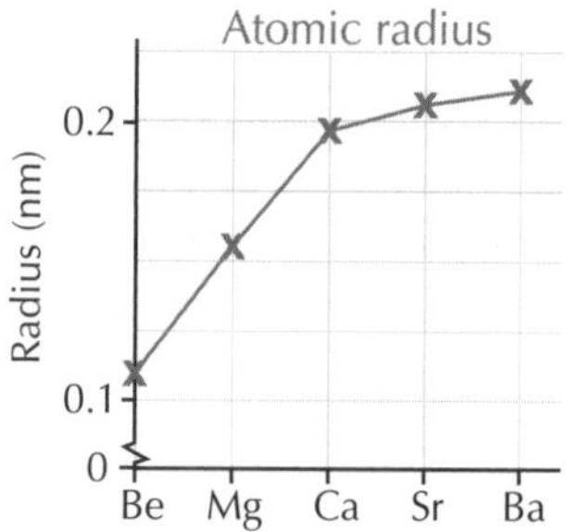

First Ionisation Energy **Decreases** Down the Group

1) Each element down Group 2 has an **extra electron shell** compared to the one above.
2) The extra inner shells **shield** the outer electrons from the attraction of the nucleus.
3) Also, the extra shell means that the outer electrons are **further away** from the nucleus, which greatly reduces the nucleus's attraction.

Mr Kelly has one final attempt at explaining electron shielding to his students...

Both of these factors make it **easier** to remove outer electrons, resulting in a **lower first ionisation energy**.

The positive charge of the nucleus does increase as you go down a group (due to the extra protons), but this effect is overridden by the effect of the extra shells.

Reactivity **Increases** Down the Group

1) As you go down the group, the **first ionisation energy** decreases. This is due to the increasing atomic radius and shielding effect (see above).
2) When Group 2 elements react they **lose electrons**, forming positive ions. The easier it is to lose electrons (i.e. the lower the first and second ionisation energies), the more reactive the element, so **reactivity increases** down the group.

Melting Points Generally **Decrease** Down the Group

1) The Group 2 elements have typical **metallic structures**, with **positive ions** in a **crystal structure** surrounded by **delocalised electrons** from the outer electron shells.
2) Going **down** the group the metal ions get **bigger**. But the number of delocalised electrons per atom doesn't change (it's always 2) and neither does the charge on the ion (it's always +2).
3) The **larger** the ionic radius, the **further away** the delocalised electrons are from the positive nuclei and the **less attraction** they feel. So it takes **less energy** to break the bonds, which means the melting points generally decrease as you go down the group. However, there's a big 'blip' at magnesium, because the crystal structure (the arrangement of the metallic ions) changes.

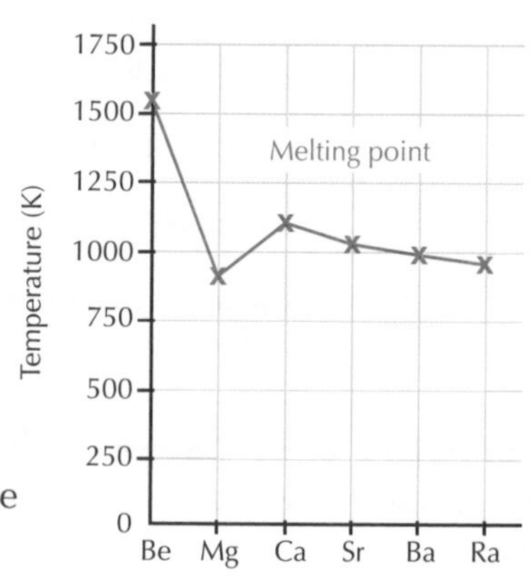

Group 2 — The Alkaline Earth Metals

Group 2 Elements React With **Water**

When Group 2 elements react, they are **oxidised** from a state of **0** to **+2**, forming M^{2+} ions.

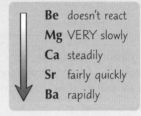

	$M \rightarrow M^{2+} + 2e^-$	E.g.	$Ca \rightarrow Ca^{2+} + 2e^-$
Oxidation state:	0 +2		0 +2

The Group 2 metals react with water to give a **metal hydroxide and hydrogen.**

$$M_{(s)} + 2H_2O_{(l)} \rightarrow M(OH)_{2(aq)} + H_{2(g)}$$

Oxidation state: 0 → +2

e.g. $$Ca_{(s)} + 2H_2O_{(l)} \rightarrow Ca(OH)_{2(aq)} + H_{2(g)}$$

The water is the oxidising agent in this reaction.

They react **more readily** down the group because the **ionisation energies** decrease.

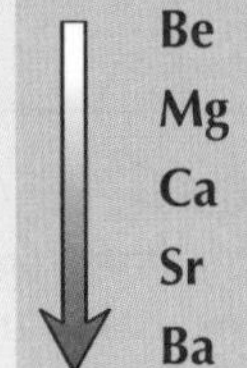

Be doesn't react
Mg VERY slowly
Ca steadily
Sr fairly quickly
Ba rapidly

Warm-Up Questions

PRACTICE QUESTIONS

Q1 Do Group 2 elements lose or gain electrons when they react? How many electrons do they lose/gain?

Q2 Which is the least reactive metal in Group 2?

Q3 Which of the following increases in size down Group 2? **atomic radius, first ionisation energy, melting point**

Q4 Why does reactivity with water increase down Group 2?

Exam Questions

Q1 a) Write out the electron configurations of magnesium and calcium. [2 marks]

b) Explain the difference between the first ionisation energies of magnesium and calcium. [3 marks]

Q2 The table shows the atomic radii of three elements from Group 2.

Element	Atomic Radius (nm)
X	0.112
Y	0.219
Z	0.194

a) Predict which element would react most rapidly with water. [1 mark]

b) Explain your answer. [2 marks]

Q3 Which element has been oxidised in the reaction below? State the change in its oxidation number.

$$Ba_{(s)} + 2H_2O_{(l)} \rightarrow Ba(OH)_{2(aq)} + H_{2(g)}$$ [2 marks]

Q4 The table shows the melting points of three elements from Group 2.

Element	Calcium	Strontium	Barium
Melting point (K)	1115	1050	1000

Explain the pattern in melting points that this table shows. [3 marks]

Bored of Group 2 trends? Me too. Let's play noughts and crosses...

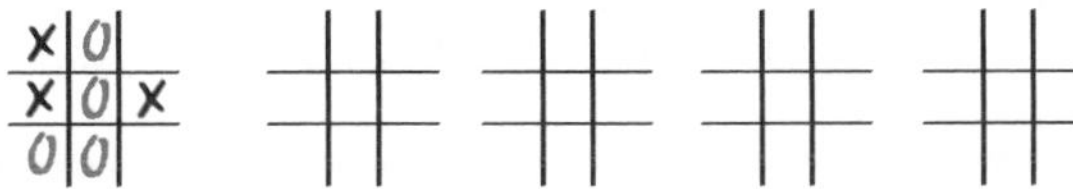

Noughts and crosses is pretty rubbish really, isn't it? It's always a draw. Ho hum. Back to Chemistry then, I guess...

Uses of the Group 2 Elements

Nice theories are all well and good but theories don't pay the bills. It's all about applications these days. So how can all this knowledge about Group 2 elements be put to good use? Read on to find out...

Solubility Trends in Group 2 Depend on the **Compound Anion**

Generally, compounds of Group 2 elements that contain **singly charged** negative ions (e.g. OH^-) **increase** in solubility down the group, whereas compounds that contain **doubly charged** negative ions (e.g. SO_4^{2-}) **decrease** in solubility down the group.

Group 2 element	hydroxide (OH^-)	sulfate (SO_4^{2-})
magnesium	least soluble	most soluble
calcium	↓	↑
strontium		
barium	most soluble	least soluble

Compounds like magnesium hydroxide, $Mg(OH)_2$, which have **very low** solubilities are said to be **sparingly soluble**. Most sulfates are soluble in water, but **barium sulfate** ($BaSO_4$) is **insoluble**. The test for sulfate ions makes use of this property...

Test for sulfate ions

If acidified barium chloride ($BaCl_2$) is added to a solution containing sulfate ions then a white precipitate of barium sulfate is formed.

$$Ba^{2+}_{(aq)} + SO_4^{2-}{}_{(aq)} \rightarrow BaSO_{4\,(s)}$$

$$\text{E.g.} \quad BaCl_{2(aq)} + FeSO_{4(aq)} \rightarrow BaSO_{4\,(s)} + FeCl_{2(aq)}$$

You need to acidify the solution with hydrochloric acid to get rid of any lurking sulfites or carbonates, which will also produce a white precipitate.

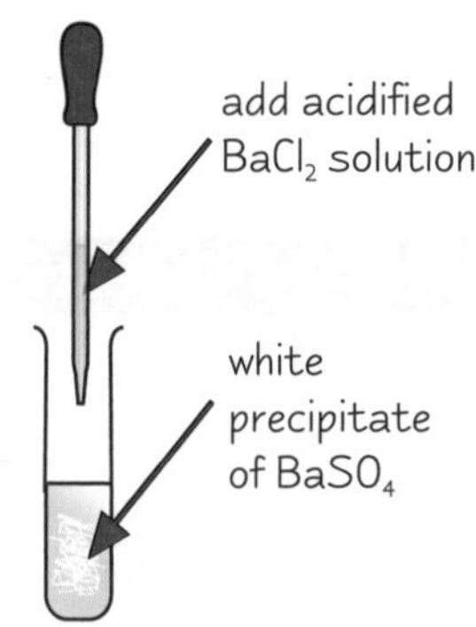

Group 2 Compounds are used to **Neutralise Acidity**

Group 2 elements are known as the **alkaline earth metals**, and many of their common compounds are used for neutralising acids. Here are a couple of common examples:

1) Calcium hydroxide (slaked lime, $Ca(OH)_2$) is used in **agriculture** to neutralise acid soils.

2) Magnesium hydroxide ($Mg(OH)_2$) is used in some indigestion tablets as an **antacid** — this is a substance which neutralises excess stomach acid.

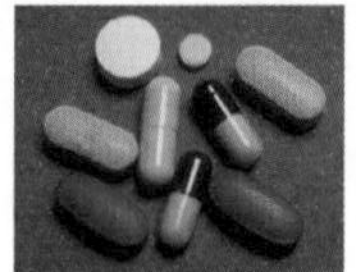

In both cases, the ionic equation for the neutralisation is

$$H^+_{(aq)} + OH^-_{(aq)} \rightarrow H_2O_{(l)}$$

Barium Sulfate is used in **'Barium Meals'**

CHRIS PRIEST / SCIENCE PHOTO LIBRARY

X-rays are great for finding broken bones, but they pass straight through soft tissue — so soft tissues, like the digestive system, don't show up on conventional X-ray pictures.

1) Barium sulfate is **opaque** to X-rays — they won't pass through it. It's used in '**barium meals**' to help diagnose problems with the oesophagus, stomach or intestines.
2) A patient swallows the barium meal, which is a suspension of **barium sulfate**. The barium sulfate **coats** the tissues, making them show up on the X-rays, showing the structure of the organs.

Uses of the Group 2 Elements

Magnesium is used in the **Extraction** of **Titanium**

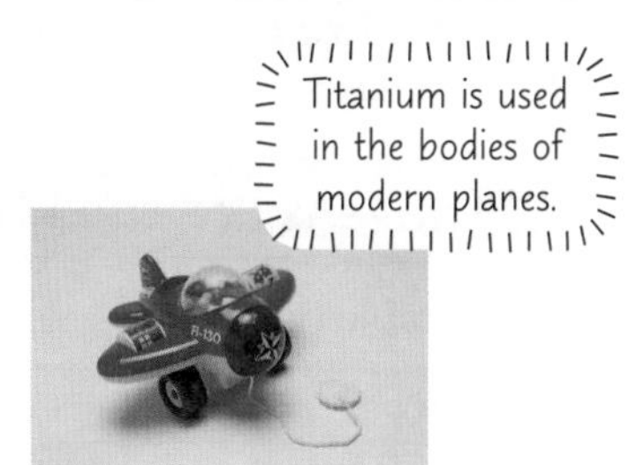

Titanium is used in the bodies of modern planes.

1) Magnesium is used as part of the process of **extracting titanium** from its ore.
2) The main titanium ore, titanium(IV) oxide (TiO_2) is first converted to **titanium(IV) chloride** ($TiCl_4$) by heating it with carbon in a stream of chlorine gas.
3) The titanium chloride is then purified by fractional distillation, before being **reduced by magnesium** in a furnace at almost 1000 °C.

$$TiCl_{4(g)} + 2Mg_{(l)} \rightarrow Ti_{(s)} + 2MgCl_{2(l)}$$

Mg is the reducing agent.

Calcium Oxide and Calcium Carbonate Remove Sulfur Dioxide

1) Burning fossil fuels to produce electricity also produces **sulfur dioxide**, which pollutes the atmosphere.
2) The acidic sulfur dioxide can be **removed** from **flue gases** by reacting with an alkali — this process is called **wet scrubbing**.
3) Powdered **calcium oxide** (lime, CaO) and **calcium carbonate** (limestone, $CaCO_3$) can both be used for this.
4) A **slurry** is made by **mixing** the calcium oxide or calcium carbonate with **water**. It's then sprayed onto the flue gases. The sulfur dioxide reacts with the alkaline slurry and produces a solid waste product, **calcium sulfite**.

Flue gases are the gases emitted from industrial exhausts and chimneys.

$$CaO_{(s)} + 2H_2O_{(l)} + SO_{2(g)} \rightarrow CaSO_{3(s)} + 2H_2O_{(l)}$$

$$CaCO_{3(s)} + 2H_2O_{(l)} + SO_{2(g)} \rightarrow CaSO_{3(s)} + 2H_2O_{(l)} + CO_{2(g)}$$

Warm-Up Questions

Q1 Which is less soluble, barium sulfate or magnesium sulfate?

Q2 How is the solubility of magnesium hydroxide often described?

Q3 Give a use of calcium hydroxide.

Q4 Which Group 2 element can be used to extract titanium from titanium chloride?

Q5 Write the equation for the removal of sulfur dioxide from flue gases by calcium oxide.

Exam Questions

Q1 Describe how you could use acidified barium chloride solution to distinguish between solutions of zinc chloride and zinc sulfate. Give the expected observations and an appropriate balanced equation including state symbols. [2 marks]

Q2 Choose the Group 2 element, labelled A-D below, which best fits each of the following descriptions.

A magnesium B calcium C strontium D barium

a) Forms hydroxide and sulfate compounds, only one of which is soluble. [1 mark]

b) Forms a hydroxide used to neutralise acidic soils. [1 mark]

c) Forms a very soluble sulfate compound but sparingly soluble hydroxide compound. [1 mark]

Q3 Describe how barium sulfate can be used to diagnose problems with the digestive system. [2 marks]

Wet scrubbing — I thought that's what you did in the shower...

The Group 2 elements and compounds have lots of uses — they're used in agriculture, medicine, for reducing pollution, saving the world... Make sure you know which compound can be used for what though — you don't want to feed limestone to someone who has a problem with their digestive system, things could get horribly clogged up.

Group 7 — The Halogens

Here comes a page jam-packed with nuggets of halogen fun. Oh yes, I kid you not. This page is a chemistry roller coaster... white-knuckle excitement all the way...

Halogen is used to describe the atom (X) or molecule (X_2). Halide is used to describe the negative ion (X^-).

Halogens are the **Highly Reactive Non-Metals** of Group 7

The table below gives some of the main properties of the first 4 halogens.

Halogen	Formula	Colour	Physical State	Electronic configuration of atom	Electronegativity
fluorine	F_2	pale yellow	gas	$1s^2\ 2s^2\ 2p^5$	increases up the group ↑
chlorine	Cl_2	green	gas	$1s^2\ 2s^2\ 2p^6\ 3s^2\ 3p^5$	
bromine	Br_2	red-brown	liquid	$1s^2\ 2s^2\ 2p^6\ 3s^2\ 3p^6\ 3d^{10}\ 4s^2\ 4p^5$	
iodine	I_2	grey	solid	$1s^2\ 2s^2\ 2p^6\ 3s^2\ 3p^6\ 3d^{10}\ 4s^2\ 4p^6\ 4d^{10}\ 5s^2\ 5p^5$	

1) **Their boiling points increase down the group.**
This is due to the increasing strength of the **van der Waals forces** as the size and relative mass of the molecules increases. This trend is shown in the changes of **physical state** from fluorine (gas) to iodine (solid).
2) **Electronegativity decreases down the group.**
Electronegativity, remember, is the tendency of an atom to **attract** a bonding pair of **electrons**. The halogens are all highly electronegative elements. But larger atoms attract electrons **less** than smaller ones. This is because the electrons are **further** from the nucleus and are **shielded** by more electrons. (See page 10 for more on shielding).

Halogens **Displace** Less Reactive Halide Ions from Solution

1) When the halogens react, they **gain an electron**. They get **less reactive down the group**, because the atoms become larger. The outer shell is further from the nucleus, so electrons are less strongly attracted to it. So you can also say that the halogens become **less oxidising** down the group.
2) The **relative oxidising strengths** of the halogens can be seen in their **displacement reactions** with the halide ions:

Halogen	Displacement reaction	Ionic equation
Cl	chlorine (Cl_2) will displace bromide (Br^-) and iodide (I^-)	$Cl_{2(aq)} + 2Br^-_{(aq)} \rightarrow 2Cl^-_{(aq)} + Br_{2(aq)}$ $Cl_{2(aq)} + 2I^-_{(aq)} \rightarrow 2Cl^-_{(aq)} + I_{2(aq)}$
Br	bromine (Br_2) will displace iodide (I^-)	$Br_{2(aq)} + 2I^-_{(aq)} \rightarrow 2Br^-_{(aq)} + I_{2(aq)}$
I	no reaction with F^-, Cl^-, Br^-	

The basic rule is:

> A **halogen** will **displace a halide** from solution if the halide is **below it** in the periodic table.

3) These displacement reactions can be used to help **identify** which halogen (or halide) is present in a solution.

	Potassium chloride solution $KCl_{(aq)}$ — colourless	Potassium bromide solution $KBr_{(aq)}$ — colourless	Potassium iodide solution $KI_{(aq)}$ — colourless
Add chlorine water $Cl_{2(aq)}$ — colourless	no reaction	orange solution (Br_2) formed	brown solution (I_2) formed
Add bromine water $Br_{2(aq)}$ — orange	no reaction	no reaction	brown solution (I_2) formed
Add iodine solution $I_{2(aq)}$ — brown	no reaction	no reaction	no reaction

Chlorine and **Sodium Hydroxide** make **Bleach**

If you mix chlorine gas with cold, dilute, aqueous sodium hydroxide you get **sodium chlorate(I) solution**, $NaClO_{(aq)}$, which just happens to be common household **bleach** (which kills bacteria).

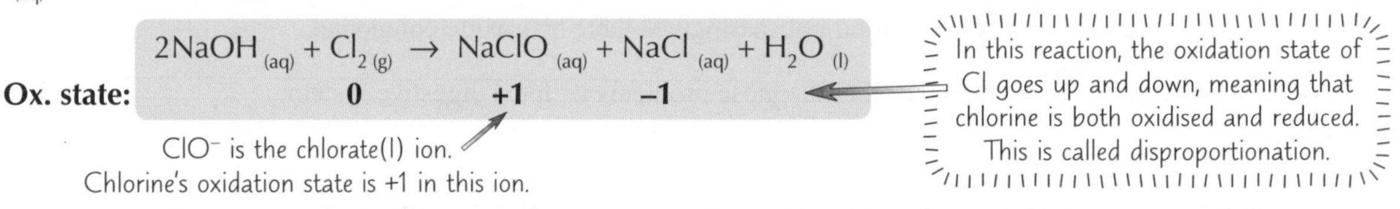

$$2NaOH_{(aq)} + Cl_{2(g)} \rightarrow NaClO_{(aq)} + NaCl_{(aq)} + H_2O_{(l)}$$

Ox. state: 0 (Cl in Cl_2), +1 (Cl in NaClO), −1 (Cl in NaCl)

ClO^- is the chlorate(I) ion. Chlorine's oxidation state is +1 in this ion.

In this reaction, the oxidation state of Cl goes up and down, meaning that chlorine is both oxidised and reduced. This is called disproportionation.

> The sodium chlorate(I) solution (bleach) has loads of uses — it's used in **water treatment**, to bleach **paper** and **textiles**... and it's good for **cleaning toilets**, too. Handy...

Group 7 — The Halogens

Chlorine is used to Kill Bacteria in Water

When you mix **chlorine** with **water**, it undergoes **disproportionation**.

You end up with a mixture of **chloride ions** and **chlorate(I) ions.**

In sunlight, chlorine can also decompose water to form chloride ions and **oxygen**.

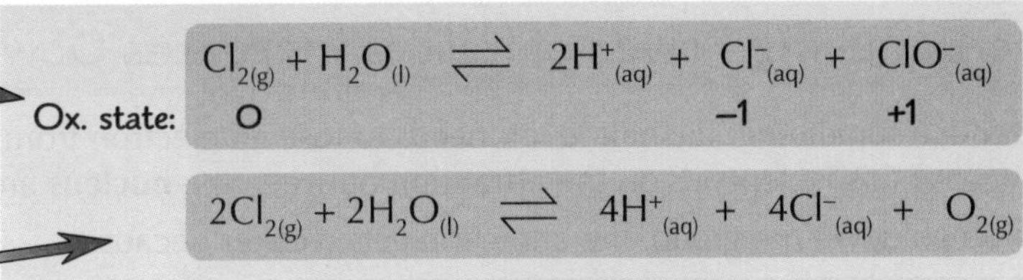

Chlorate(I) ions **kill bacteria**. So, **adding chlorine** (or a compound containing chlorate(I) ions) to water can make it safe to **drink** or **swim** in. On the downside, chlorine is toxic.

1) In the UK our drinking water is **treated** to make it safe. **Chlorine** is an important part of water treatment:

- It **kills disease-causing microorganisms**.
- Some chlorine persists in the water and **prevents reinfection** further down the supply.
- It prevents the growth of **algae**, eliminating **bad tastes** and **smells**, and **removes discolouration** caused by organic compounds.

2) However, there are risks from using chlorine to treat water:

- **Chlorine gas** is **very harmful** if it's breathed in — it irritates the **respiratory system**. **Liquid chlorine** on the skin or eyes causes severe **chemical burns**. Accidents involving chlorine could be really serious, or fatal.
- Water contains a variety of organic compounds, e.g. from the decomposition of plants. Chlorine reacts with these compounds to form **chlorinated hydrocarbons**, e.g. chloromethane (CH_3Cl), and many of these chlorinated hydrocarbons are carcinogenic (cancer-causing). However, this increased cancer risk is small compared to the risks from untreated water — a cholera epidemic, say, could kill thousands of people.

3) We have to weigh up these risks and benefits when making decisions about whether we should add chemicals to drinking water supplies.

Warm-Up Questions

Q1 Place the halogens F, Cl, Br and I in order of increasing: a) boiling point, b) electronegativity.

Q2 What would be seen when chlorine water is added to potassium iodide solution?

Q3 How is common household bleach formed?

Exam Questions

Q1 a) Write an ionic equation for the reaction between iodine solution and sodium astatide (NaAt). [1 mark]

b) For the equation in a), state which substance is oxidised. [1 mark]

Q2 a) Describe and explain the trends in:

i) the boiling points of Group 7 elements as you move down the Periodic Table. [3 marks]

ii) electronegativity of Group 7 elements as you move down the Periodic Table. [3 marks]

b) Which halogen is the most powerful oxidising agent? [1 mark]

Q3 Chlorine is added to the water in public swimming baths in carefully controlled quantities.

a) Write an equation for the reaction of chlorine with water to form chlorate(I) ions. [1 mark]

b) Why is chlorine added to the water in swimming baths, and why must the quantity added be carefully controlled? [2 marks]

Remain seated until the page comes to a halt. Please exit to the right...

Oooh, what a lovely page, if I do say so myself. There's nowt too taxing here — you just need to learn the colours of the solutions, all the equations, the advantages and disadvantages of adding chlorine to water supplies... it never ends.

Halide Ions

OK, a quick reminder of the basics first. Halides are compounds with the –1 halogen ion (e.g. Cl^-, Br^-, I^-) like KI, HCl and NaBr. They all end in "-ide" — chloride, bromide, iodide. Got that? Good. Now, you're ready to go in...

The **Reducing Power** of Halides **Increases** Down the Group...

To reduce something, the halide ion needs to lose an electron from its outer shell.
How easy this is depends on the **attraction** between the **nucleus** and the outer **electrons**.

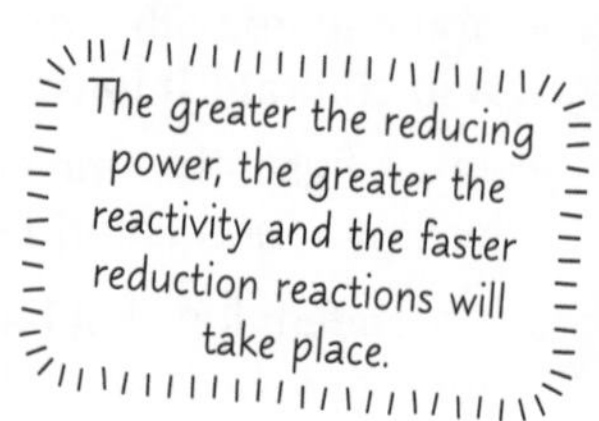

The greater the reducing power, the greater the reactivity and the faster reduction reactions will take place.

As you go down the group, the attraction gets **weaker** because:

1) the ions get bigger, so the electrons are **further** away from the positive nucleus,
2) there are extra inner electron shells, so there's a greater **shielding** effect.

So, the further down the group the halide ion is, the easier it loses electrons and the greater its reducing power.

A good example of halogens doing a bit of reduction is the good old halogen / halide displacement reactions (the ones you learned on page 62... yes, those ones). And here come some more examples to learn...

...which Explains their Reactions with **Sulfuric Acid**

All the halides react with concentrated sulfuric acid to give a **hydrogen halide** as a product to start with. But what happens next depends on which halide you've got...

Reaction of NaF or NaCl with H_2SO_4

$$NaF_{(s)} + H_2SO_{4(l)} \rightarrow NaHSO_{4(s)} + HF_{(g)}$$

$$NaCl_{(s)} + H_2SO_{4(l)} \rightarrow NaHSO_{4(s)} + HCl_{(g)}$$

1) Hydrogen fluoride (HF) or hydrogen chloride gas (HCl) is formed. You'll see misty fumes as the gas comes into contact with moisture in the air.
2) But HF and HCl aren't strong enough reducing agents to reduce the sulfuric acid, so the reaction stops there.
3) It's not a redox reaction — the oxidation states of the halide and sulfur stay the same (–1 and +6).

Reaction of NaBr with H_2SO_4

$$NaBr_{(s)} + H_2SO_{4(l)} \rightarrow NaHSO_{4(s)} + HBr_{(g)}$$

$$2HBr_{(aq)} + H_2SO_{4(l)} \rightarrow Br_{2(g)} + SO_{2(g)} + 2H_2O_{(l)}$$

ox. state of S: +6 → +4 reduction
$6HI_{(g)} + SO_{2(g)} \rightarrow H_2S_{(g)} + 3I_{2(s)} + 2H_2O_{(l)}$
ox. state of Br: –1 → 0 oxidation

1) The first reaction gives misty fumes of hydrogen bromide gas (HBr).
2) But the HBr is a stronger reducing agent than HCl and reacts with the H_2SO_4 in a redox reaction.
3) The reaction produces choking fumes of SO_2 and orange fumes of Br_2.

Reaction of NaI with H_2SO_4

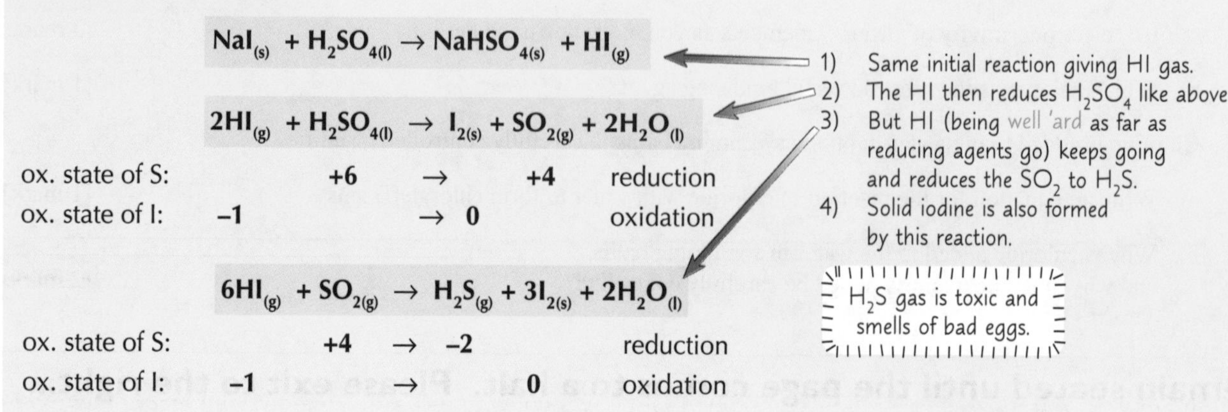

1) Same initial reaction giving HI gas.
2) The HI then reduces H_2SO_4 like above.
3) But HI (being well 'ard as far as reducing agents go) keeps going and reduces the SO_2 to H_2S.
4) Solid iodine is also formed by this reaction.
H_2S gas is toxic and smells of bad eggs.

Halide Ions

Silver Nitrate Solution is used to **Test for Halides**

The test for halides is dead easy. First you add **dilute nitric acid** to remove ions which might interfere with the test. Then you just add a few drops of **silver nitrate solution** ($AgNO_{3(aq)}$). A **precipitate** is formed (of the silver halide).

$$Ag^+_{(aq)} + X^-_{(aq)} \rightarrow AgX_{(s)}$$ ...where X is F, Cl, Br or I

1) The **colour** of the precipitate identifies the halide.

SILVER NITRATE TEST FOR HALIDE IONS...		
Fluoride F^-:	no precipitate	
Chloride Cl^-:	white precipitate	forms slowest
Bromide Br^-:	cream precipitate	↓
Iodide I^-:	yellow precipitate	forms fastest

2) Then to be extra sure, you can test your results by adding **ammonia solution**. Each silver halide has a different solubility in ammonia.

SOLUBILITY OF SILVER HALIDE PRECIPITATES IN AMMONIA...		
Chloride Cl^-:	white precipitate, dissolves in dilute $NH_{3(aq)}$	most soluble
Bromide Br^-:	cream precipitate, dissolves in conc. $NH_{3(aq)}$	↑
Iodide I^-:	yellow precipitate, insoluble in conc. $NH_{3(aq)}$	least soluble

Warm-Up Questions

Q1 Give two reasons why a bromide ion is a more powerful reducing agent than a chloride ion.

Q2 Name the gaseous products formed when sodium bromide reacts with concentrated sulfuric acid.

Q3 What is produced when sodium iodide reacts with concentrated sulfuric acid?

Q4 How would you test whether an aqueous solution contained chloride ions?

Exam Questions

Q1 Describe the test you would carry out in order to distinguish between solid samples of sodium chloride and sodium bromide using silver nitrate solution and aqueous ammonia. State your observations. [6 marks]

Q2 The halogen below iodine in Group 7 is astatine (At).

a) Which of the following shows the products that would form when concentrated sulfuric acid is added to a solid sample of sodium astatide.

A $NaHSO_{4(aq)}$, $At_{2(g)}$, $SO_{2(g)}$, $2H_2O_{(l)}$

B $NaHSO_{4(aq)}$, $HAt_{(s)}$, $H_2S_{(g)}$, $2H_2O_{(l)}$

C $NaHSO_{4(aq)}$, $At_{2(s)}$, $H_2S_{(g)}$, $2H_2O_{(l)}$

D $NaHSO_{4(aq)}$, $At_{2(s)}$, $HAt_{(g)}$, $2H_2O_{(l)}$ [1 mark]

b) Predict what would be observed if silver astatide was added to a concentrated ammonia solution. Explain your answer. [2 marks]

Testing times — for the halides and for you...

Chemistry exams. What a bummer, eh... No one ever said it was going to be easy. Not even your teacher would be that cruel. There are plenty more equations on this page to learn. As well as that, make sure you really understand everything... the trend in the reducing power of halides... and the reactions with sulfuric acid...

Tests for Ions

It is a truth universally acknowledged that chemistry students need to know how to work out which ions are hanging around in a random ionic solution. Here are some tests that will help. (You have met a few of them before, thankfully...)*

**OK, I admit it, 'universally acknowledged' is probably a slight exaggeration...*

You Can Use **Chemical Tests** To **Identify Positive Ions**

Positive ions (or **cations**) include things like the ions of **Group 2 metals** and **ammonium ions.**
Here are the **chemical tests** that you need to know to help you identify them:.

Use **Flame Tests** to Identify **Group 2 Ions**

Compounds of some **Group 2 metals** burn with characteristic **colours.**
You can identify them using a **flame test**. Here's how to do them:

1) Dip a **nichrome wire loop** in concentrated hydrochloric acid.
2) Then dip the wire loop into the **unknown compound.**
3) Hold the loop in the clear blue part of a Bunsen burner flame.
4) Observe the **colour change** in the flame.

Metal ion	Flame colour
Calcium, Ca^{2+}	**brick red**
Strontium, Sr^{2+}	**red**
Barium, Ba^{2+}	**pale green**

Use **Red Litmus Paper** and **NaOH** to Test for **Ammonium Ions**

1) **Ammonia gas** (NH_3) is alkaline — so you can test for it using a damp piece of **red litmus paper.** (The litmus paper needs to be damp so the ammonia gas can dissolve). If there's ammonia present, the paper will turn **blue.**
2) If you add **hydroxide ions** to (OH^-) a solution containing **ammonium ions** (NH_4^+), they will react to produce **ammonia gas** and water, like this:

$$NH_4^+{}_{(aq)} + OH^-{}_{(aq)} \rightarrow NH_{3(g)} + H_2O_{(l)}$$

3) You can use this reaction to test whether a substance contains **ammonium ions** (NH_4^+). Add some dilute **sodium hydroxide** solution to your mystery substance in a test tube and **gently heat** the mixture. If there's ammonia given off, ammonium ions must be present.

You Can Use **Chemical Tests** To **Identify Negative Ions** Too

Negative ions (or **anions**) include things like **halide ions, hydroxide ions, sulfate ions** and **carbonate ions.**
Here are the **chemical tests** for these ions:

Test for **Sulfates** with HCl and **Barium Chloride**

You've already met this test back on page 60, but here's a quick reminder in case you've forgotten.

To identify a **sulfate** ion (SO_4^{2-}), you add a little dilute hydrochloric acid, followed by **barium chloride solution,** $BaCl_{2(aq)}$.

$$Ba^{2+}{}_{(aq)} + SO_4^{2-}{}_{(aq)} \rightarrow BaSO_{4\,(s)}$$

If a **white precipitate** of **barium sulfate** forms, it means the original compound contained a sulfate.

The hydrochloric acid is added to get rid of any traces of carbonate ions before you do the test. (These would also produce a precipitate, so they'd confuse the results.)

Use a **pH Indicator** to Test for **Hydroxides**

Hydroxide ions make solutions alkaline. So if you think a solution might contain hydroxide ions, you can use a **pH indicator** to test it. For example:

1) Dip a piece of **red litmus paper** into the solution.
2) If hydroxide ions are present, the paper will turn **blue.**

Tests for Ions

Test for **Halides** with **Silver Nitrate** Solution

To test for **chloride** (Cl^-), **bromide** (Br^-) or **iodide** (I^-) ions, you just add dilute **nitric acid** (HNO_3), followed by **silver nitrate** solution ($AgNO_3$).

A **chloride** gives a **white** precipitate of **silver chloride**.

A **bromide** gives a **cream** precipitate of **silver bromide**.

An **iodide** gives a **yellow** precipitate of **silver iodide**.

There's more info about this test on page 65.

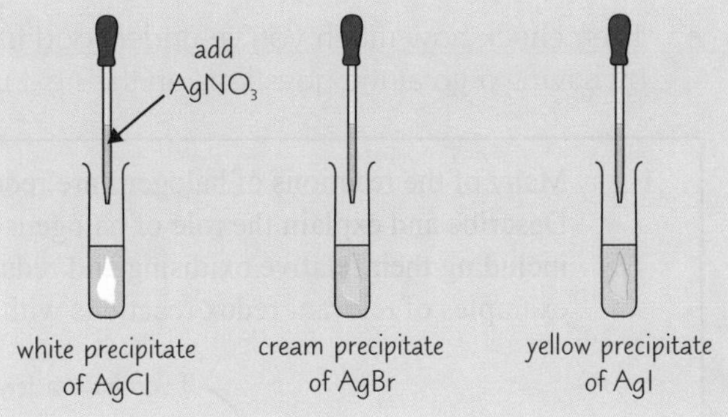

Hydrochloric Acid Can Help Detect **Carbonates**

You can test to see if a solution contains carbonate ions (CO_3^{2-}) by adding an acid. Here's how to do it:

When you add dilute **hydrochloric acid**, a solution containing **carbonate ions** will fizz. This is because the carbonate ions react with the hydrogen ions in the acid to give **carbon dioxide**:

$$CO_3^{2-}{}_{(s)} + 2H^+_{(aq)} \rightarrow CO_{2(g)} + H_2O_{(l)}$$

You can test for carbon dioxide using **limewater**. Carbon dioxide **turns limewater cloudy** — just bubble the gas through a test tube of limewater and watch what happens. If the limewater goes cloudy, your solution contains **carbonate ions**.

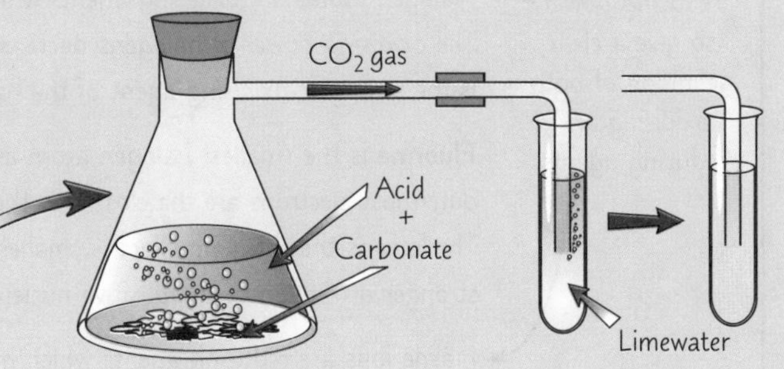

Warm-Up Questions

Q1 Describe how to carry out a flame test.

Q2 What colour would damp, red litmus paper turn in the presence of ammonia gas?

Q3 Describe how you could test a solution to see if it contained hydroxide ions.

Exam Questions

Q1 A student adds dilute nitric acid and silver nitrate to a solution of an unknown ionic compound. A yellow precipitate forms. Which anion is present in the solution?

A Bromide B Carbonate C Sulfate D Iodide [1 mark]

Q2 A student has a solution of an unknown ionic compound. He performs a flame test on a sample of the solution and notes that the compound burns with a pale green flame. He then reacts another sample of the solution with dilute hydrochloric acid. The reactants fizz and the gas produced turns limewater cloudy. What is the formula of the ionic compound? [2 marks]

Q3 You are given a sample of an ionic compound in solution and asked to confirm that the compound is ammonium sulfate. Describe the tests that you could perform to confirm the identity of the compound. [4 marks]

I've got my ion you...

...and you better have your ion these pages. There are lots of tests to learn and you best not get them all muddled up. Go through each test and make sure you know all the reagents you'd need to do the test, how you'd actually do it, and what a positive result looks like. Then once you know them all, treat yourself with a biscuit — that's a positive result too.

Extra Exam Practice

You've done it. You've reached the end of Unit 2 Sections 1 and 2. You'll get the chance to practise questions covering a range of sections later on, but first, let's see how much of the last couple has sunk in.

- Have a look at this example of how to answer a tricky exam question.
- Then check how much you've understood from Unit 2 Sections 1 and 2 by having a go at the questions on the next page.

1 Many of the reactions of halogens are redox reactions.
Describe and explain the role of halogens and halide ions in redox reactions, including their relative oxidising and reducing power. You should include examples of relevant redox reactions with their equations in your answer.

(6 marks)

If you have a few things to write about, it's worth spending a few seconds making a rough plan of everything you need to include.

1

- Generally halogens are oxidising agents and halide ions are reducing agents (discuss factors for relative reducing/oxidising power here).
- Reactions: displacement reactions of halogens, reduction of conc. sulfuric acid (explain what happens in terms of redox for each reaction).

Halogen atoms are oxidising agents which means **they gain electrons**. The oxidising power of halogens **decreases** as you go down Group 7, so fluorine is the strongest oxidising agent of the halogens.

Fluorine is the smallest halogen atom as it has the fewest electron shells, so its outermost electrons are the closest to the nucleus compared to the other halogens. This means the shielding effect is smaller and the outermost electrons have a stronger attraction to the positive nucleus, making it is easier to gain an electron.

Halide ions are reducing agents which means **they lose electrons**. The reducing power of halides **increases** as you go down Group 7, so fluoride ions are the weakest reducing agents of the halides.

Fluoride ions are the smallest halides so it is hardest for them to lose an electron. This is because their outer shell is relatively close to the nucleus and there is less shielding, so the outermost electrons are more tightly held to the nucleus.

Halogen molecules have an oxidation state of zero and can be reduced to halide ions. Halide ions have an oxidation state of –1 and can be oxidised to halogens.

Displacement reactions of halogens show that chlorine can oxidise aqueous bromide or iodide ions to form bromine or iodine. Chlor**ine** is simultaneously reduced to chlor**ide** ions. For example: $Cl_2 + 2Br^- \rightarrow Br_2 + 2Cl^-$

Chloride ions do not have enough reducing power to reduce concentrated sulfuric acid. Bromide ions and iodide ions do have enough reducing power to reduce concentrated sulfuric acid to sulfur dioxide They are oxidised and form bromine and iodine in the process.
For example: $2HI + H_2SO_4 \rightarrow I_2 + SO_2 + 2H_2O$

Iodide ions are stronger reducing agents than bromide ions so can reduce the sulfur dioxide further to hydrogen sulfide: $6HI + SO_2 \rightarrow H_2S + 3I_2 + 2H_2O$

You've been asked to consider oxidising and reducing power so give a clear definition of both oxidising and reducing agents.

Clearly state the trends in oxidising and reducing power of halogens and halides, making sure you go on to give an explanation of each.

You could also explain the relative oxidising/reducing power in relation to size in terms of any of the halides and halogens.

Including these two points will show you have a good understanding of the role of both species in redox reactions.

Be careful not to get halogens (-ine) and halides (-ide) mixed up.

Remember to include equations if the question has asked for them.

You could also write a full equation showing, for example, KBr and KCl.

It's not necessary to show an equation for the reaction between chloride ions and conc. sulfuric acid since it's not a redox reaction — it's an acid-base reaction.

This is an extended response question, so you should write clearly and coherently to gain full marks. It's worth 6 marks, so you should know that you're expected to give a lot of information in your answer. Don't waffle on though, you won't get marks for information that isn't relevant to the question.

Extra Exam Practice

2 Barium nitrate can be used to test for the presence of sulfate ions, and silver nitrate can be used to test for the presence of halide ions. Prior to the addition of these reagents, dilute nitric acid is added to the sample solutions to be tested.

2.1 Suggest what would be observed if dilute nitric acid, followed by barium nitrate solution, was added to a solution containing both sodium sulfate and sodium carbonate.

(2 marks)

2.2 Dilute nitric acid, followed by silver nitrate solution, is added to a solution containing both sodium chloride and sodium hydroxide.
Write the simplest ionic equation for each of the two reactions that occur.

(2 marks)

2.3 A solution containing a mixture of sodium halides was acidified with dilute nitric acid. Silver nitrate solution was then added to it.
The result was a pale yellow precipitate that partly dissolved in dilute ammonia solution.
Suggest the composition of the solution, giving reasons for your answer.

(3 marks)

3 A student is researching the properties of the Period 3 elements.

Figure 1 shows the melting and boiling points of sulfur, chlorine and argon.

Figure 1

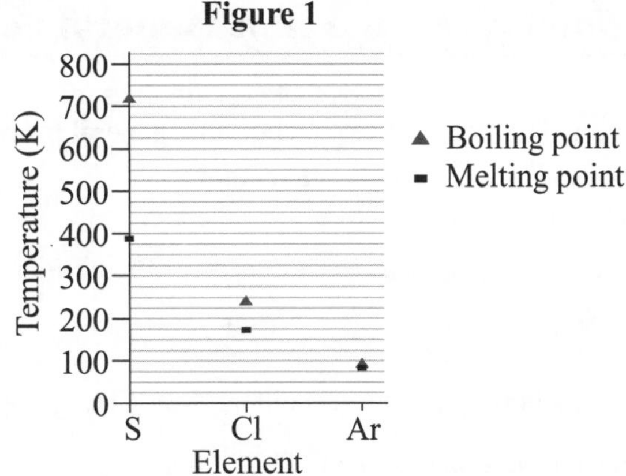

3.1 Use your knowledge of the structure and bonding of Period 3 elements to explain why chlorine is the only element shown in **Figure 1** that is a liquid at 200 K.

(6 marks)

3.2 Use your knowledge of the structure and bonding of Period 3 elements to predict a value for the melting point of phosphorus.

(1 mark)

3.3 State and explain how the atomic radius of magnesium would compare with the atomic radius of argon.

(2 marks)

3.4 The student adds a small amount of magnesium hydroxide powder to a test tube and anhydrous magnesium sulfate powder to a second test tube. Both test tubes contain hot water. She agitates the mixtures before filtering the resulting contents of each test tube and then examining the filter paper.

Suggest what the student will observe in each case. Explain your answer.

(2 marks)

Basic Stuff

Organic chemistry is all about carbon compounds. There are loads of them, and you're mainly made up of them, so they're fairly important. Chemists have organised them into families, which makes them a tad easier to cope with.

There are **Loads of Ways** of **Representing** Organic Compounds

TYPE OF FORMULA	WHAT IT SHOWS YOU	FORMULA FOR BUTAN-1-OL
General formula	An algebraic formula that can describe **any member** of a family of compounds.	$C_nH_{2n+1}OH$ (for all alcohols)
Empirical formula	The **simplest ratio** of atoms of each element in a compound (cancel the numbers down if possible). (So ethane, C_2H_6, has the empirical formula CH_3.)	$C_4H_{10}O$
Molecular formula	The **actual** number of atoms of each element in a molecule.	$C_4H_{10}O$
Structural formula	Shows the atoms **carbon by carbon**, with the attached hydrogens and functional groups.	$CH_3CH_2CH_2CH_2OH$
Skeletal formula	Shows the **bonds** of the carbon skeleton **only**, with any functional groups. The hydrogen and carbon atoms aren't shown. This is handy for drawing large complicated structures, like cyclic hydrocarbons.	(zigzag) OH
Displayed formula	Shows how all the atoms are **arranged**, and all the bonds between them.	H–C(H)(H)–C(H)(H)–C(H)(H)–C(H)(H)–O–H

Homologous Compounds have the Same **General Formulas**

1) A **homologous series** is a group of compounds that contain the same functional group. They can all be represented by the same **general formula**.
2) You can use a general formula to work out the **molecular formula** of any member of a homologous series.

A functional group is a reactive part of a molecule — it gives it most of its chemical properties.

Example: The alkanes have the general formula C_nH_{2n+2}. What's the formula of the alkane with six carbons?

n = 6, so the formula is $C_6H_{(2 \times 6) + 2} = \mathbf{C_6H_{14}}$

3) Each **successive member** of a homologous series differs by a '$\mathbf{CH_2}$' group.

Example: Alcohols have the general formula $C_nH_{2n+1}OH$.
What are the first six alcohols in the homologous series?

Each alcohol has one more **CH_2 group** than the one before:

Methanol	Ethanol	Propanol	Butanol	Pentanol	Hexanol
CH_3OH	C_2H_5OH	C_3H_7OH	C_4H_9OH	$C_5H_{11}OH$	$C_6H_{13}OH$

4) Here are the **homologous series** that you might need to know about:

Homologous series	Prefix or suffix	Example
alkanes	–ane	propane, $CH_3CH_2CH_3$
branched alkanes	alkyl– (–yl)	methylpropane, $CH_3CH(CH_3)CH_3$
alkenes	–ene	propene, $CH_3CH{=}CH_2$
halogenoalkanes	fluoro– / chloro– / bromo– / iodo–	chloroethane, CH_3CH_2Cl
alcohols	–ol	ethanol, CH_3CH_2OH
aldehydes	–al	ethanal, CH_3CHO
ketones	–one	propanone, CH_3COCH_3
cycloalkanes	cyclo– –ane	cyclohexane, C_6H_{12}
carboxylic acids	–oic acid	ethanoic acid, CH_3COOH

Don't worry if you don't recognise all of these yet — you'll meet them by the end of the unit.

Basic Stuff

Nomenclature is a Fancy Word for the Naming of Organic Compounds

You can name any organic compound using these **rules** of nomenclature:

1) Count the carbons in the **longest continuous chain** that contains the functional group— this gives you the stem:

Number of carbons	1	2	3	4	5	6
Stem	meth–	eth–	prop–	but–	pent–	hex–

Don't forget — the longest carbon chain may be bent.

2) The **main functional group** of the molecule usually gives you the end of the name (the **suffix**) — see the table on the previous page.

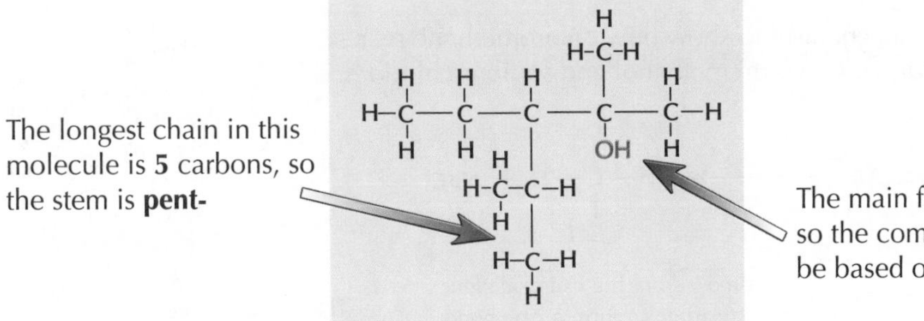

3) Number the carbons in the **longest** carbon chain so that the carbon with the main functional group attached has the lowest possible number. If there's more than one longest chain, pick the one with the **most side-chains**.

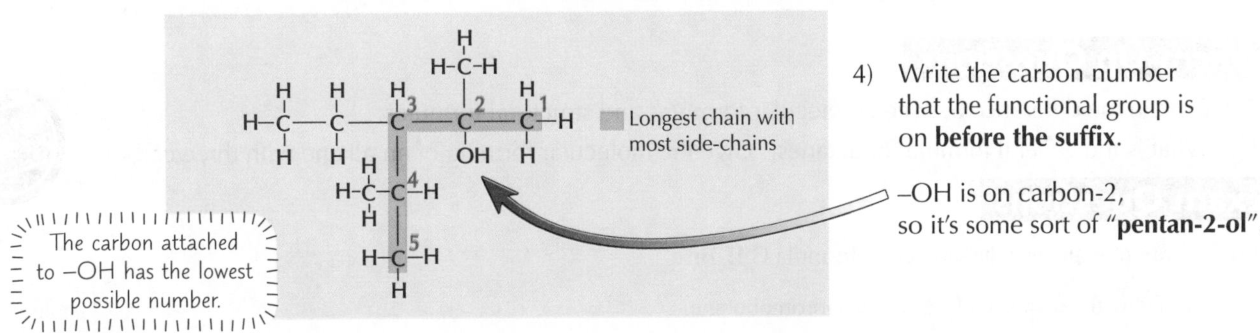

4) Write the carbon number that the functional group is on **before the suffix**.

–OH is on carbon-2, so it's some sort of "**pentan-2-ol**".

5) Any side-chains or less important functional groups are added as prefixes at the start of the name. Put them in **alphabetical** order, with the **number** of the carbon atom each is attached to.

6) If there's more than one **identical** side-chain or functional group, use **di-** (2), **tri-** (3) or **tetra-** (4) before that part of the name — but ignore this when working out the alphabetical order.

There's an ethyl group on carbon-3, and methyl groups on carbon-2 and carbon-4, so it's **3-ethyl-2,4-dimethylpentan-2-ol**

IUPAC Rules Help Avoid Confusion

Fancy a cup of tea? Tea, you know... Brown stuff. Oh come on, don't just sit there looking confused..."

1) The **IUPAC system** for naming organic compounds is the agreed **international language** of chemistry. Years ago, organic compounds were given whatever names people fancied, such as acetic acid and ethylene. But these names caused **confusion** between different countries.
2) The IUPAC system means scientific ideas can be communicated **across the globe** more effectively. So it's easier for scientists to get on with testing each other's work, and either confirm or dispute new theories.

Basic Stuff

A Mechanism Breaks Down a Reaction into Individual Stages

1) It's all very well knowing the outcome of a reaction, but it can also be useful to know **how** a reaction happens.
2) **Mechanisms** are diagrams that break reactions down into individual stages.
They show how molecules react together by using **curly arrows** to show which **bonds** are made or broken.

Curly Arrows Show How Electron Pairs Move Around

In order to make or break a bond in a reaction, **electrons** have to move around.
A **curly arrow** shows where a **pair** of electrons goes during a reaction. They look like this:

The arrow starts at the bond or lone pair where the electrons are at the beginning of the reaction. The arrow points to where the new bond is formed at the end of the reaction.

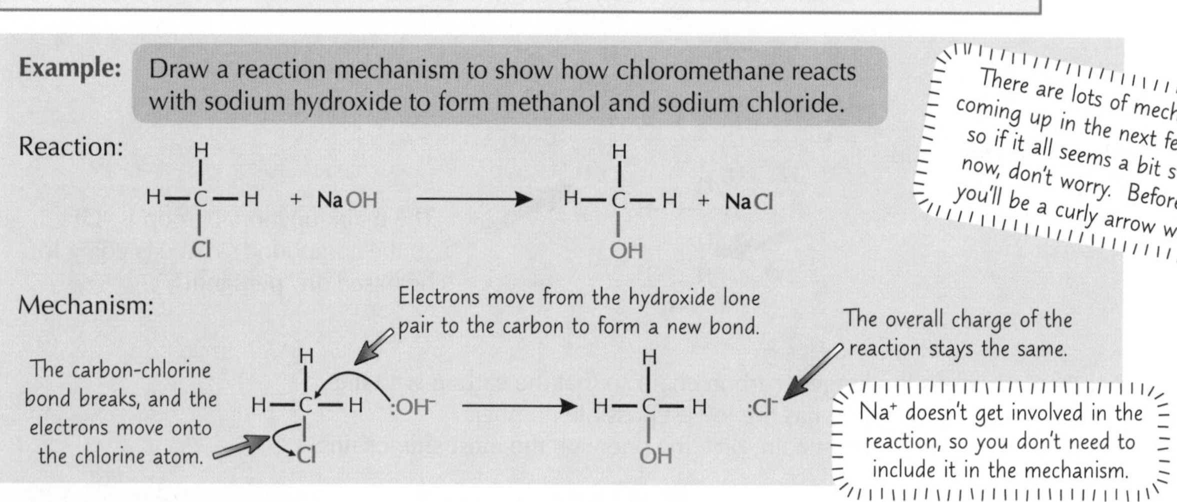

Example: Draw a reaction mechanism to show how chloromethane reacts with sodium hydroxide to form methanol and sodium chloride.
Reaction:
H
H—C—H + NaOH → H—C—H + NaCl
Cl
OH
Mechanism:
Electrons move from the hydroxide lone pair to the carbon to form a new bond.
The overall charge of the reaction stays the same.
The carbon-chlorine bond breaks, and the electrons move onto the chlorine atom.
H—C—H :OH⁻ → H—C—H :Cl⁻
Cl
OH

There are lots of mechanisms coming up in the next few pages, so if it all seems a bit strange now, don't worry. Before long you'll be a curly arrow wizard.

Na^+ doesn't get involved in the reaction, so you don't need to include it in the mechanism.

Warm-Up Questions

Q1 Explain the difference between molecular formulas and structural formulas.

Q2 What is the general formula for alkanes? Give the molecular formula of an alkane with three carbons.

PRACTICE QUESTIONS

Exam Questions

Q1 1-bromobutane has the molecular formula C_4H_9Br.

a) Draw the displayed formula of 1-bromobutane. [1 mark]

b) Which homologous series does 1-bromobutane belong to? [1 mark]

c) 1-bromobutane can be made from the molecule shown on the right. Name the molecule. [1 mark]

$$\mathrm{H{-}CH_2{-}CH_2{-}CH{=}CH_2}$$

Q2 a) Alkanes are an example of a homologous series. What is a homologous series? [1 mark]

b) i) Write down the molecular formula for the alkane molecule that has five carbon atoms. [1 mark]

ii) What is the IUPAC name of this molecule? [1 mark]

Q3 A molecule has the structural formula CH_2ClCH_2Cl. Give each of the following:

a) Its IUPAC name. [1 mark]

b) Its displayed formula. [1 mark]

c) Its skeletal formula. [1 mark]

I hope all that hasn't sent iu-packing...

I know it's a pain that there are about a gazillion different ways of describing the same molecule but examiners love asking you to draw molecules from their IUPAC name or formula and vice versa. You'll only be able to do this quickly if you practise. So choose a molecule and write down all its different representations. That's right. Every. Single. One.

Isomerism

Isomers are great fun — they're all about putting the same atoms together in different ways to make completely different molecules. It's like playing with plastic building bricks, but it hurts less when you tread on one by accident.

Isomers Have the Same Molecular Formula

1) Two molecules are isomers of one another if they have the same **molecular formula** but the atoms are arranged **differently**.
2) There are two types of isomers you need to know about — **structural isomers** and **stereoisomers**.

Structural Isomers have different Structural Arrangements of Atoms

In structural isomers the atoms are **connected** in different ways.
So they have the **same molecular formula** but different **structural formulas**.

There are **three types** of structural isomers:

Chain Isomers

Chain isomers have different arrangements of the **carbon skeleton**. Some are **straight chains** and others **branched** in different ways.

butane

methylpropane

Positional Isomers

Positional isomers have the **same skeleton** and the **same atoms or groups of atoms** attached.

The difference is that the atom or group of atoms is attached to a **different carbon atom**.

1-chlorobutane

2-chlorobutane

Functional Group Isomers

Functional group isomers have the same atoms arranged into **different functional groups**.

hex-1-ene

cyclohexane

You can never turn one isomer into the other by rotating the bonds in a molecule.

Stereoisomers Have Different Arrangements in Space

Stereoisomers have the same structural formula but a **different arrangement** in space.
(Just bear with me for a moment... that will become clearer, I promise.)

Double Bonds Can't Rotate

1) Carbon atoms in a C=C double bond and the atoms bonded to these carbons all lie in the **same plane** (they're **planar**).
2) Another important thing about C=C double bonds is that atoms **can't rotate** around them like they can around single bonds. In fact, double bonds are fairly **rigid** — they don't bend much either.
3) The **restricted rotation** around the C=C double bond causes a type of stereoisomerism called **E/Z isomerism** (more about this on the next page).

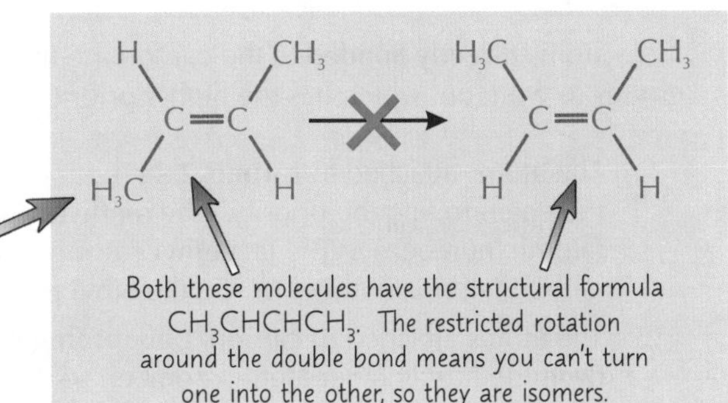

Both these molecules have the structural formula $CH_3CHCHCH_3$. The restricted rotation around the double bond means you can't turn one into the other, so they are isomers.

Isomerism

Alkenes Show **E/Z** Isomerism

(You might see E/Z isomerism being called geometric isomerism.)

1) **Alkenes** have **restricted rotation** around their carbon-carbon double bonds.
2) This means that if both of the double-bond carbons have **different atoms** or **groups** attached to them, the arrangement of those groups around the double bond becomes important — you get two **stereoisomers.**
3) One of these isomers is called the **'E-isomer'** and the other is called the **'Z-isomer'**.
4) The **Z-isomer** has the same groups either **both above** or **both below** the double bond. The **E-isomer** has the same groups positioned **across** the double bond.

E stands for 'entgegen', the German for 'opposite'. Z stands for 'zusammen', the German for 'together'.

For example, here are the two stereoisomers of **but-2-ene**:

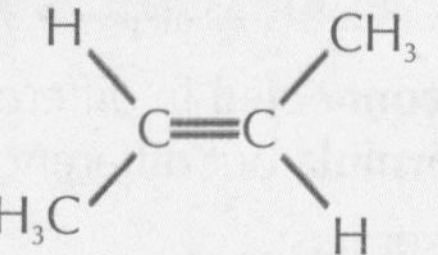

Here, the same groups are both **above** the double bond so it's the **Z-isomer**. This molecule is **Z-but-2-ene**.

Here, the same groups are **across** the double bond so it's the **E-isomer**. This molecule is **E-but-2-ene**.

One way to remember which isomer is which is to say that in the Z-isomer the matching groups are on 'ze zame zide', but in the E-isomer, they are 'enemies'.

The **E/Z System** Works Even When the Groups Are **Different**

A molecule that has a C=C bond surrounded by **3 or 4 different groups** still has an E- and a Z-isomer — it's just harder to work out which is which. But you can solve this problem using the **Cahn-Ingold-Prelog (CIP) priority rules**:

Example: Using the **Cahn-Ingold-Prelog Priority Rules** to Identify an **E/Z Isomer**

1) The first step is to **assign a priority** to the two atoms attached to each carbon in the double bond.
2) To do this, you look at the atoms that are **directly bonded** to each of the C=C carbon atoms. The atom with the higher **atomic number** on each carbon is given the higher **priority**.

Here's one of the stereoisomers of 1-bromo-1-chloro-2-fluoro-ethene:

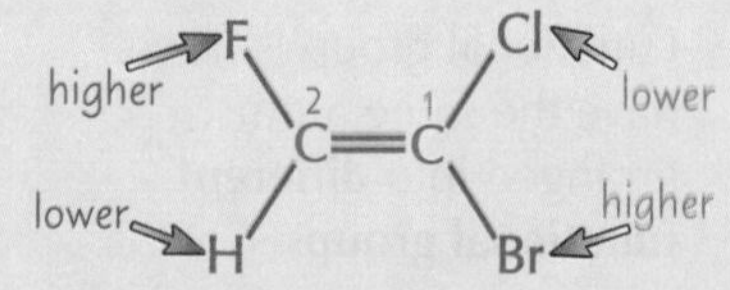

- The atoms directly attached to **carbon-2** are fluorine and hydrogen. **Fluorine** has an atomic number of **9** and **hydrogen** has an atomic number of **1**. So **fluorine** is the higher priority group.
- The atoms directly attached to **carbon-1** are bromine and chlorine. **Bromine** has an atomic number of **35** and **chlorine** has an atomic number of **17**. So **bromine** is the higher priority group.

3) Now to work out which isomer you have, just look at how the **two higher priority groups** are arranged.

In the stereoisomer shown above, the two higher priority groups (**Br** and **F**) are positioned **across** the double bond from one another — so this is the **E-isomer** of 1-bromo-1-chloro-2-fluoro-ethene.

Be careful if you're doing this for an alkene with only **3 different groups**. The E/Z system gives the positions of the **highest priority group** on each carbon, which aren't always the **matching groups.**

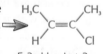

E-2-chlorobut-2-ene

You May Have to Look **Further** Along a **Chain** to work out **Priorities**

If the atoms **directly bonded** to the carbon are the **same**, then you have to look at the **next** atom in the groups to work out which has the higher priority. For example, look at this branched alkene molecule:

1) The atoms attached to **carbon-2** are both carbons, so go a step **along** the chain to find the priority. The **methyl** carbon is joined to hydrogen (atomic number 1). The first **ethyl** carbon is joined to another carbon (atomic number 6). So the **ethyl group** has higher priority.
2) The atoms attached to **carbon-1** are bromine and chlorine. **Bromine** has a higher atomic number, so it is the higher priority group.
3) Both higher priority groups are **below** the double bond — so this molecule is a **Z-isomer**.

Isomerism

Don't be Fooled — What Looks Like an Isomer Might Not Be

Beware — sometimes what looks like an isomer, isn't. If you can **switch** between two drawings of a molecule, either by rotating the **C-C single bonds** or rotating the **entire molecule**, then you've drawn the same isomer twice.

E.g. There are only **two** chain or positional isomers of C_3H_7Br.

① 1-bromopropane — 1-bromopropane again... — ... and again 1-bromopropane — ... and again 1-bromopropane

② 2-bromopropane — 2-bromopropane again...

But-2-ene only has **two** stereoisomers.

① E-but-2-ene — Still E-but-2-ene

② Z-but-2-ene — Another Z-but-2-ene

Warm-Up Questions

PRACTICE QUESTIONS

Q1 What are structural isomers?

Q2 Define the term 'stereoisomers'.

Q3 What property of alkenes gives rise to E/Z isomerism?

Q4 Which group would have a higher priority under the CIP priority rules: a bromine atom or an –OH group?

Exam Questions

Q1 There are four halogenoalkanes with the molecular formula C_4H_9Cl.

a) Give the names of all four of these halogenoalkanes. [4 marks]

b) Identify a pair of positional isomers from your answer to part a). [1 mark]

c) Identify a pair of chain isomers from your answer to part a). [1 mark]

Q2 1-bromopropene has the structural formula $CH_3CH{=}CHBr$.

a) Draw the structure of E-1-bromopropene. [1 mark]

b) Draw the structures of two isomers of 1-bromopropene that do not exhibit E/Z isomerism. [2 marks]

Q3 a) Draw and name the E/Z isomers of pent-2-ene. [2 marks]

b) Explain why alkenes can have E/Z isomers but alkanes cannot. [2 marks]

I just love my new surround-sound stereoisomer...

IMPORTANT FACT: If the two groups connected to one of the double-bonded carbons in an alkene are the same, then it won't have geometric isomers. So neither propene nor but-1-ene have E/Z isomers. Try drawing them out if you're not sure. And then draw out all the structural isomers of butene. Just to prove you've got this completely sussed.

Alkanes and Petroleum

Alkanes are the first set of organic chemicals you need to know about. They're what petroleum's mainly made of.

Alkanes are **Saturated Hydrocarbons**

1) Alkanes have the **general formula C_nH_{2n+2}**.
2) They only contain **carbon** and **hydrogen** atoms, so they're **hydrocarbons**.
3) Every carbon atom in an alkane has **four single bonds** with other atoms. It's **impossible** for carbon to make more than four bonds, so alkanes are **saturated** (they only contain **single bonds**).

   Here are a few examples of alkanes:

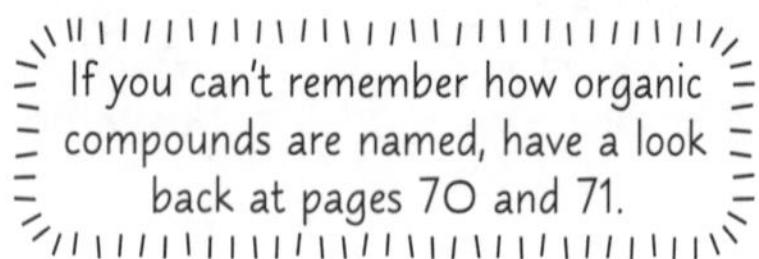

If you can't remember how organic compounds are named, have a look back at pages 70 and 71.


```
   H            H  H             H  H  H
   |            |  |             |  |  |
H— C —H     H— C — C —H      H—C— C — C —H
   |            |  |             |  |  |
   H            H  H             H  H  H
Methane        Ethane           Propane
```

4) You can get **cycloalkanes** too. They have a ring of carbon atoms with two hydrogens attached to each carbon.
5) Cycloalkanes have a **different general formula** from that of normal alkanes (C_nH_{2n}, assuming they have only one ring), but they are still **saturated**.

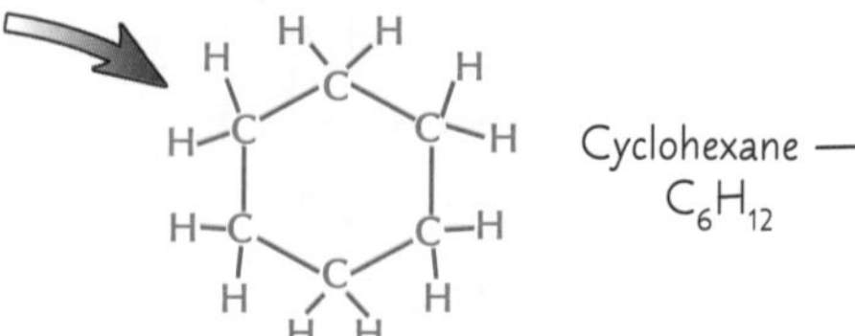

Crude Oil is Mainly **Alkanes**

1) **Petroleum** is just a fancy word for **crude oil** — the sticky black stuff they get out of the ground with oil wells.
2) Petroleum is a mixture of **hydrocarbons**. It's mostly made up of **alkanes**. They range from **small alkanes**, like pentane, to **massive alkanes** of more than 50 carbons.
3) Crude oil isn't very useful as it is, but you can **separate** it out into useful bits (**fractions**) by **fractional distillation**.

Here's how fractional distillation works — don't try this at home.

1) First, the crude oil is **vaporised** at about 350 °C.
2) The vaporised crude oil goes into a **fractionating column** and rises up through the trays. The largest hydrocarbons don't **vaporise** at all, because their boiling points are too high — they just run to the bottom and form a gooey **residue**.
3) As the crude oil vapour goes up the fractionating column, it gets **cooler**. Because the alkane molecules have different chain lengths, they have different **boiling points**, so each fraction **condenses** at a different temperature. The fractions are **drawn off** at different levels in the column.
4) The hydrocarbons with the **lowest boiling points** don't condense. They're drawn off as **gases** at the top of the column.

You might do fractional distillation in the lab, but if you do you'll use a safer crude oil substitute instead.

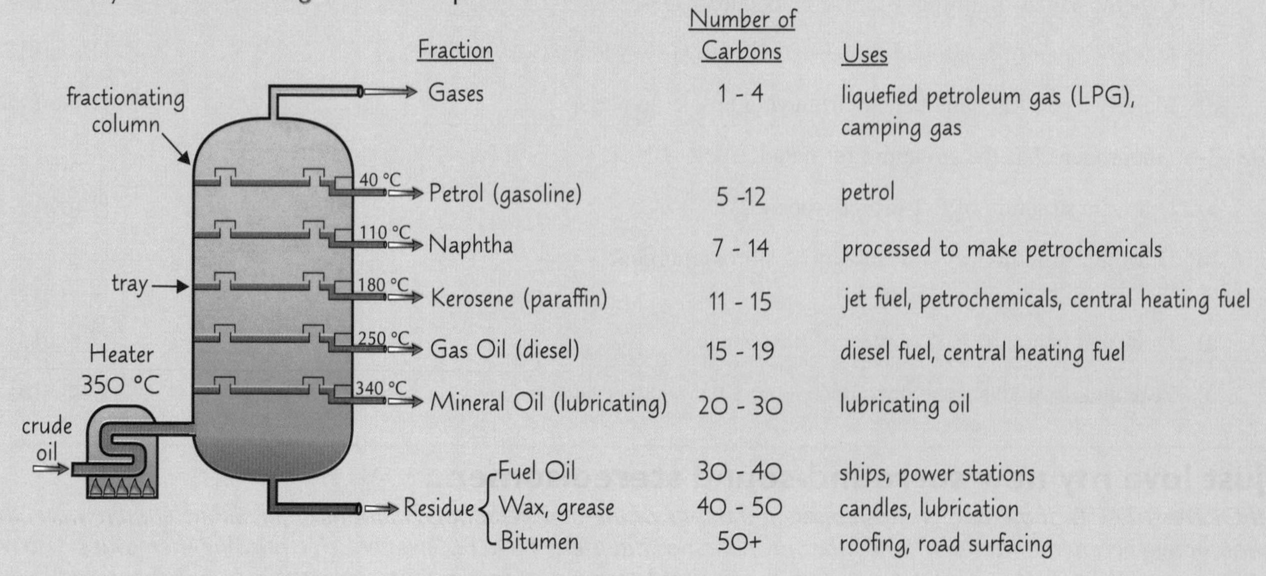

Fraction	Number of Carbons	Uses
Gases	1 - 4	liquefied petroleum gas (LPG), camping gas
Petrol (gasoline)	5 -12	petrol
Naphtha	7 - 14	processed to make petrochemicals
Kerosene (paraffin)	11 - 15	jet fuel, petrochemicals, central heating fuel
Gas Oil (diesel)	15 - 19	diesel fuel, central heating fuel
Mineral Oil (lubricating)	20 - 30	lubricating oil
Residue: Fuel Oil	30 - 40	ships, power stations
Residue: Wax, grease	40 - 50	candles, lubrication
Residue: Bitumen	50+	roofing, road surfacing

Alkanes and Petroleum

Heavy Fractions can be 'Cracked' to Make Smaller Molecules

1) People want loads of the **light** fractions of crude oil, like petrol and naphtha. They don't want so much of the **heavier** stuff like bitumen though. Stuff that's in high demand is much more **valuable** than the stuff that isn't.
2) To meet this demand, the less popular heavier fractions are **cracked**. Cracking is **breaking** long-chain alkanes into **smaller** hydrocarbons (which can include alkenes). It involves breaking the **C–C bonds**.

For example, **decane** could crack like this:

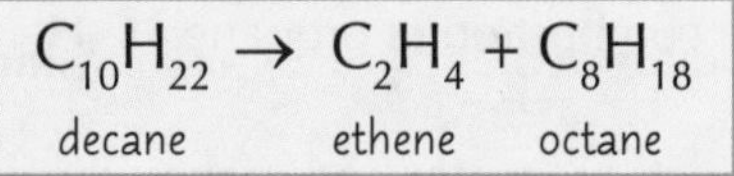

Where the chain breaks is random, so you'll get a different mixture of products every time you crack a hydrocarbon.

There are **two types** of **cracking** you need to know about:

Thermal cracking:
- This takes place at **high temperature** (up to 1000 °C) and **high pressure** (up to 70 atm).
- It produces a lot of **alkenes**.
- These **alkenes** are used to make heaps of valuable products, like **polymers** (plastics). A good example is **poly(ethene)**, which is made from ethene.

Catalytic cracking:
- Catalytic cracking uses something called a **zeolite catalyst** (**hydrated aluminosilicate**), at a **slight pressure** and **high temperature** (about 450 °C).
- It mostly produces **aromatic** hydrocarbons and **motor fuels**.

  Aromatic compounds contain benzene rings. Benzene rings have six carbon atoms with three double bonds. They're pretty stable because the electrons are delocalised around the carbon ring.
- Using a catalyst **cuts costs**, because the reaction can be done at a **low** pressure and a **lower** temperature. The catalyst also **speeds** up the reaction, saving time (and time is money).

Warm-Up Questions

Q1 What is the general formula for alkanes?

Q2 Alkanes are saturated hydrocarbons — explain what the term 'saturated' means.

Q3 What is cracking?

Q4 What type of organic chemical does thermal cracking produce?

Exam Questions

Q1 Crude oil contains many different alkane molecules.
These are separated using a process called fractional distillation.

a) Why do the components of crude oil need to be separated? [1 mark]

b) What physical property of the molecules is used to separate them? [1 mark]

c) A typical alkane found in the petrol fraction has 8 carbon atoms.

i) Give the molecular formula for this alkane. [1 mark]

ii) Would you find the petrol fraction near the top or the bottom of the fractionating column?
Explain your answer. [2 marks]

Q2 Crude oil is a source of fuels and petrochemicals. It can be vaporised and separated into fractions by fractional distillation. Some heavier fractions are processed using cracking.

a) Give one reason why cracking is carried out. [1 mark]

b) An alkane containing 12 carbon atoms is cracked to produce hexane, butene and ethene.
Write a balanced equation for this reaction. [1 mark]

Crude oil — not the kind of oil you could take home to meet your mother...

This isn't the most exciting topic in the history of the known universe. Although in a galaxy far, far away there may be lots of pages on more boring topics. But, that's neither here nor there, because you've got to learn the stuff anyway. Get fractional distillation and cracking straight in your brain and make sure you know why people bother to do it.

Alkanes as Fuels

Alkanes are absolutely fantastic as fuels. Except for the fact that they produce loads of nasty pollutant gases.

Alkanes are Useful **Fuels**

1) If you burn (**oxidise**) alkanes (and other hydrocarbons) with **plenty of oxygen**, you get **carbon dioxide** and water — it's a **combustion reaction**.

   For example, here's the equation for the combustion of propane: $C_3H_{8(g)} + 5O_{2(g)} \rightarrow 3CO_{2(g)} + 4H_2O_{(g)}$

2) This is **complete combustion** — the only products are **water** and **carbon dioxide**. (There's also incomplete combustion, which is really bad — see below.)
3) Alkanes make great **fuels** — burning just a small amount releases a humongous amount **of energy**.
4) They're burnt in power stations, central heating systems and, of course, to power car engines.
5) They do have a downside though — burning alkanes also produces lots of **pollutants**. Handily, that's what the rest of this topic is all about...

Incomplete Combustion Happens When There's Not Enough **Oxygen**

If there's not enough oxygen around, hydrocarbons combust **incompletely**.
This changes the **products** of the reaction and can lead to some nasty side effects.

Carbon Monoxide

- When a hydrocarbon undergoes incomplete combustion, you can get **carbon monoxide** gas instead of, or as well as, carbon dioxide. For example:

$$CH_{4(g)} + 1\tfrac{1}{2}O_{2(g)} \rightarrow CO_{(g)} + 2H_2O_{(g)}$$

$$C_8H_{18(g)} + 10\tfrac{1}{2}O_{2(g)} \rightarrow 4CO_{2(g)} + 4CO_{(g)} + 9H_2O_{(g)}$$

- This is bad news because carbon monoxide gas is **poisonous**. Carbon monoxide molecules bind to the same sites on **haemoglobin molecules** in red blood cells as oxygen molecules. So **oxygen** can't be carried around the body.
- Luckily, carbon monoxide can be removed from exhaust gases by **catalytic converters** on cars.

Carbon

- **Carbon particles** (**soot**) can also be formed by incomplete combustion. For example:

$$CH_4 + O_2 \rightarrow C + 2H_2O$$

- Soot is thought to cause **breathing problems**. It can also build up in **engines**, meaning they don't work properly.

Burning Fossil Fuels Contributes to **Global Warming**

1) Burning fossil fuels produces **carbon dioxide**. Carbon dioxide is a **greenhouse gas**.
2) The greenhouse gases in our atmosphere are really good at absorbing **infrared energy** (**heat**). They emit some of the energy they absorb back towards the Earth, keeping it warm. This is called the **greenhouse effect**.
3) Most scientists agree that by **increasing** the amount of carbon dioxide in our atmosphere, we are making the Earth **warmer**.
4) This process is known as **global warming**.

Marjorie loved her new green-house effect.

Alkanes as Fuels

Unburnt Hydrocarbons and Oxides of Nitrogen Can Cause Smog

1) Engines **don't burn** all of the fuel molecules. Some of them will come out as **unburnt hydrocarbons**.
2) **Oxides of nitrogen** (NO_x) are produced when the high **pressure** and **temperature** in a car engine cause the nitrogen and oxygen atoms from the air to react together.
3) Hydrocarbons and nitrogen oxides react in the presence of sunlight to form **ground-level ozone** (O_3), which is a major component of **smog**. **Ground-level ozone** irritates people's eyes, aggravates respiratory problems and even causes lung damage (ozone isn't nice stuff, unless it is high up in the atmosphere as part of the ozone layer).
4) **Catalytic converters** on cars remove unburnt hydrocarbons and oxides of nitrogen from the exhaust.

As if That's Not Bad Enough...Acid Rain is Caused by Sulfur Dioxide

1) Some fossil fuels contain **sulfur**. When they are burnt, the sulfur reacts to form **sulfur dioxide gas** (SO_2).
2) Sulfur dioxide is a bit of a nasty beast. If it gets into the atmosphere, it dissolves in the moisture and is converted into **sulfuric acid**. This is what causes **acid rain**.
3) Acid rain destroys **trees** and **vegetation**, as well as **corroding buildings** and **statues** and **killing fish** in lakes.

The same process occurs when nitrogen oxides escape into the atmosphere — nitric acid is produced.

Fortunately, sulfur dioxide can be **removed** from power station flue gases before it gets into the atmosphere. Powdered **calcium carbonate** (limestone) or **calcium oxide** is mixed with water to make an **alkaline slurry**. When the flue gases mix with the alkaline slurry, the **acidic sulfur dioxide** gas reacts with the calcium compounds to form a harmless salt (**calcium sulfate**) — see page 61 for more on this.

Warm-Up Questions

Q1 Which two compounds are produced when an alkane burns completely?

Q2 Under what conditions does incomplete combustion of a fuel take place?

Q3 Name four pollutants that can be produced when a fuel is burnt.
For each pollutant you have named, give one environmental problem that it causes.

Q4 Describe how burning fossil fuels causes acid rain.

Exam Questions

Q1 Heptane, C_7H_{16}, is an alkane present in some fuels.

a) Write a balanced equation for the complete combustion of heptane. [1 mark]

b) Fuels often contain compounds called oxygenates which are added to ensure that the fuel burns completely.

i) What poisonous compound is produced by incomplete combustion of alkanes like heptane? [1 mark]

ii) Apart from adding oxygenates, how else can this compound be removed from exhaust gases? [1 mark]

Q2 Burning fossil fuels produces a variety of gaseous pollutants, such as oxides of nitrogen and sulfur dioxide.

a) Explain how oxides of nitrogen are produced in car engines. [2 marks]

b) Explain how sulfur dioxide can be removed from power station flue gases using calcium carbonate. [2 marks]

Burn, baby, burn — so long as the combustion is complete...

Don't you just hate it when you come up with a great idea, then everyone picks holes in it? Just imagine you were the one who thought of burning alkanes for fuel... it seemed like such a good idea at the time. Despite all the problems, we still use them — and until we find some suitable alternatives, we all have to deal with the negative consequences.

Chloroalkanes and CFCs

For a while, everyone thought CFCs were the bee's knees. That was until they started destroying the ozone layer...

Free Radicals Have Unpaired Electrons

1) A **free radical** is a particle with an **unpaired electron**.
2) Free radicals form when a covalent bond splits **equally**, giving **one electron** to each atom.
3) The unpaired electron makes them **very reactive**.
4) You can show something's a free radical in a mechanism by putting a dot next to it, like this
   The dot represents the unpaired electron.

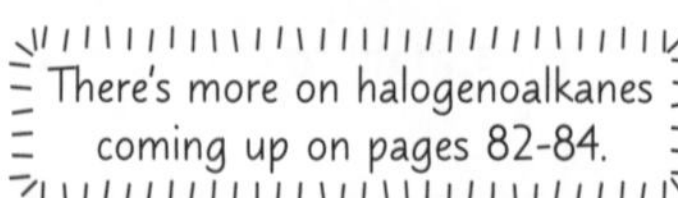

There's more on halogenoalkanes coming up on pages 82-84.

Halogens React with Alkanes to form Halogenoalkanes

1) Halogens react with alkanes in **photochemical** reactions — reactions that are started by **ultraviolet** light.
2) A hydrogen atom is **substituted** (replaced) by chlorine or bromine. This is a **free-radical substitution reaction**.

Example: Reacting Chlorine With Methane

Chlorine and **methane** react with a bit of a bang to form **chloromethane**:

$$CH_4 + Cl_2 \xrightarrow{UV} CH_3Cl + HCl$$

The **reaction mechanism** has three stages.

Stage 1: Initiation reactions — free radicals are produced.

1) Sunlight provides enough energy to break the Cl-Cl bond — this is **photodissociation**.

$$Cl_2 \xrightarrow{UV} 2Cl\bullet$$

2) The bond splits **equally** and each atom gets to keep one electron.
   The atom becomes a highly reactive **free radical**, Cl•, because of its **unpaired electron**.

Stage 2: Propagation reactions — free radicals are used up and created in a chain reaction.

1) Cl• attacks a **methane** molecule: $Cl\bullet + CH_4 \rightarrow CH_3\bullet + HCl$
2) The new **methyl free radical**, $CH_3\bullet$, can attack another Cl_2 molecule: $CH_3\bullet + Cl_2 \rightarrow CH_3Cl + Cl\bullet$
3) The new Cl• can attack **another** CH_4 molecule, and so on, until all the Cl_2 or CH_4 molecules are used up.

Stage 3: Termination reactions — free radicals are mopped up.

1) If two free radicals join together, they make a **stable molecule**.
   The two unpaired electrons form a covalent bond.
2) There are **heaps** of possible termination reactions. Here's a couple of them to give you the idea:

$$Cl\bullet + CH_3\bullet \rightarrow CH_3Cl \qquad CH_3\bullet + CH_3\bullet \rightarrow C_2H_6$$

What happens after this depends on whether there's more **chlorine** or **methane** around:

1) If the **chlorine's** in excess, Cl• free radicals will start attacking chloromethane, producing **dichloromethane** CH_2Cl_2, **trichloromethane** $CHCl_3$, and even **tetrachloromethane** CCl_4.
2) **But** if the **methane's** in excess, then the product will mostly be **chloromethane**.

Chlorofluorocarbons Contain No Hydrogen

Chlorofluorocarbons (**CFCs**) are halogenoalkane molecules where all of the hydrogen atoms have been replaced by **chlorine** and **fluorine** atoms.

```
      Cl                  F
      |                   |
  Cl—C—Cl             F—C—F
      |                   |
      F                   Cl
trichlorofluoromethane   chlorotrifluoromethane
```

Chloroalkanes and CFCs

Chlorine Atoms are Destroying The **Ozone Layer**

1) Ozone (O_3) in the upper atmosphere acts as a **chemical sunscreen**. It absorbs a lot of **ultraviolet radiation** from the Sun, stopping it from reaching us. Ultraviolet radiation can cause **sunburn** or even **skin cancer**.
2) Ozone's **formed naturally** when an oxygen molecule (O_2) is **broken down** into two **free radicals** by **ultraviolet radiation**. The free radicals **attack** other oxygen molecules forming **ozone**. Just like this:

$$O_2 \xrightarrow{UV} O\bullet + O\bullet \quad \text{then} \quad O_2 + O\bullet \rightarrow O_3$$

You've probably heard that **CFCs** are creating **holes** in the **ozone layer**. Well, here's what's happening.

1) **Chlorine free radicals** (Cl•) are formed in the upper atmosphere when C–Cl bonds in **CFCs** are broken down by **ultraviolet radiation**. E.g. $CCl_3F \xrightarrow{UV} CCl_2F\bullet + Cl\bullet$
2) These free radicals are **catalysts**. They react with **ozone** to form an **intermediate** (ClO•) and an oxygen molecule.

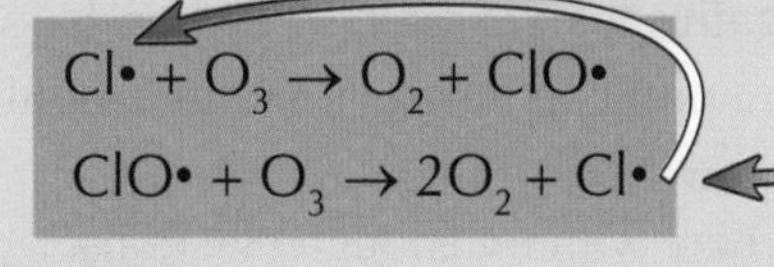

The chlorine free radical is regenerated and can go straight on to attack another ozone molecule. So it only takes one chlorine free radical to destroy loads of ozone molecules.

3) So the **overall reaction** is... $2O_3 \rightarrow 3O_2$ ... and Cl• is the **catalyst**.

CFCs Are Now **Banned**

1) CFCs are pretty **unreactive**, **non-flammable** and **non-toxic**. They used to be used as coolant gas in fridges, as solvents, and as propellants in aerosols.
2) In the 1970s research by several different scientific groups demonstrated that CFCs were causing **damage** to the **ozone layer**. The **advantages** of CFCs couldn't outweigh the **environmental problems** they were causing, so they were **banned**.
3) Chemists have developed safer **alternatives** to CFCs which contain no **chlorine** such as **HFCs (hydrofluorocarbons)** and **hydrocarbons.**

Warm-Up Questions

PRACTICE QUESTIONS

Q1 What is a free radical?

Q2 Write an overall equation for the reaction of methane with chlorine in the presence of UV light.

Q3 Explain why having ozone in the upper atmosphere is beneficial to humans.

Q4 Name two past uses for CFCs. Name one type of compound that is used as an alternative to CFCs today.

Exam Questions

Q1 In the upper atmosphere, chlorine free radicals are produced by the action of ultraviolet light on CFC molecules. Chlorine free radicals can catalyse the breakdown of ozone (O_3), damaging the ozone layer.

Write two equations to show how a chlorine free radical catalyses the breakdown of an ozone molecule. [2 marks]

Q2 The alkane ethane (C_2H_6) will react with chlorine in a photochemical reaction.

a) Give the name for this type of reaction. [1 mark]

b) Write equations to show the mechanism for the reaction of ethane (C_2H_6) with chlorine. Your mechanism should include an initiation reaction, propagation reactions and an example of one possible termination reaction that produces an organic compound. [4 marks]

This stuff is like...totally radical, man...

Mechanisms are an absolute pain in the neck to learn, but unfortunately reactions are what Chemistry's all about. If you don't like it, you should have taken art — no mechanisms in that, just pretty pictures. Ah well, there's no going back now. You've just got to sit down and learn the stuff. Keep hacking away at it, till you know it all off by heart.

Halogenoalkanes

Don't worry if you see halogenoalkanes called haloalkanes. It's a government conspiracy to confuse you.

Halogenoalkanes are **Alkanes** with **Halogen** Atoms

A **halogenoalkane** is an alkane with at least one **halogen atom** in place of a hydrogen atom.

E.g.

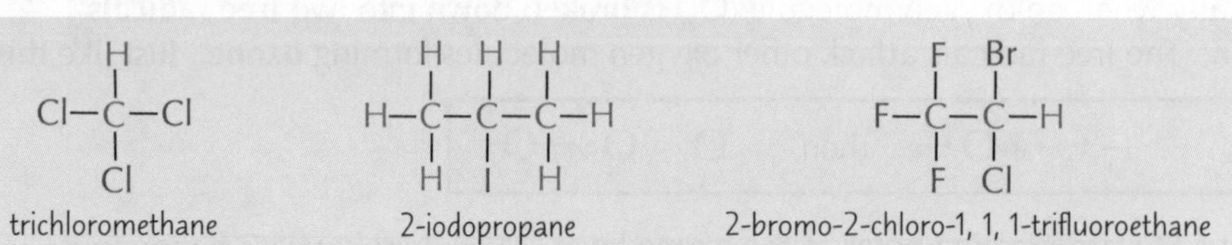

There's more about how to name organic compounds, including halogenoalkanes, on pages 70-71.

The **Carbon–Halogen Bond** in Halogenoalkanes is **Polar**

1) Halogens are much more **electronegative** than carbon, so carbon-halogen bonds are **polar**.
2) The δ+ charge on the carbon makes it prone to attacks from **nucleophiles**.
3) A nucleophile is an **electron-pair donor**.
   It donates an electron pair to somewhere without enough electrons.
4) **OH^-**, **CN^-** and **NH_3** are all **nucleophiles** that can react with halogenoalkanes.

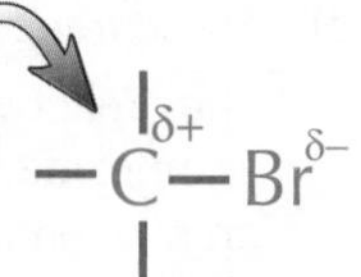

Halogenoalkanes Can Undergo **Nucleophilic Substitution** Reactions

1) A nucleophile can react with a polar molecule by kicking out the functional group and taking its place.
2) This is called a **nucleophilic substitution reaction**. It works like this:

Curly arrows show the movement of electron pairs. If you can't remember how they work, look back at page 72.

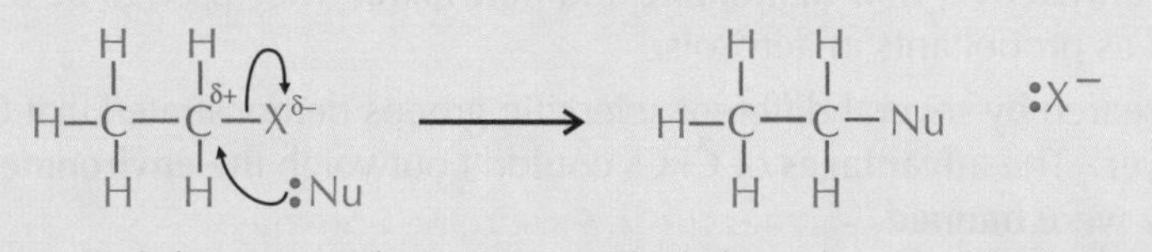

The lone pair of electrons on the nucleophile attacks the δ+ carbon. The C–X bond breaks.

The halogen leaves, taking both electrons with it. A new bond forms between the carbon and the nucleophile.

X stands for one of the halogens (F, Cl, Br or I). **Nu** stands for a nucleophile.

3) The **product** of these reactions depends on what the **nucleophile** is...

Halogenoalkanes React with **Hydroxides** to Form **Alcohols**

For example, bromoethane can react to form ethanol. You have to use **warm aqueous sodium** or **potassium hydroxide** — it's a **nucleophilic substitution reaction**.

This is sometimes called hydrolysis, because exactly the same reaction will happen with water. (Hydrolysis means splitting a molecule apart by reacting it with water.)

Here's how it happens:

$$CH_3CH_2Br + {:}OH^- \longrightarrow CH_3CH_2OH + {:}Br^-$$

The δ+ carbon attracts a lone pair of electrons from the OH^- ion. The C–Br bond breaks.

The bromine leaves, taking both electrons to become Br^-. A new bond forms between the carbon and the OH^- ion, making an alcohol.

Nitriles Are Formed by Reacting Halogenoalkanes with **Cyanide**

Nitriles have –C≡N groups.

If you **warm** a halogenoalkane with **ethanolic potassium cyanide** (potassium cyanide dissolved in ethanol) you get a **nitrile**. It's yet another **nucleophilic substitution reaction** — the **cyanide ion**, CN^-, is the **nucleophile**.

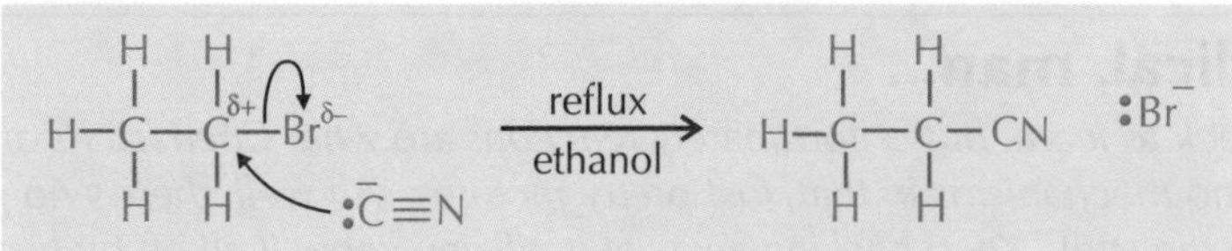

This follows the same pattern — the lone pair of electrons on the CN^- ion attacks the δ+ carbon, the C–Br bond breaks and the bromine leaves.

Halogenoalkanes

Reacting Halogenoalkanes with **Ammonia** Forms **Amines**

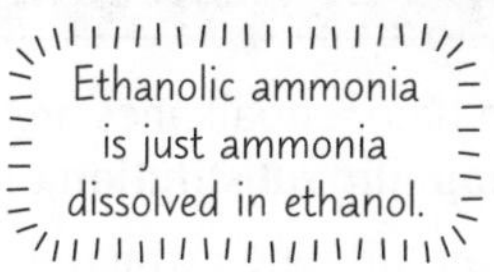

Ethanolic ammonia is just ammonia dissolved in ethanol.

1) If you **warm** a halogenoalkane with excess **ethanolic** ammonia, the **ammonia** swaps places with the **halogen** — yes, it's another one of these **nucleophilic substitution reactions**.

The first step is the same as the mechanism on the previous page, except this time the nucleophile is NH_3.

In the second step, an ammonia molecule removes a hydrogen from the NH_3 group, forming an amine and an ammonium ion (NH_4^+).

2) The ammonium ion can react with the bromine ion to form ammonium bromide. So the overall reaction looks like this:

$$CH_3CH_2Br + 2NH_3 \xrightarrow{\text{ethanol}} CH_3CH_2NH_2 + NH_4Br$$

3) The **amine group** in the product still has a lone pair of electrons. This means that it can also act as a **nucleophile** — so it may react with halogenoalkane molecules itself, giving a mixture of products.

Iodoalkanes React **Fastest**, Fluoroalkanes React **Slowest**

1) The **carbon-halogen bond strength** (or enthalpy) decides **reactivity**. For any reaction to occur the carbon-halogen bond needs to **break**.
2) The **C–F bond** is the **strongest** — it has the highest **bond enthalpy**. So **fluoroalkanes** undergo nucleophilic substitution reactions **more slowly** than other halogenoalkanes.
3) The **C–I bond** has the **lowest bond enthalpy**, so it's easier to break. This means that **iodoalkanes** are substituted more **quickly**.

bond	bond enthalpy kJ mol^{-1}
C–F	467
C–Cl	346
C–Br	290
C–I	228

Faster substitution as bond enthalpy decreases (the bonds are getting weaker).

Halogenoalkanes also Undergo **Elimination Reactions**

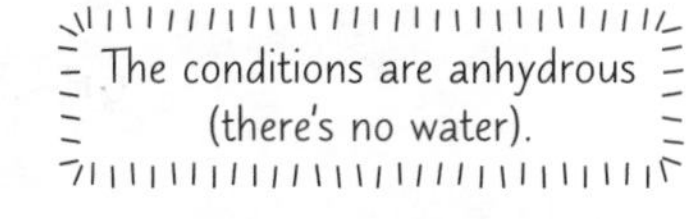

The conditions are anhydrous (there's no water).

1) If you warm a halogenoalkane with hydroxide ions dissolved in **ethanol** instead of water, an **elimination reaction** happens, and you end up with an **alkene**.
2) You have to heat the mixture **under reflux** or you'll lose volatile stuff.
3) Here's how the reaction works:

1) OH^- acts as a base and takes a proton, H^+, from the carbon on the left. This makes water.
2) The left carbon now has a spare electron, so it forms a double bond with the middle carbon.
3) To form the double bond, the middle carbon has to let go of the Br, which drops off as a Br^- ion.

4) If you use 2-bromopropane and potassium hydroxide, the equation for the reaction will look like this:

$$CH_3CHBrCH_3 + KOH \xrightarrow[\text{reflux}]{\text{ethanol}} CH_2CHCH_3 + H_2O + KBr$$

5) This is an example of an **elimination reaction**. In an elimination reaction, a **small group** of atoms breaks away from a molecule. This group is **not replaced** by anything else (whereas it would be in a substitution reaction). For example, in the reaction above, H and Br have been eliminated from $CH_3CHBrCH_3$ to leave CH_2CHCH_3.

Halogenoalkanes

The **Type of Reaction** Depends on the **Conditions**

Bob's reaction to the sight of a golf course was not affected by the conditions.

1) When halogenoalkanes are reacted with **hydroxides**, they may undergo either **nucleophilic substitution** or **elimination**. The two reactions are said to be **competing**.
2) You can influence which reaction will happen the most by **changing the conditions**.

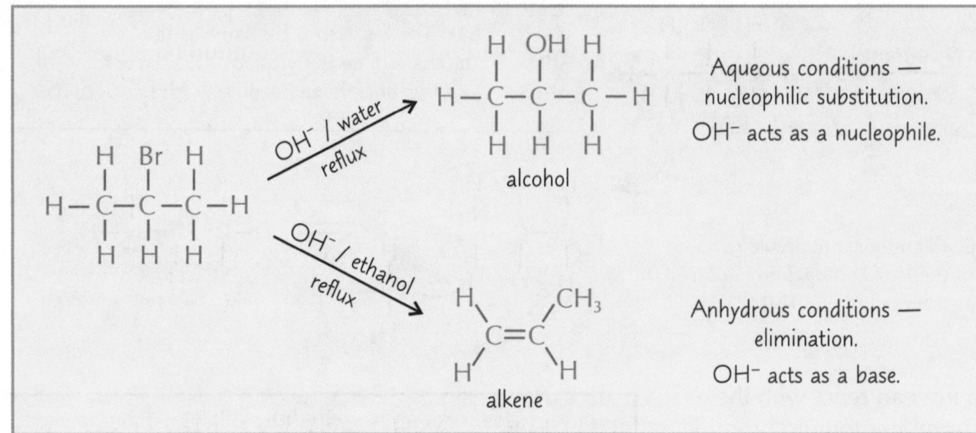

3) If you use a **mixture** of water and ethanol as the solvent, **both** reactions will happen and you'll get a mixture of the two products.

Warm-Up Questions

Q1 Why are carbon-halogen bonds polar?

Q2 What is a nucleophile?

Q3 Name the type of organic compound formed by the reaction of a halogenoalkane with:
a) aqueous potassium hydroxide b) potassium cyanide c) ethanolic ammonia

Q4 Why does iodoethane react faster than chloroethane with nucleophiles?

Q5 Draw the mechanism for the reaction of bromoethane with potassium hydroxide dissolved in ethanol.

Exam Questions

Q1 Three reactions of 2-bromopropane, $CH_3CHBrCH_3$, are shown below.

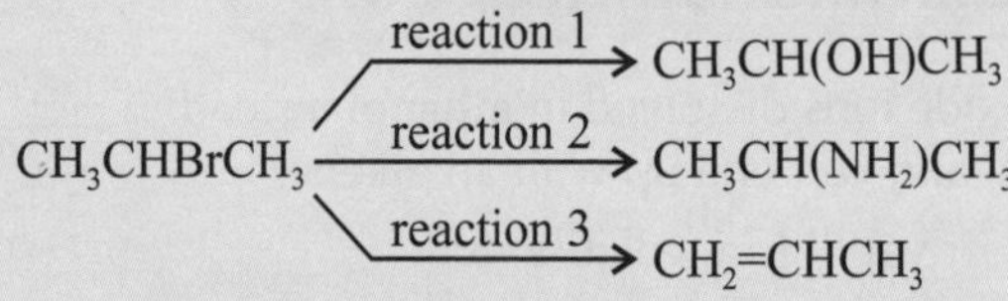

$CH_3CHBrCH_3 \xrightarrow{\text{reaction 1}} CH_3CH(OH)CH_3$

$CH_3CHBrCH_3 \xrightarrow{\text{reaction 2}} CH_3CH(NH_2)CH_3$

$CH_3CHBrCH_3 \xrightarrow{\text{reaction 3}} CH_2{=}CHCH_3$

a) For each reaction, name the reagent and the solvent used. [6 marks]

b) Under the same conditions, 2-iodopropane was used in reaction 1 in place of 2-bromopropane. What difference (if any) would you expect in the rate of the reaction? Explain your answer. [2 marks]

Q2 Which of the following statements about bromoethane is true?

A The carbon attached to the bromine atom has a partial negative charge.

B It reacts with KCN dissolved in ethanol to form CH_3CH_2CN.

C It reacts with KOH in aqueous conditions to form $CH_2{=}CH_2$.

D It reacts with nucleophiles at a slower rate than chloroethane.

[1 mark]

If you don't learn this — you will be eliminated. Resistance is nitrile...

Polar bonds get into so many bits of chemistry. If you still think they're something to do with bears or mints, flick back to page 30 and have a read. Make sure you learn all these reactions and mechanisms, as well as which halogenoalkanes react fastest. This stuff's always coming up in exams, so make sure it's filed away in your brain for when you need it.

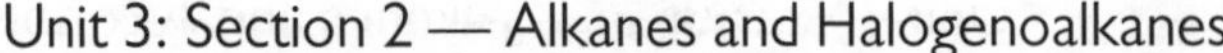

Alkenes

I'll warn you now — some of this stuff gets a bit heavy — but stick with it, as it's pretty important.

Alkenes are **Unsaturated Hydrocarbons**

Alkenes with more than one double bond have fewer Hs than the general formula suggests.

1) Alkenes have the **general formula C_nH_{2n}**. They're just made of carbon and hydrogen atoms, so they're **hydrocarbons**.
2) Alkene molecules **all** have at least one **C=C double covalent bond**. Molecules with C=C double bonds are **unsaturated** because they can make more bonds with extra atoms in **addition** reactions.
3) Because there are two pairs of electrons in the C=C double bond, it has a really **high electron density**. This makes alkenes pretty reactive. Here are a few pretty diagrams of **alkenes**:

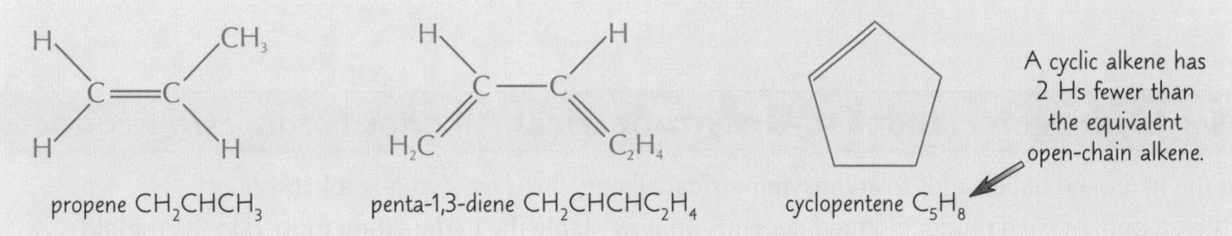

propene CH_2CHCH_3
penta-1,3-diene $CH_2CHCHC_2H_4$
cyclopentene C_5H_8
A cyclic alkene has 2 Hs fewer than the equivalent open-chain alkene.

Electrophilic Addition Reactions Happen to Alkenes

Electrophilic addition reactions aren't too complicated...

1) The **double bonds** open up and atoms are **added** to the carbon atoms.
2) Electrophilic addition reactions happen because the double bond has got plenty of **electrons** and is easily attacked by **electrophiles**.

Electrophiles are **electron-pair acceptors** — they're usually a bit short of electrons, so they're **attracted** to areas where there are lots of them about.
Here are a few examples:

- **Positively charged ions**, like H^+ and NO_2^+.
- **Polar molecules** — the δ+ atom is attracted to places with lots of electrons.

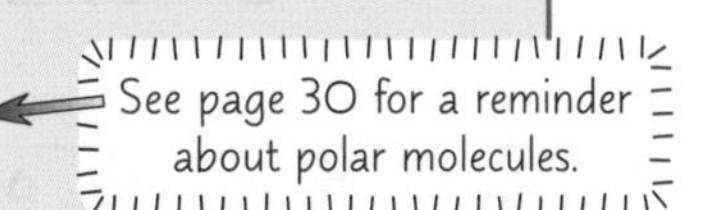

See page 30 for a reminder about polar molecules.

Eric Trofill — double bond hunter. Between you and me, he's a few electrons short of an atom.

Use **Bromine Water** to Test for **Unsaturation**

When you shake an alkene with **orange bromine water**, the solution quickly **decolourises** (goes from **orange** to **colourless**). Bromine is added across the C=C double bond to form a colourless **dibromoalkane** — this happens by **electrophilic addition**. Here's the mechanism...

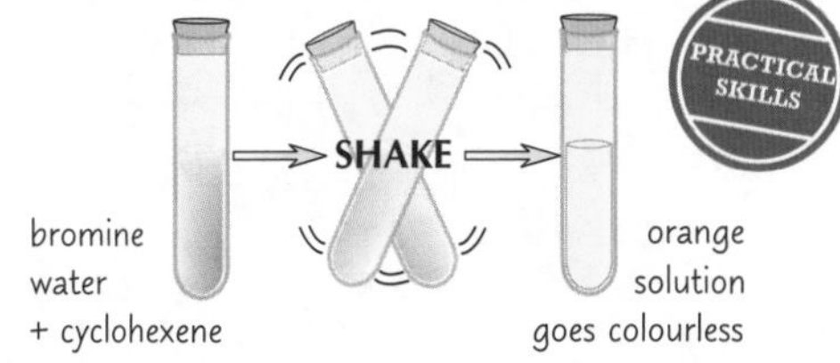

orange solution goes colourless

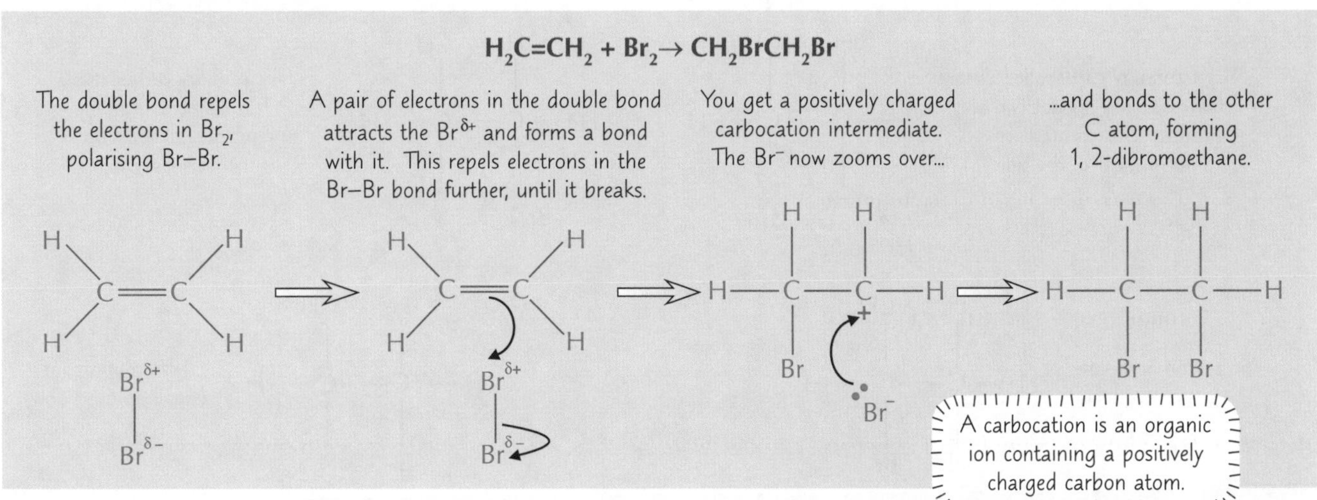

...and bonds to the other C atom, forming 1, 2-dibromoethane.

Alkenes

Alkenes also Undergo **Addition** with **Hydrogen Halides**

Alkenes also undergo **electrophilic addition** reactions with hydrogen halides — to form **halogenoalkanes**. This is the reaction between **ethene** and **hydrogen bromide**, to form **bromoethane**.

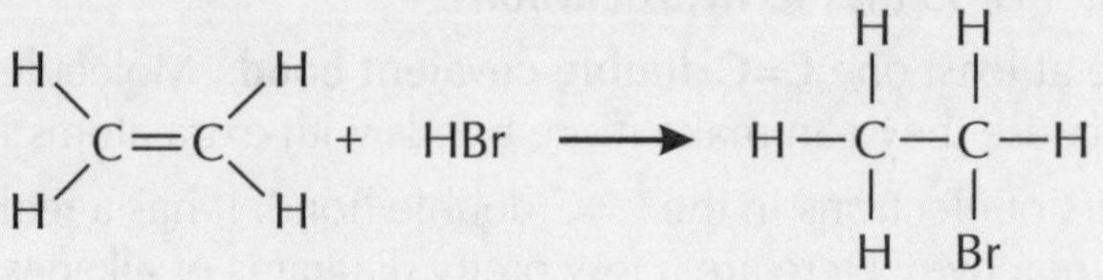

$$C_2H_4 + HBr \rightarrow C_2H_5Br$$

Other alkenes react in a similar way.

Adding **Hydrogen Halides** to **Unsymmetrical Alkenes** Forms **Two Products**

1) If the hydrogen halide adds to an **unsymmetrical** alkene, there are two possible products.
2) The amount of each product formed depends on how **stable** the **carbocation** formed in the middle of the reaction is — this is known as the **carbocation intermediate**.
3) Carbocations with more **alkyl groups** are more stable because the alkyl groups feed **electrons** towards the positive charge. The **more stable carbocation** is much more likely to form.

R = alkyl group

→ = electron donation

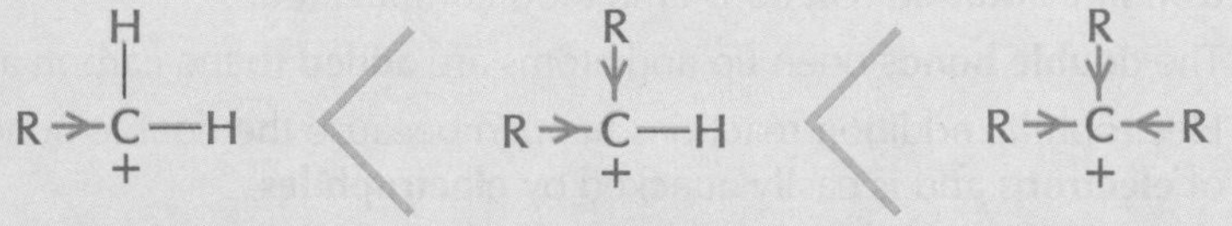

Alkyl groups are alkanes with a hydrogen removed, e.g. methyl, CH_3^-.

primary carbocation (one R group) — Least stable

secondary carbocation (two R groups)

tertiary carbocation (three R groups) — Most stable

Here's how **Hydrogen Bromide** Reacts with **Propene**

$H_2C{=}CHCH_3 \rightarrow CH_3CHBrCH_3$
2-bromopropane (major product)

$H_2C{=}CHCH_3 \rightarrow CH_2BrCH_2CH_3$
1-bromopropane (minor product)

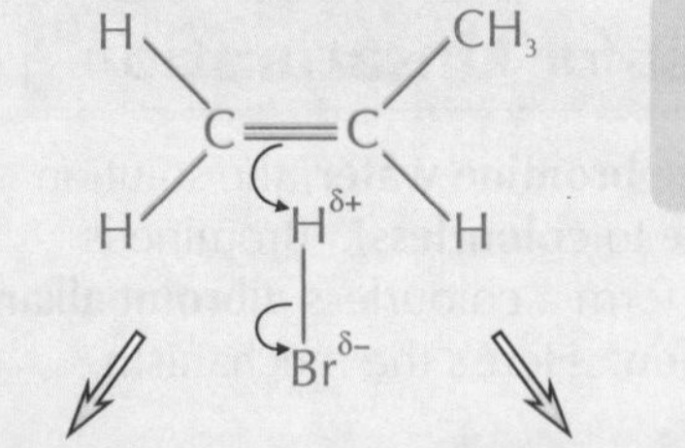

The secondary carbocation's more stable because it's got two alkyl groups. This carbocation will form most of the time.

The primary carbocation's less stable as it's only got one alkyl group. It forms less often.

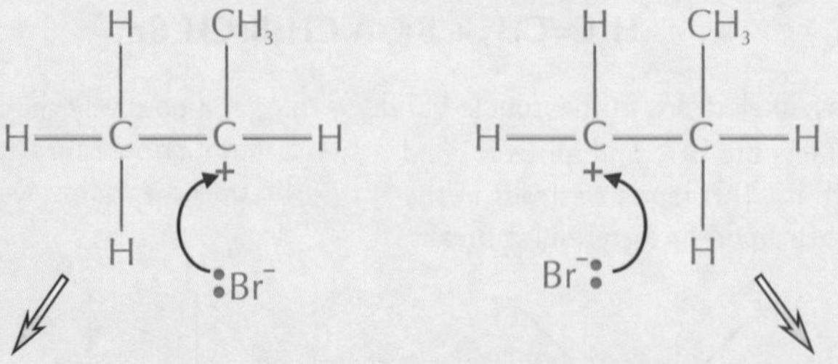

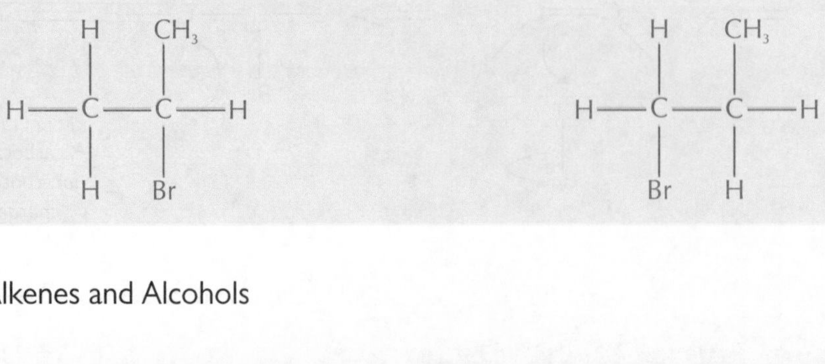

2-bromopropane (major product)

1-bromopropane (small amount only)

Alkenes

Alkenes also Undergo **Electrophilic Addition Reactions** with H_2SO_4

Alkenes will react with **cold concentrated sulfuric acid** to form **alkyl hydrogen sulfates**. You can then convert the alkyl hydrogen sulfates formed into **alcohols** by adding water and warming the reaction mixture. For example:

1) Cold concentrated **sulfuric acid** reacts with an alkene in an **electrophilic addition** reaction.

$$H_2C{=}CH_2 + H_2SO_4 \rightarrow CH_3CH_2OSO_2OH$$

ethene, sulfuric acid, ethyl hydrogen sulfate

2) If you then add cold **water** and warm the product, it **hydrolyses** to form an alcohol.

$$CH_3CH_2OSO_2OH + H_2O \rightarrow CH_3CH_2OH + H_2SO_4$$

ethyl hydrogen sulfate, ethanol

3) The **sulfuric acid** isn't used up — it acts as a **catalyst**.

$+ H_2O$

warm

This step is a hydrolysis reaction (see p.82).

If you're using this reaction to produce ethanol, then the equation for the overall reaction looks like this:

$$H_2C = CH_2 + H_2O \xrightarrow{H_2SO_4} C_2H_5OH$$

Just as with hydrogen halides on the previous page, if you do this reaction with an **unsymmetrical alkene**, you get a **mixture of products**. The one that's formed via the **most stable** carbocation intermediate will be the **major product**.

Warm-Up Questions

Q1 What is the general formula for an alkene?

Q2 Why do alkenes react with electrophiles?

Q3 What is an electrophile?

Q4 What is a carbocation?

Exam Questions

Q1 But-1-ene is an alkene. Alkenes contain at least one C=C double bond.

a) Describe how bromine water can be used to test for C=C double bonds. [2 marks]

b) Name the reaction mechanism involved in the above test. [1 mark]

c) Hydrogen bromide will react with but-1-ene by this mechanism, producing two isomeric products.

i) Draw a mechanism for the reaction of HBr with $CH_2{=}CHCH_2CH_3$, showing the formation of the major product only. Name the product. [4 marks]

ii) Explain why it is the major product for this reaction. [2 marks]

Q2 Cold concentrated sulfuric acid is mixed with propene. Cold water is then added to the mixture, and the mixture is warmed. What are the end products of this procedure?

A $C_3H_7OH + H_2SO_4$

B $C_3H_7SO_4H + H_2O$

C $C_3H_8 + H_2SO_4 + H_2O$

D $C_3H_8OH + H_2SO_4$

[1 mark]

Got an unsymmetrical alkene? I'd get that looked at...

Wow... these pages really are packed. There's not one, not two, but three mechanisms to learn. They mightn't be as handy in real life as a tin opener, but you won't need a tin opener in the exam. Get the book shut and scribble them out. Make sure your arrows start at the electron pair and finish exactly where the electrons are going.

Addition Polymers

Polymers are long, stringy molecules made by joining lots of little molecules together. They're made up of one unit repeated over and over and over and over and over and over and over and over again. Get the idea? Let's get started.

Polymers are Formed from **Monomers**

1) **Polymers** are long chain molecules formed when lots of small molecules, called **monomers**, join together.
2) Polymers can be **natural**, like DNA and proteins, or **synthetic** (man-made), like poly(ethene).
3) People have been using **natural polymers**, like silk, cotton and rubber, for hundreds of years.
4) In the **19th century**, research concentrated on modifying the properties of natural polymers — for example **hardening rubber**, to make it more suitable for machine parts and car tyres.
5) The **20th century** saw the invention and production of **synthetic polymers**, like **nylon** and **Kevlar®**.
6) Scientists are still developing **new polymers**, with new properties, all the time.

Addition Polymers are Formed from **Alkenes**

Alkenes can act as monomers and form polymers because their double bonds can open up and join together to make long chains. These type of polymers are called **addition polymers**.

Addition polymers made from alkenes are called polyalkenes.

Poly(phenylethene) is formed from **phenylethene**.

the double bond opens up

'n' means there are lots of these units

phenylethene monomer → poly(phenylethene) polymer

This is what a section of the chain would look like:

section of poly(phenylethene) polymer

Polyalkene chains are **saturated** molecules (they only contain single bonds in the carbon chain). The main carbon chain of a polyalkene is also **non-polar**. These factors result in addition polymers being very **unreactive**.

The **Properties** of Polyalkenes Depend on Their **Intermolecular Forces**

1) Polyalkene chains are usually **non-polar** — so the chains are only held together by **Van der Waals forces** (see page 31).
2) The **longer** the polymer chains are and the **closer** together they can get, the **stronger** the Van der Waals forces between the chains will be.
3) This means that polyalkenes made up of **long**, **straight chains** tend to be **strong** and **rigid**, while polyalkenes that are made up of **short**, **branched chains** tend to be **weaker** and more **flexible**.

Polymers that contain electronegative atoms (like Cl) can be polar. These polymers will have permanent dipole-dipole forces.

You Can **Modify** The Properties of Polymers Using **Plasticisers**

Adding a **plasticiser** to a polymer makes it more flexible. The plasticiser molecules get **between** the polymer chains and push them apart. This **reduces** the strength of the **intermolecular forces** between the chains — so they can slide around more, making the polymer easy to **bend**.

Poly(chloroethene), PVC is formed from **chloroethene**.

n $CH_2{=}CHCl$ → $-(CH_2-CHCl)_n-$

chloroethene monomer → poly(chloroethene) polymer

1) PVC has long, closely packed polymer chains, making it hard but brittle at room temperature. **Rigid PVC** is used to make **drainpipes** and **window frames**.
2) **Plasticised PVC** is much more flexible than rigid PVC. It's used to make **electrical cable insulation, flooring tiles** and **clothing**.

Pretty Polymer.

Addition Polymers

You can Draw the Repeating Unit from a Monomer or Polymer

Polymers are made up of **repeating units** (a bit of molecule that repeats over and over again). The repeating units of addition polymers look very similar to the monomer, but with the double bond opened out.

1) To draw the **repeating unit** of an addition polymer from its **monomer**, first draw the two alkene carbons. Replace the double bond with a single bond. Add a single bond coming out from each of the carbons.
2) Then just fill in the rest of the groups in the same way they surrounded the double bond.

Example: Draw the repeating unit of the polymer formed from ethene, C_2H_4.

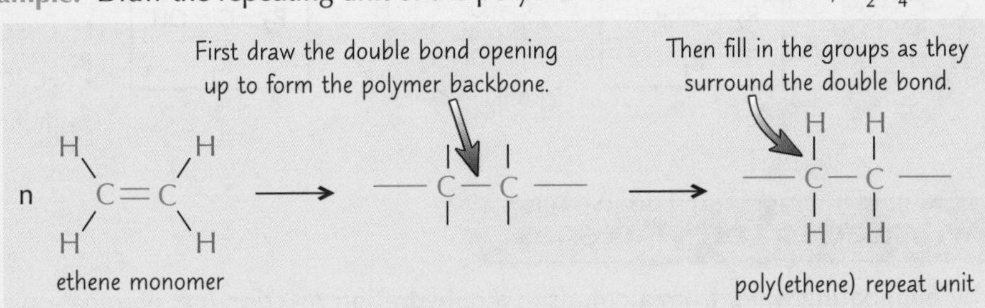

To write the name of an addition polymer, you write the name of the alkene monomer, put brackets around it and stick 'poly' in front. For example, the polymer made from ethene is poly(ethene).

3) To draw the **repeating unit** from its **polymer**, you just need to look at the chain and work out which part is repeating. For an addition polymer, the repeating unit should be **two** carbons long (so it looks like the alkene monomer). Once you have the repeating unit, you can easily draw the **monomer** by adding a double bond.

Example: Draw the repeating unit and monomer of the polymer chain Teflon® (poly(tetrafluoroethene)).

section of Teflon® polymer → Teflon® repeat unit → Teflon® monomer

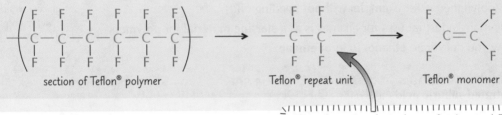

The polymer is only made up of carbon and fluorine atoms, so the repeating unit is just two carbons, surrounded by fluorines.

Warm-Up Questions

Q1 What is a polymer?

Q2 What type of polymers do alkenes form?

Q3 Explain why polyalkenes with long, straight chains are stronger than those with short, branched chains.

Q4 Give two typical uses of rigid PVC.

Exam Questions

PRACTICE QUESTIONS

Q1 The diagram on the right shows a section of the polymer poly(propene).

a) Draw the structure of the monomer that forms this polymer. [1 mark]

b) Draw the structure of the repeating unit of poly(propene). [1 mark]

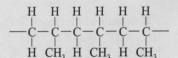

Q2 The polymer poly(chloroethene) (PVC) is made from chloroethene, shown right.

a) Draw the structure of the repeating unit of poly(chloroethene). [1 mark]

b) Explain how the properties of PVC change when you add a plasticiser. [3 marks]

c) Give two typical uses of plasticised PVC. [2 marks]

Never miss your friends again — form a polymer...

These polymers are really useful — drainpipes, clothing, electrical cable insulation... you couldn't do without them. And someone had to invent them. Just think, you could be the next mad inventor, working for the biggest secret agency in the world. And you'd have a really fast car, which obviously would turn into a yacht with the press of a button...

Alcohols

Alcohol — evil stuff, it is. I could start preaching, but I won't, because this page is enough to put you off alcohol for life...

Alcohols are **Primary, Secondary** or **Tertiary**

1) The **functional group** in the **alcohol** homologous series is the **hydroxyl** group, **-OH**.
2) An alcohol is **primary**, **secondary** or **tertiary**, depending on which carbon atom the **-OH** group is bonded to...

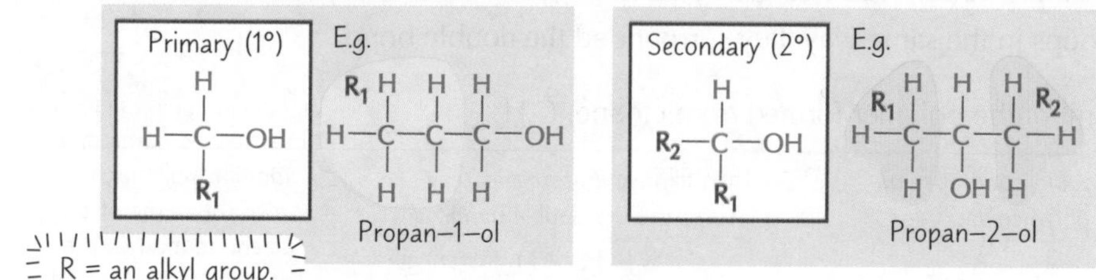

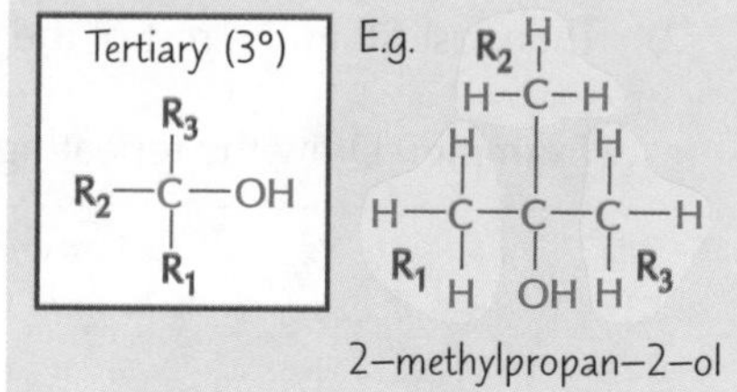

R = an alkyl group.

Alcohols can be **Dehydrated** to Form **Alkenes**

1) You can make alkenes by **eliminating** water from **alcohols** in a **dehydration reaction** (i.e. elimination of **water**).

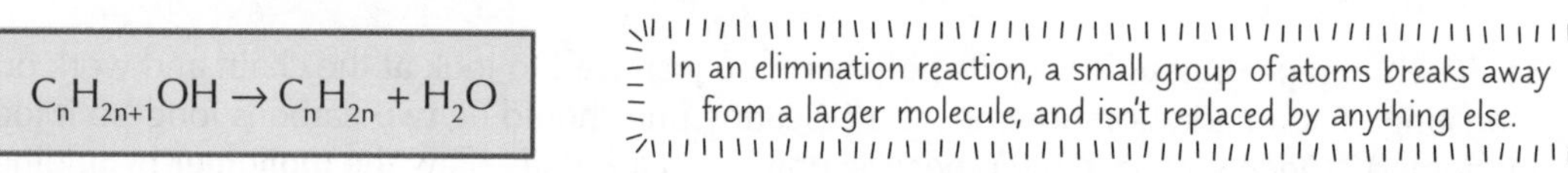

$C_nH_{2n+1}OH \rightarrow C_nH_{2n} + H_2O$
In an elimination reaction, a small group of atoms breaks away from a larger molecule, and isn't replaced by anything else.

2) This reaction allows you to produce alkenes from **renewable** resources.
3) This is important, because it means that you can produce **polymers** (poly(ethene), for example) **without** needing **oil**.
4) One of the main industrial uses for alkenes is as a **starting material** for **polymers**.

Because you can produce ethanol by fermentation of glucose, which you can get from plants.

Here's how you dehydrate **ethanol** to form **ethene**:

Ethanol is heated with a **concentrated sulfuric acid** catalyst: $C_2H_5OH \xrightarrow{H_2SO_4} C_2H_4 + H_2O$

Phosphoric acid (H_3PO_4) can also be used as a catalyst for this reaction. Often, the two are used together.

The product is usually in a **mixture** with water, acid and reactant in it so the alkene has to be **separated** out.

And here's the mechanism for the elimination of water from ethanol...

$+ H_2O$ $+ H^+$

A **lone pair of electrons** from the oxygen bonds to an **H⁺** from the acid. The alcohol is **protonated**, giving the oxygen a **positive charge**.

The positively charged oxygen **pulls** electrons away from the carbon. An **H_2O molecule** leaves, creating an **unstable carbocation intermediate**.

The carbocation **loses an H⁺**...

...and the **alkene** is formed.

Dehydration of more complicated alcohols can have **more than one possible product** — the double bond can form either side of the carbon with the –OH group attached. For example:

$+ H_2SO_4$ ⟹ ... and ...

Alcohols

Distillation is Used to Separate Chemicals

1) The products of organic reactions are often **impure** — so you've got to know how to **purify** them.
2) In the dehydration of alcohols to form alkenes, the **mixture** at the end contains the **product**, the **reactant**, **acid** and **water**. To get a **pure alkene**, you need a way to **separate** it from the other substances.
3) Distillation is a technique which uses the fact that different chemicals have **different boiling points** to separate them. Often further **separation and purification** is needed though. Here's an example of how to produce an **alkene** from an **alcohol** and separate out the product.

Producing cyclohexene from cyclohexanol

Stage 1 — distillation

1) Add concentrated H_2SO_4 and H_3PO_4 to a **round-bottom flask** containing cyclohexanol. Mix the solution by swirling the flask and add 2-3 **carborundum boiling chips** (these make the mixture boil more calmly).
2) The mixture should be gently heated to around 83 °C (the boiling point of cyclohexene) using a **water bath** or **electric heater**.
3) Chemicals with boiling points up to 83 °C will evaporate. The warm gas will rise out of the flask and into the **condenser**, which has cold water running through the outside, turning it into a liquid.
4) The product can then be collected in a **cooled flask**.

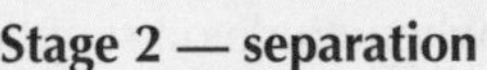

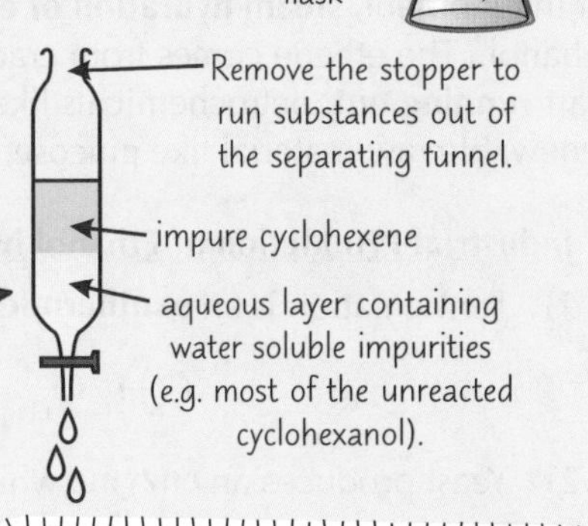

Stage 2 — separation

1) The product collected after distillation will still contain impurities.
2) Transfer the product mixture to a **separating funnel** and add water to **dissolve** water soluble impurities and create an aqueous solution.
3) Allow the mixture to settle into layers. Drain the aqueous lower layer, leaving the impure cyclohexene.

Stage 3 — purification

1) Drain the cyclohexene into a round-bottomed flask.
2) Add anhydrous $CaCl_2$ (a drying agent) and stopper the flask. Let the mixture dry for at least 20 minutes with occasional swirling.
3) The cyclohexene will still have small amounts of impurities so **distil** the mixture one last time.

In this example, the impurities are removed from the separating funnel first, but sometimes the desired product will be in the lower (more dense) layer.

Warm-Up Questions

Q1 What is the general formula for an alcohol?

Q2 Draw out the mechanism for the elimination of water from ethanol.

Exam Questions

Q1 Butanol C_4H_9OH has four chain and positional isomers.

a) Class each one as a primary, secondary or tertiary alcohol.

i) ii) iii) iv)

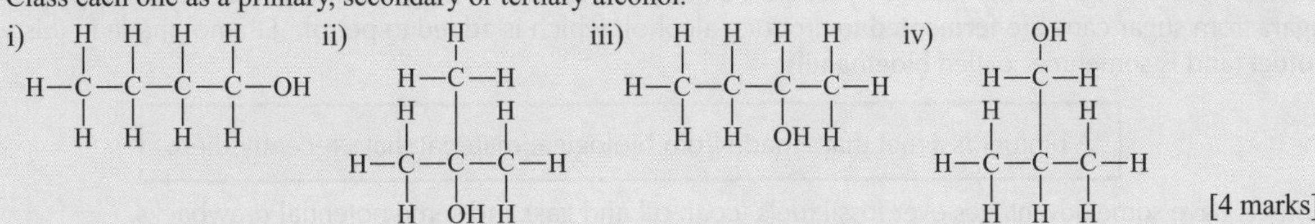

[4 marks]

b) Draw the organic product formed when each of the molecules above reacts with concentrated H_2SO_4. [4 marks]

Q2 Explain how distillation can help separate a liquid product from liquid by-products. [2 marks]

Euuurghh, what a page... I think I need a drink...

Not much to learn here — a few basic definitions, an industrial process and a three-step experimental process... Like I said, not much here at all. Think I'm going to faint. [THWACK]

Ethanol Production

Humans have been making ethanol for thousands of years. We've gotten pretty good at it.

Alcohols are Produced by Hydration of Alkenes

1) The standard industrial method for producing alcohols is to **hydrate** an **alkene** using **steam** in the presence of an **acid catalyst.**

$$C_nH_{2n} + H_2O \overset{H^+}{\rightleftharpoons} C_nH_{2n+1}OH$$

2) Here's the general mechanism for this type of reaction. (It's the reverse of the dehydration mechanism from page 90.)

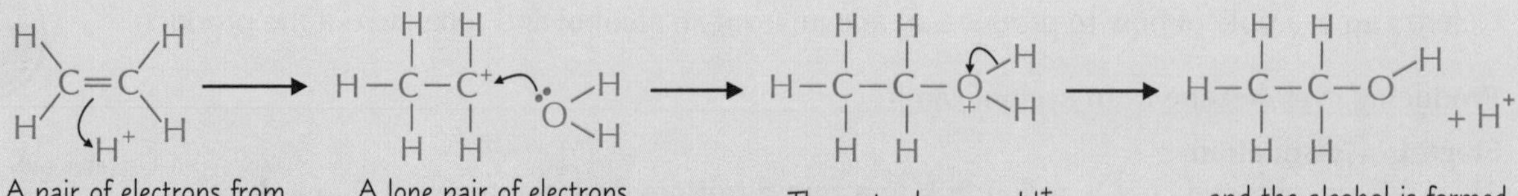

A pair of electrons from the double bond bonds to an H^+ from the acid. — A lone pair of electrons from a water molecule bonds to the carbocation. — The water loses an H^+... — ...and the alcohol is formed.

3) **Ethanol** can be produced by the **hydration** of **ethene** by **steam** at 300 °C and a pressure of 60 atm. It needs a solid **phosphoric(V) acid catalyst.**

This is similar to the reaction of an alkene with sulfuric acid from page 87, but because the reaction conditions are different the mechanism's slightly different too.

Ethanol can be Produced Industrially by Fermentation

At the moment, **steam hydration of ethene** is the most widely used technique in the industrial production of ethanol. The ethene comes from cracking heavy fractions of crude oil. But in the future, when crude oil supplies start **running out**, petrochemicals like ethene will be expensive — so producing ethanol by **fermentation**, using a renewable raw material like glucose, will become much more important...

Industrial Production of Ethanol by Fermentation of Glucose

1) Fermentation is an **exothermic** process, carried out by **yeast** in **anaerobic conditions** (without oxygen).

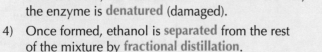

$$C_6H_{12}O_{6(aq)} \xrightarrow[\text{yeast}]{30\text{-}40\ °C} 2C_2H_5OH_{(aq)} + 2CO_{2(g)}$$

2) Yeast produces an **enzyme** which converts sugars, such as glucose, into **ethanol** and **carbon dioxide**.
3) The enzyme works at an **optimum** (ideal) temperature of **30-40 °C**. If it's too cold, the reaction is **slow** — if it's too hot, the enzyme is **denatured** (damaged).
4) Once formed, ethanol is **separated** from the rest of the mixture by **fractional distillation**.
5) Fermentation is **low-tech**. It uses cheap equipment and **renewable resources**. But the fractional distillation step that is needed to **purify** the ethanol produced using this method takes extra time and money.

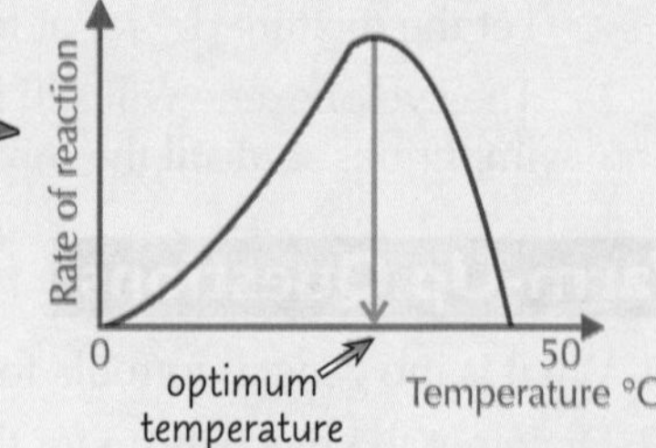

Ethanol is a Biofuel

Ethanol is increasingly being used as a **fuel**, particularly in countries with few oil reserves. For example, in Brazil, **sugars** from sugar cane are **fermented** to produce alcohol, which is added to petrol. Ethanol made in this way is a **biofuel** (and is sometimes called **bioethanol**).

A biofuel is a fuel that's made from biological material that's recently died.

Biofuels have some advantages over fossil fuels (coal, oil and gas) and some potential drawbacks.

1) Biofuels are **renewable** energy sources. Unlike fossil fuels, biofuels won't run out, so they're more **sustainable**.
2) Biofuels do produce CO_2 when they're burnt, but it's CO_2 that the plants **absorbed** while growing, so **biofuels** are usually still classed as **carbon neutral** (see next page).
3) But one problem with switching from fossil fuels to biofuels in transport is that **petrol car engines** would have to be **modified** to use fuels with high ethanol concentrations.
4) Also, when you use land used to grow crops for fuel, that land can't be used to grow **food**. If countries start using land to grow biofuel crops instead of food, they may be unable to feed everyone in the country.

Ethanol Production

Bioethanol Production is **Almost Carbon Neutral**... But **Not Quite**

1) Just like burning the hydrocarbons from fossil fuels, burning ethanol produces **carbon dioxide** (CO_2). Carbon dioxide is a **greenhouse gas** — it contributes to **global warming** (see pages 78 and 101).
2) But the plants that are grown to produce bioethanol **take in carbon dioxide** from the **atmosphere** when they're growing. As they grow, they take in the same amount of carbon dioxide as burning the bioethanol you produce from them gives out. So it could be argued that burning ethanol as a fuel is **carbon neutral**.

   Here are the **chemical equations** to support that argument...

   Plants take in **carbon dioxide** from the atmosphere to produce **glucose** by **photosynthesis**...

   $$6CO_2 + 6H_2O \rightarrow C_6H_{12}O_6 + 6O_2$$

   6 moles of carbon dioxide are taken from the atmosphere to produce 1 mole of glucose.

   In the **fermentation** process, **glucose** is converted into **ethanol**...

   $$C_6H_{12}O_6 \rightarrow 2C_2H_5OH + 2CO_2$$

   2 moles of carbon dioxide are released into the atmosphere when 1 mole of glucose is converted to 2 moles of ethanol.

   When **ethanol** is **burned**, **carbon dioxide** and water are produced...

   $$2C_2H_5OH + 6O_2 \rightarrow 4CO_2 + 6H_2O$$

   4 moles of carbon dioxide are released into the atmosphere when 2 moles of ethanol are burned completely.

   If you **combine** all three of these equations, you'll find that exactly **6 moles of CO_2** are taken in...
   ...and exactly **6 moles of CO_2** are given out.

3) However, **fossil fuels** will need to be burned to power the machinery used to make **fertilisers** for the crops, **harvest the crops** and **refine and transport** the bioethanol. Burning the fuel to power this machinery produces carbon dioxide. So using bioethanol made by fermentation **isn't completely carbon neutral**.

Warm-Up Questions

Q1 What is the standard method of producing alcohols from alkenes?

Q2 Why should the fermentation of glucose not be carried out at more than 40 °C?

Q3 What is a biofuel?

Q4 Write down one advantage and one disadvantages of replacing fossil fuels with biofuels.

Exam Questions

Q1 Industrially, ethanol can be produced by fermentation of glucose, $C_6H_{12}O_6$.

a) Write a balanced equation for this reaction. [1 mark]

b) State the conditions used for the industrial fermentation of glucose. [3 marks]

c) How is the ethanol separated from the reaction mixture? [1 mark]

Q2 In a classroom debate on the future of fuels, one student states that bioethanol is "carbon neutral". Another student argues that bioethanol is not really a carbon neutral fuel.

a) Explain why bioethanol is sometimes described as a carbon neutral fuel. [1 mark]

b) Explain why bioethanol cannot really be considered a carbon neutral fuel [2 marks]

Steam hydration or fermentation? Come on, everyone has a favourite...

The hydration reaction here is just the opposite of the elimination reaction a couple of pages back. Make sure that you know the fermentation reaction (including the conditions) inside out. Biofuels are a relatively simple idea to get your head round — then it's just a matter of learning about the pros and cons of the hydration and fermentation processes.

Oxidation of Alcohols

Another couple of pages of alcohol reactions. Probably not what you wanted for Christmas... But at least you're almost at the end of the section... and your wits, probably.

How Much an Alcohol can be **Oxidised** Depends on its **Structure**

1) The simple way to oxidise alcohols is to burn them. But you don't get the most exciting products by doing this. If you want to end up with something more interesting, you need a more sophisticated way of oxidising...
2) You can use the **oxidising agent acidified potassium dichromate(VI)**, $K_2Cr_2O_7$, to **mildly** oxidise alcohols. The **orange** dichromate(VI) ion, $Cr_2O_7^{2-}$, is reduced to the **green** chromium(III) ion, Cr^{3+}.

- **Primary** alcohols are oxidised to **aldehydes** and then to **carboxylic acids**.
- **Secondary** alcohols are oxidised to **ketones** only.
- **Tertiary** alcohols aren't oxidised.

Learn What **Aldehydes, Ketones** and **Carboxylic Acids** are

Aldehydes and **ketones** are **carbonyl** compounds — they have the functional group C=O. Their general formula is $\mathbf{C_nH_{2n}O}$. **Carboxylic acids** have the functional group COOH and have the general formula $\mathbf{C_nH_{2n+1}COOH}$.

ALDEHYDES

1) Have a **hydrogen** and **one alkyl group** attached to the carbonyl carbon atom.
2) Their suffix is **-al**. You don't have to say which carbon the functional group is on — it's always on carbon-1.

propanal
CH_3CH_2CHO

KETONES

1) Have **two alkyl groups** attached to the carbonyl carbon atom.
2) Their suffix is **-one**. For ketones with five or more carbons, you always have to say which carbon the functional group is on.

propanone
CH_3COCH_3

pentan-2-one
$CH_3COC_3H_7$

CARBOXYLIC ACIDS

1) Have a **COOH group** at the end of their carbon chain.
2) Their suffix is **-oic acid**.

propanoic acid
CH_3CH_2COOH

Primary Alcohols will Oxidise to **Aldehydes** and **Carboxylic Acids**

[O] = oxidising agent

$R{-}CH_2{-}OH + [O] \longrightarrow R{-}CHO + H_2O$
primary alcohol → aldehyde

then

$R{-}CHO + [O] \xrightarrow{\text{reflux}} R{-}COOH$
aldehyde → carboxylic acid

You can control how **far** the alcohol is oxidised by controlling the **reaction conditions**:

1) Gently heating ethanol with potassium dichromate(VI) and sulfuric acid in a test tube produces ethanal (an aldehyde). However, it's tricky to control the heat and the aldehyde is usually oxidised to form ethanoic acid.
2) To get just the aldehyde, you need to get it out of the oxidising solution as soon as it forms. You do this using distillation apparatus, so the aldehyde (which boils at a lower temperature than the alcohol) is distilled off immediately.
3) To produce the carboxylic acid, the alcohol has to be vigorously oxidised. The alcohol is mixed with excess oxidising agent and heated under reflux.
4) Heating under reflux means you can increase the temperature of an organic reaction without losing volatile solvents, reactants or products. Any vaporised compounds cool, condense and drip back into the reaction mixture. So the aldehyde stays in the reaction mixture and is oxidised to carboxylic acid.

Reflux apparatus

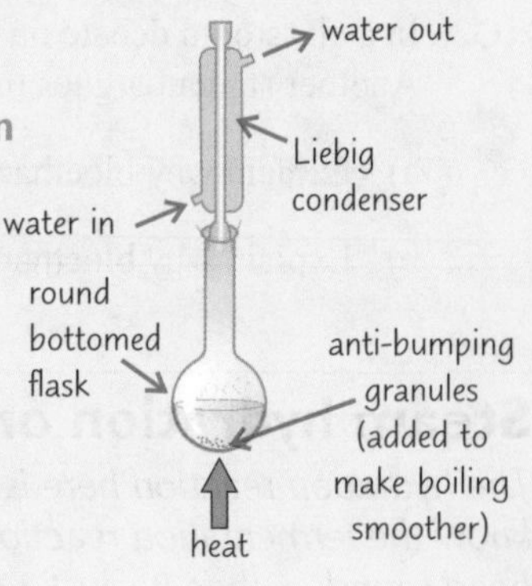

Oxidation of Alcohols

Secondary Alcohols will Oxidise to **Ketones**

$$R_1-\underset{R_2}{\overset{H}{C}}-OH + [O] \xrightarrow{\text{reflux}} R_1R_2C{=}O + H_2O$$

1) Refluxing a secondary alcohol, e.g. propan-2-ol, with acidified dichromate(VI) will produce a **ketone**.
2) Ketones can't be oxidised easily, so even prolonged refluxing won't produce anything more.

Tertiary Alcohols **can't** be Oxidised Easily

Tertiary alcohols don't react with potassium dichromate(VI) at all — the solution stays orange. The only way to oxidise tertiary alcohols is by **burning** them.

Use Oxidising Agents to **Distinguish** Between **Aldehydes** and **Ketones**

Aldehydes and ketones can be distinguished using **oxidising agents**. Aldehydes are easily oxidised but ketones aren't.

1) **Fehling's solution** and **Benedict's solution** are both deep blue Cu^{2+} complexes, which reduce to brick-red Cu_2O when warmed with an aldehyde, but stay blue with a ketone.
2) **Tollens' reagent** is $[Ag(NH_3)_2]^+$ — it's reduced to **silver** when warmed with an aldehyde, but not with a ketone. The silver will coat the inside of the apparatus to form a **silver mirror**.

There's more details on test you can use to distinguish between aldehydes and ketones on pages 96-97.

Warm-Up Questions

PRACTICE QUESTIONS

Q1 What is the colour change when potassium dichromate(VI) is reduced?

Q2 What's the difference between the structure of an aldehyde and a ketone?

Q3 What will acidified potassium dichromate(VI) oxidise secondary alcohols to?

Q4 Describe two tests you can use to distinguish between a sample of an aldehyde and a sample of a ketone.

Exam Question

Q1 A student wanted to produce the aldehyde propanal from propanol, and set up a reflux apparatus using a suitable oxidising agent.

a) i) Suggest an oxidising agent that the student could use. [1 mark]

ii) Draw the displayed formula of propanal. [1 mark]

b) The student tested his product and found that he had not produced propanal.

i) Describe a test for an aldehyde. [1 mark]

ii) What is the student's product? [1 mark]

iii) Write equations to show the two-stage reaction. Use [O] to represent the oxidising agent. [2 marks]

iv) What technique should the student have used to form propanal? [1 mark]

c) The student also tried to oxidise 2-methylpropan-2-ol, unsuccessfully.

i) Draw the skeletal formula for 2-methylpropan-2-ol. [1 mark]

ii) Why is it not possible to oxidise 2-methylpropan-2-ol with an oxidising agent? [1 mark]

I.... I .... just can't do it, R2...

Don't give up now. Only as a fully-trained Chemistry Jedi, with the force as your ally, can you take on the Examiner. If you quit now, if you choose the easy path as Wader did, all the marks you've fought for will be lost. Be strong.

Tests for Functional Groups

There's no escaping all these alcohols, aldehydes, alkenes, carboxylic acids. As well as knowing all about them and their reactions, you need to be able to carry out tests to distinguish between them. These pages should help...

You Can **Test** Whether You've Got a **Primary, Secondary** or **Tertiary** Alcohol

You've already seen how to **oxidise alcohols** using **acidified potassium dichromate (VI)** on pages 94 to 95. You can use that reaction to test which sort of alcohol you've got — **primary**, **secondary**, or **tertiary**. Here's what you do:

1) Add 10 drops of the alcohol to 2 cm^3 of acidified potassium dichromate solution in a test tube.
2) Warm the mixture gently in a hot water bath.
3) Then watch for a colour change:

PRIMARY – the **orange** solution slowly turns **green** as an aldehyde forms.
(If you carry on heating, the aldehyde will be oxidised further to give a carboxylic acid.)
SECONDARY – the **orange** solution slowly turns **green** as a ketone forms.
TERTIARY – nothing happens — boring, but easy to remember.

You can also test for alcohols using sodium metal. If you add a small piece of sodium to a pure alcohol, it will fizz as it gives off H_2 gas.

The colour change is the orange dichromate(VI) ion ($Cr_2O_7^{2-}$) being reduced to the green chromium(III) ion (Cr^{3+}).

The problem with this test is that it shows the **same result** for **primary** and **secondary alcohols**.
To find out which one you started with, you'll have to repeat the experiment and collect some of the **product**:

1) Add excess alcohol to 2 cm^3 of acidified potassium dichromate solution in a round bottomed flask.
2) Set up the flask as part of distillation apparatus (see the picture on the right).
3) Gently heat the flask. The alcohol will be oxidised and the product will be distilled off immediately so you can collect it.

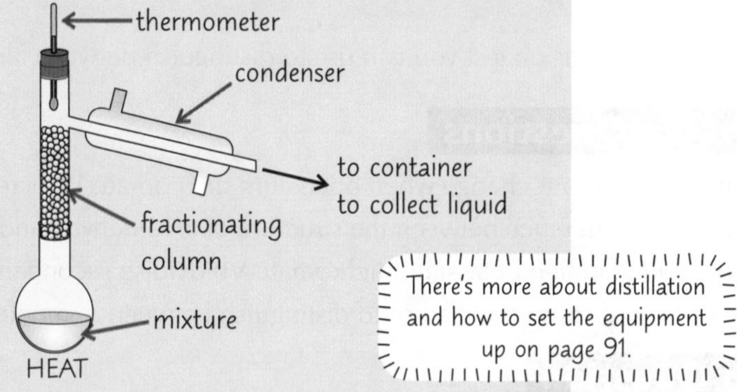

There's more about distillation and how to set the equipment up on page 91.

Once you've collected the product, you'll need to test it to find out if it's an **aldehyde** or a **ketone**.
Handily, what's coming up next is how to do just that...

You Can **Test** Whether You've Got an **Aldehyde** or a **Ketone**

There are three main reagents you can use to distinguish between **aldehydes** and **ketones** — Fehling's solution, Benedict's solution and Tollens' reagent.

Fehling's Solution and **Benedict's Solution**

Fehling's solution and Benedict's solution work in exactly the same way.

1) Add 2 cm^3 of Fehling's or Benedict's solution to a test tube. (Whichever one you use, it should be a clear blue solution.)
2) Add 5 drops of the aldehyde or ketone to the test tube.
3) Put the test tube in a hot water bath to warm it for a few minutes.

ALDEHYDE – the blue solution will give a **brick red precipitate**.
KETONE – nothing happens.

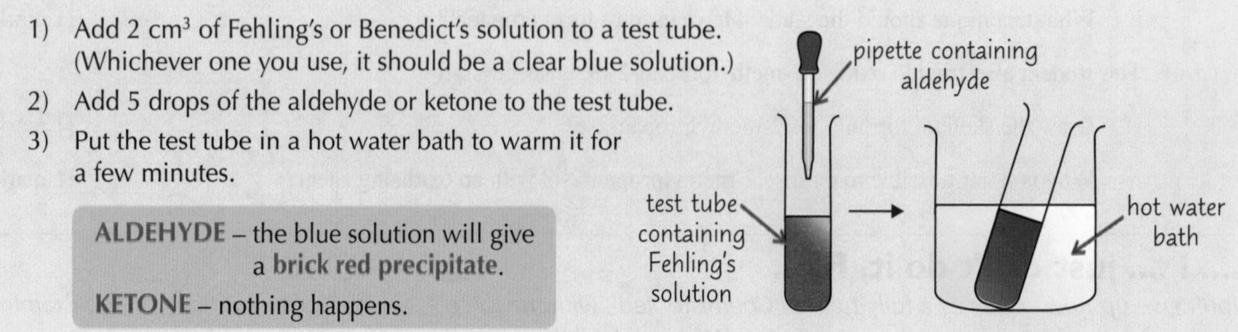

Tests for Functional Groups

Tollens' Reagent

You'd think that two reagents you could use to test for aldehydes and ketones would be enough, but there's one more to go. This one's a bit more tricky, because you have to start by making up the Tollens' reagent yourself.

1) Put 2 cm^3 of 0.10 mol dm^{-3} silver nitrate solution in a test tube.

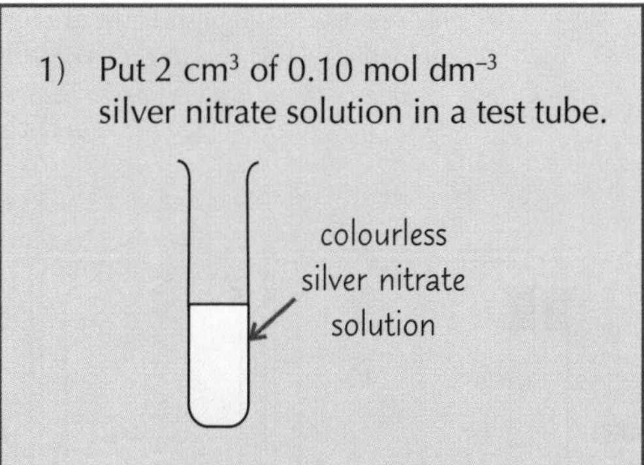

2) Add a few drops of dilute sodium hydroxide solution. A light brown precipitate should form.

light brown precipitate

3) Add drops of dilute ammonia solution until the brown precipitate dissolves completely.

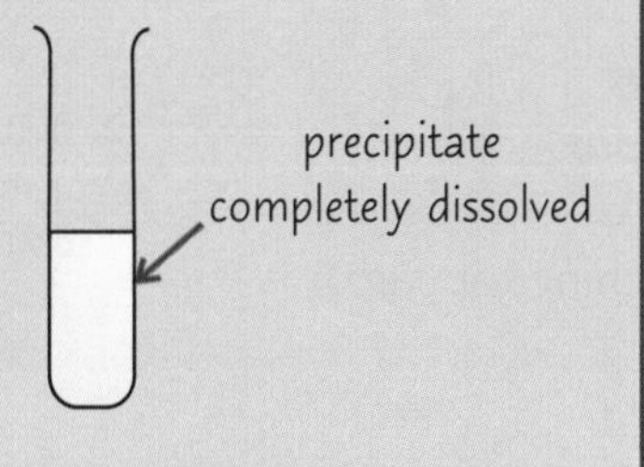

The solution you've made at the end of step 3) is Tollens' reagent.

4) Place the test tube in a hot water bath and add 10 drops of aldehyde or ketone. Wait for a few minutes.

ALDEHYDE – a **silver mirror** (a thin coating of silver) forms on the walls of the test tube.

KETONE – nothing happens.

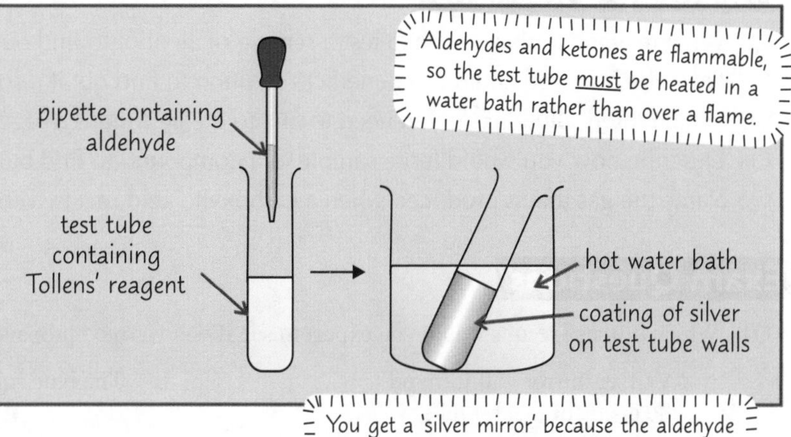

Aldehydes and ketones are flammable, so the test tube must be heated in a water bath rather than over a flame.

You get a 'silver mirror' because the aldehyde reduces the Ag^+ ions to silver atoms.

Use **Bromine Water** to Test for **Alkenes**

Here's another test that you've come across before (on page 85). This one allows you to test a solution to find out if it's an **alkene** — what you're actually testing for is the presence of **double bonds**. Here's what you do:

1) Add 2 cm^3 of the solution that you want to test to a test tube.
2) Add 2 cm^3 of bromine water to the test tube.
3) Shake the test tube.

ALKENE – the solution will decolourise (go from **orange** to **colourless**).

NOT ALKENE – nothing happens.

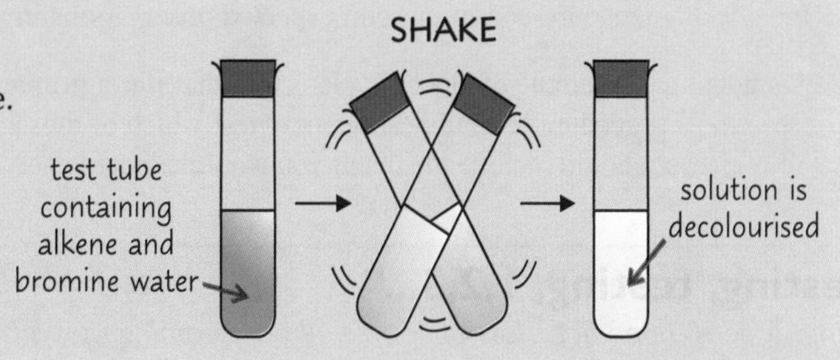

Tests for Functional Groups

Use **Sodium Carbonate** to Test for **Carboxylic Acids**

1) Another thing you might be asked to test for is **carboxylic acids**. You met carboxylic acids on page 94, so have a look back if you can't remember what they are.
2) Carboxylic acids react with **carbonates** to form a salt, carbon dioxide and water. You can use this reaction to test whether a solution is a carboxylic acid, like this:

Be careful though — this test will give a positive result with any acid, so you can only use it to distinguish between organic compounds when you already know that one of them is a carboxylic acid.

1) Add 2 cm^3 of the solution that you want to test to a test tube.
2) Add 1 small spatula of solid sodium carbonate (or 2 cm^3 of sodium carbonate solution).
3) If the solution begins to fizz, bubble the gas that it produces through some limewater in a second test tube.

CARBOXYLIC ACID – the solution will fizz. The carbon dioxide gas that is produced will turn limewater cloudy.
NOT CARBOXYLIC ACID – nothing happens.

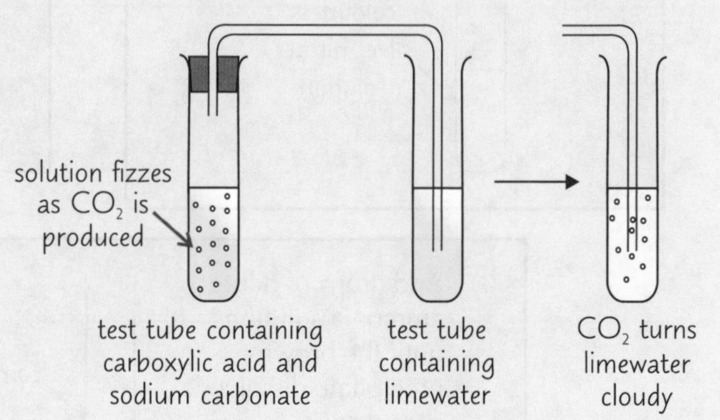

Warm-Up Questions

Q1 What reagent could you use to test a sample of alcohol to find out whether it was a tertiary alcohol?
Q2 Describe how you could use Benedict's solution to find out if a solution was an aldehyde or a ketone.
Q3 Which three solutions do you need to mix to create Tollens' reagent?
Q4 Describe how you would test a sample of a compound to find out if it was an alkane or an alkene.
Q5 Name the gas that is produced when a carboxylic acid reacts with sodium carbonate.

PRACTICE QUESTIONS

Exam Questions

Q1 Which of these results would you expect to see if you warmed propanone with Fehling's solution?

A A silver mirror will form on the inside of the test tube.
B The blue solution will give a brick red precipitate.
C The orange solution will decolourise.
D Nothing will happen.
[1 mark]

Q2 Which of these statements about cyclohexene is correct?

A It produces a brick red precipitate with Fehling's solution.
B It decolourises bromine water.
C It turns limewater cloudy.
D It forms a silver mirror with Tollens' reagent.
[1 mark]

Q3 Describe a chemical test you could use to show that a solution is a carboxylic acid.
Include any reagents, conditions and expected observations in your answer.
[3 marks]

Q4 A student has a sample of alcohol. He is told that it is a primary or secondary alcohol.
Describe a procedure he could carry out to test which of these it is.
Your answer should include the result you would expect to see in each case.
[5 marks]

"Testing, testing, 1,2,3..."

Fehling, Tollens, Benedict... lots of people all busy coming up with different ways to test for ketones and aldehydes. You'd think they could've found something better to do with their time. Unfortunately for you, they didn't, and you could actually be asked to do these tests yourself. So make sure you learn how to do each one, you won't regret it. Honest.

Analytical Techniques

Get ready for some thrilling pages featuring the return of mass spectrometry and the dramatic first appearance of infrared spectroscopy — and watch out for the big twist at the end...

Mass Spectrometry Can Help to Identify Compounds

1) You saw on page 7 that **mass spectrometry** can be used to find the **relative molecular mass** (M_r) of a compound.
2) In the mass spectrometer, a **molecular ion** (M^+) is formed when a molecule loses an **electron**.
3) The molecular ion produces a **molecular ion peak** on the mass spectrum of the compound.
4) For any compound, the **mass/charge** (m/z) value of the molecular ion peak will be the same as the **molecular mass** of the compound.

Assuming the ion has a 1+ charge, which it normally will have.

Example: The mass spectrum of a straight chain alkane contained a molecular ion peak with m/z = 72.0. Identify the compound.

1) The m/z value of the molecular ion peak is **72.0** — so the M_r of the compound must be 72.0.
2) If you calculate the molecular masses of the first few straight-chain alkanes, you'll find that the one with a molecular mass of 72.0 is pentane (C_5H_{12}):
   M_r of pentane = (5 × 12.0) + (12 × 1.0) = 72.0
3) So the compound must be **pentane**.

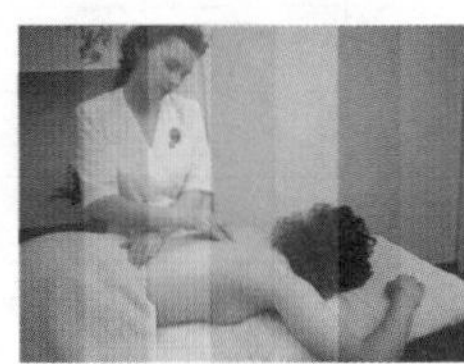
A massage spectrum

High Resolution Mass Spectrometry

1) Some mass spectrometers can measure atomic and molecular masses **extremely accurately** (to several decimal places). These are known as **high resolution mass spectrometers**.
2) This can be useful for identifying compounds that appear to have the **same M_r** when they're **rounded** to the nearest whole number.
3) For example, propane (C_3H_8) and ethanal (CH_3CHO) both have an M_r of 44 to the nearest whole number. But on a high resolution mass spectrum, propane has a molecular ion peak with m/z = 44.0624 and ethanal has a molecular ion peak with m/z = 44.0302.

Example: On a high resolution mass spectrum, a compound had a molecular ion peak of 98.0448.
What was its molecular formula?

A $C_5H_{10}N_2$
B $C_6H_{10}O$
C C_7H_{14}
D $C_5H_6O_2$

Use these precise atomic masses to work out your answer:
^{1}H — 1.0078 ^{12}C — 12.0000 ^{14}N — 14.0064 ^{16}O — 15.9990

1) Work out the precise molecular mass of each compound:
   $C_5H_{10}N_2$: M_r = (5 × 12.0000) + (10 × 1.0078) + (2 × 14.0064) = 98.0908
   $C_6H_{10}O$: M_r = (6 × 12.0000) + (10 × 1.0078) + 15.9990 = 98.0770
   C_7H_{14}: M_r = (7 × 12.0000) + (14 × 1.0078) = 98.1092
   $C_5H_6O_2$: M_r = (5 × 12.0000) + (6 × 1.0078) + (2 × 15.9990) = 98.0448
2) So the answer is **D**, $C_5H_6O_2$.

On a normal (low resolution) mass spectrum, all of these molecules would show up as having an M_r of 98.

Analytical Techniques

Infrared Spectroscopy Helps You Identify Organic Molecules

1) In infrared (IR) spectroscopy, a beam of **IR radiation** is passed through a sample of a chemical.
2) The IR radiation is absorbed by the **covalent bonds** in the molecules, increasing their **vibrational** energy.
3) **Bonds between different atoms** absorb **different frequencies** of IR radiation. Bonds in different **places** in a molecule absorb different frequencies too — so the O–H group in an **alcohol** and the O–H in a **carboxylic acid** absorb different frequencies. This table shows what **frequencies** different bonds absorb:

Bond	Where it's found	Wavenumber (cm^{-1})
N–H (amines)	amines (e.g. methylamine, CH_3NH_2)	3300 - 3500
O-H (alcohols)	alcohols	3230 - 3550
C–H	most organic molecules	2850 - 3300
O–H (acids)	carboxylic acids	2500 - 3000
C≡N	nitriles (e.g. ethanenitrile, CH_3CN)	2220 - 2260
C=O	aldehydes, ketones, carboxylic acids, esters	1680 - 1750
C=C	alkenes	1620 - 1680
C–O	alcohols, carboxylic acids	1000 - 1300
C–C	most organic molecules	750 - 1100

Wavenumber is the measure used for the frequency — it's just $\frac{1}{\text{wavelength (cm)}}$

You <u>don't</u> need to learn this data (but you do need to understand how to use it).

4) An infrared spectrometer produces a **graph** that shows you what frequencies of radiation the molecules are absorbing. So you can use it to identify the **functional groups** in a molecule:

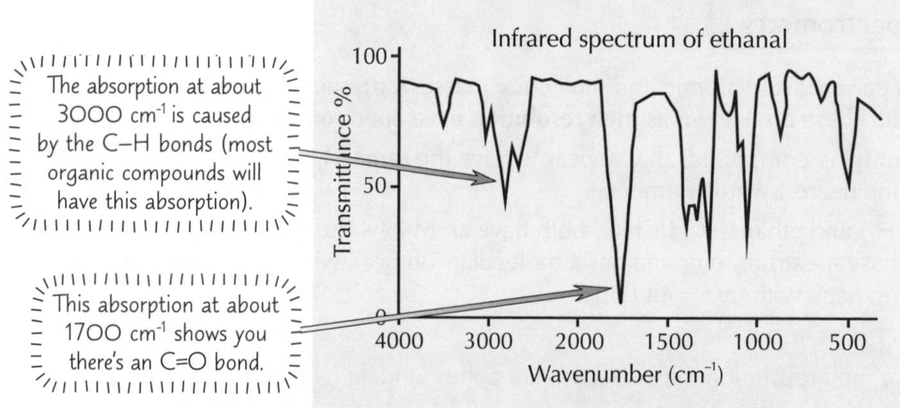

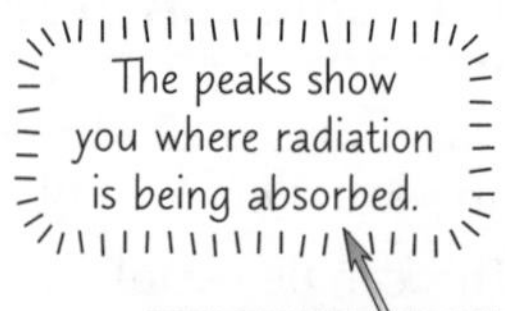

The peaks show you where radiation is being absorbed.

The 'peaks' on IR spectra point downwards.

The Fingerprint Region Identifies a Molecule

1) The region between **500 cm^{-1} and 1500 cm^{-1}** is called the **fingerprint** region. It's **unique** to a **particular compound**. You can use a computer database to check this region of an unknown compound's IR spectrum against those of known compounds. If it **matches** one of them, you know what the molecule is.

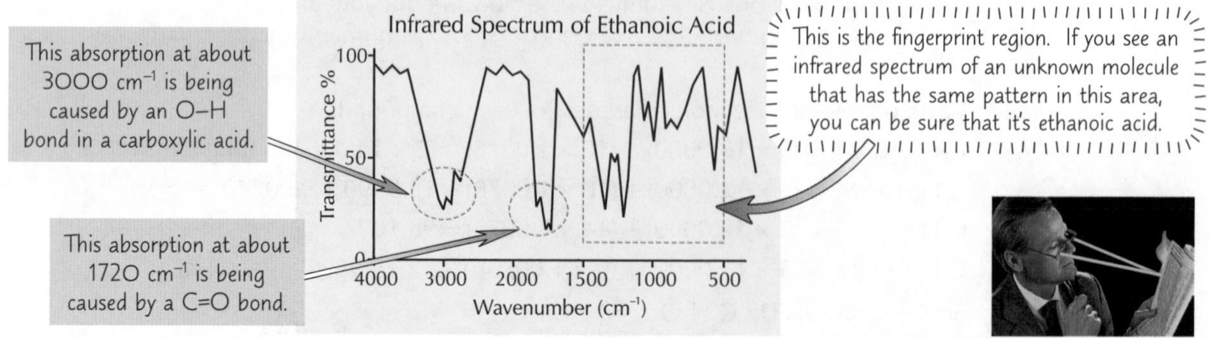

This absorption at about 3000 cm⁻¹ is being caused by an O–H bond in a carboxylic acid.
This absorption at about 1720 cm⁻¹ is being caused by a C=O bond.
Infrared Spectrum of Ethanoic Acid
Transmittance %
100
50
0
4000
3000
2000
1500
1000
500
Wavenumber (cm⁻¹)
This is the fingerprint region. If you see an infrared spectrum of an unknown molecule that has the same pattern in this area, you can be sure that it's ethanoic acid.

Clark began to regret having an infrared mechanism installed in his glasses.

2) Infrared spectroscopy can also be used to find out how **pure** a compound is, and identify any impurities. Impurities produce **extra peaks** in the fingerprint region.

Analytical Techniques

Infrared Radiation **Absorption** is Linked to **Global Warming**

1) Some of the electromagnetic radiation emitted by the **Sun** reaches the Earth and is absorbed. The Earth then re-emits some of it as **infrared radiation** (heat).
2) Molecules of **greenhouse gases**, like **carbon dioxide**, **methane** and **water vapour**, in the atmosphere absorb this infrared radiation. Then they re-emit some of it back towards the Earth, keeping us warm. This is called the '**greenhouse effect**'.
3) Human activities, such as burning fossil fuels and leaving rubbish to rot in landfill sites, have caused a **rise** in **greenhouse gas concentrations**.
4) This means more heat is being trapped and the Earth is getting warmer — this is **global warming**.

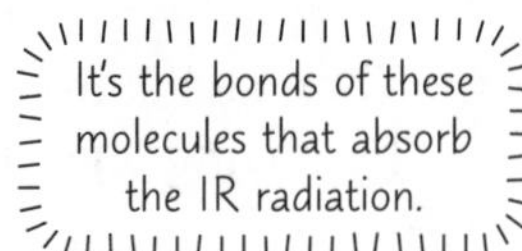

It's the bonds of these molecules that absorb the IR radiation.

Warm-Up Questions

Q1 In mass spectrometry, what is meant by a molecular ion?

Q2 Explain how you could find the molecular mass of a compound by looking at its mass spectrum.

Q3 Which parts of a molecule absorb infrared radiation?

Q4 On an infrared spectrum, what is meant by the 'fingerprint region'?

Q5 Explain how increasing the amount of carbon dioxide in the atmosphere leads to global warming.

Exam Questions

Q1 Use the following precise atomic masses to answer this question:
^{1}H — 1.0078 ^{12}C — 12.0000 ^{14}N — 14.0064 ^{16}O — 15.9990

a) The high resolution mass spectrum of a compound has a molecular ion peak with m/z = 74.0908. Which of the following could be the molecular formula of the compound?
A $C_3H_6O_2$ B $C_4H_{10}O$ C $C_3H_{10}N_2$ D $C_2H_6N_2O$ [1 mark]

b) Explain why low resolution mass spectrometry would not allow you to distinguish between the options given in part a). [1 mark]

c) The high resolution mass spectrum of 2-fluoroethanol (CH_2FCH_2OH) produced a molecular ion peak with m/z = 64.0364. Use this information to find the precise atomic mass of fluorine. [1 mark]

Q2 An organic molecule with a molecular mass of 74 produces the IR spectrum shown below.

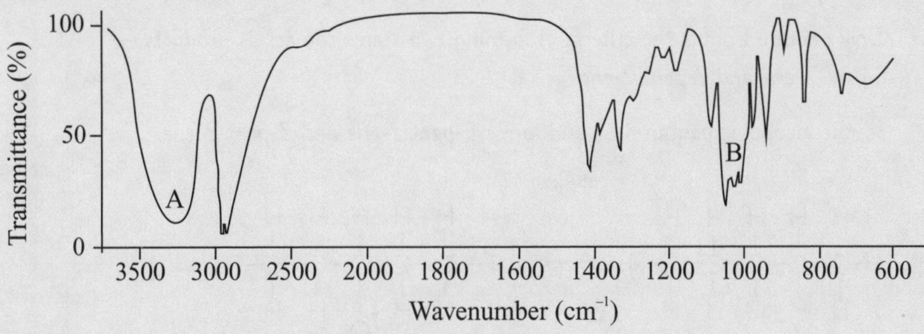

a) Identify the bonds that are responsible for causing the peaks labelled A and B. Use the data table on page 100 to help. [2 marks]

b) Suggest the molecular formula of this molecule. Explain your answer. [3 marks]

I wonder what the infrared spectrum of a fairy cake would look like...

Very squiggly I imagine. Luckily you don't have to be able to remember what any infrared spectrum graphs look like. But you definitely need to know how to interpret them. And don't worry, I haven't forgotten I said there was twist at the end... erm... hydrogen was my sister all along... and all the elements went to live in Jamaica. The End.

Extra Exam Practice

There we are, the end of Unit 3 Sections 1-4. All that's left now is to find out how well you remember it all by doing a few questions. These will be based on the material you've covered in the last four sections, but in the exams you could be asked about topics from different parts of the course.

- Have a look at this example of how to answer a tricky exam question.
- Then check how much you've understood from Unit 3 Sections 1-4 by having a go at the questions on the next page.

Don't worry, this isn't the last of the practice exam questions — there are synoptic questions covering the whole AS-level/Year 1 course on p.112-114.

1 A saturated five-carbon secondary alcohol is heated with a concentrated acid catalyst. An elimination reaction takes place that can form two possible organic products. These two possible organic products are stereoisomers.

Deduce the name of the secondary alcohol and the two stereoisomers it can form. Include the mechanism of the elimination reaction forming one of the stereoisomer products in your answer.

(5 marks)

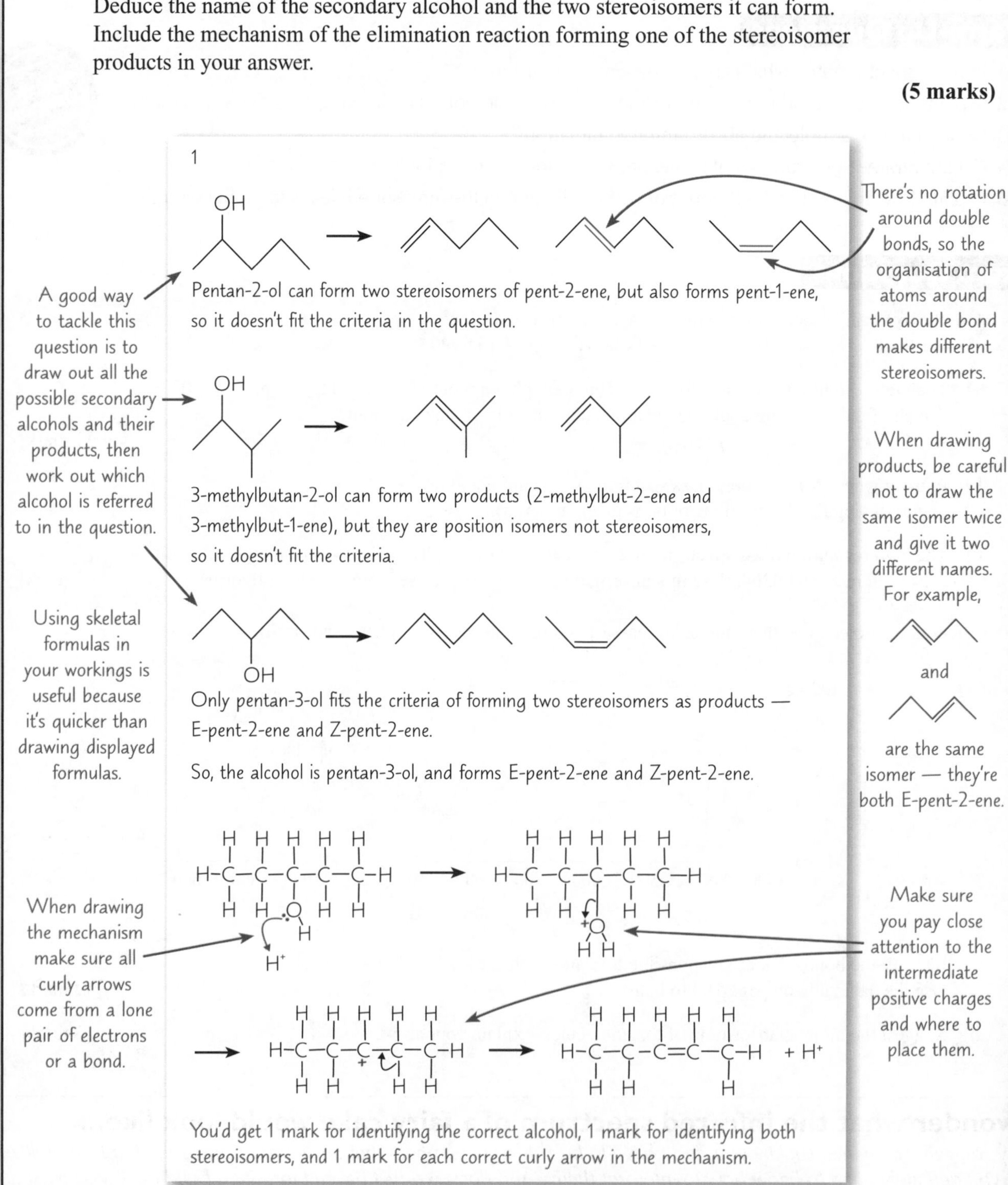

1
OH
Pentan-2-ol can form two stereoisomers of pent-2-ene, but also forms pent-1-ene, so it doesn't fit the criteria in the question.
OH
3-methylbutan-2-ol can form two products (2-methylbut-2-ene and 3-methylbut-1-ene), but they are position isomers not stereoisomers, so it doesn't fit the criteria.
OH
Only pentan-3-ol fits the criteria of forming two stereoisomers as products — E-pent-2-ene and Z-pent-2-ene.
So, the alcohol is pentan-3-ol, and forms E-pent-2-ene and Z-pent-2-ene.
H⁺
+ H⁺
You'd get 1 mark for identifying the correct alcohol, 1 mark for identifying both stereoisomers, and 1 mark for each correct curly arrow in the mechanism.
A good way to tackle this question is to draw out all the possible secondary alcohols and their products, then work out which alcohol is referred to in the question.
Using skeletal formulas in your workings is useful because it's quicker than drawing displayed formulas.
When drawing the mechanism make sure all curly arrows come from a lone pair of electrons or a bond.
There's no rotation around double bonds, so the organisation of atoms around the double bond makes different stereoisomers.
When drawing products, be careful not to draw the same isomer twice and give it two different names. For example,
and
are the same isomer — they're both E-pent-2-ene.
Make sure you pay close attention to the intermediate positive charges and where to place them.

Extra Exam Practice

2 **Figure 1** shows the conversion of 2-chloropropane into other substances by a variety of reactions.

Figure 1

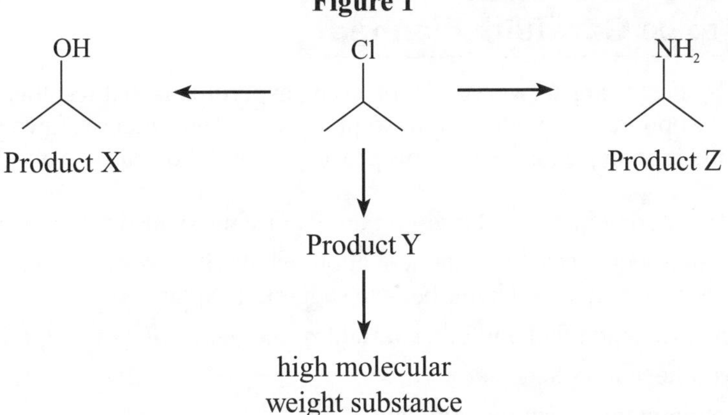

2.1 Describe the formation of the high molecular weight substance from 2-chloropropane. Include the displayed formulas of Product Y and the high molecular weight substance in your answer.

(4 marks)

2.2 Product X can be formed from an alkene using steam in the presence of an acid catalyst. Draw the mechanism for this reaction and explain how it shows that the acid is acting as a catalyst.

(5 marks)

2.3 The structure of Compound W is shown in **Figure 2**.

Figure 2

OH

Outline a method that could be used to distinguish a sample of Compound W from Product X. Include any observations in your answer.

(5 marks)

2.4 **Table 1** shows the frequencies of infrared radiation absorbed by different bonds.

Table 1

Bond	Wavenumber / cm^{-1}
N–H (amines)	3300 - 3500
O–H (alcohols)	3230 - 3550
C–H	2850 - 3300
O–H (acids)	2500 - 3000
C≡N	2220 - 2260
C=O	1680 - 1750
C=C	1620 - 1680

Explain whether the data in **Table 1** could be used to differentiate between the IR spectra of Product X and that of Product Z.

(2 marks)

2.5 2-chloropropane is warmed with excess ethanolic ammonia to produce Product Z and a salt. Draw the mechanism for this reaction and name the salt that is formed.

(5 marks)

Planning Experiments

As well as doing practical work in class, you can get asked about it in your exams too. Harsh I know, but I'm afraid that's how it goes. You need to be able to plan experiments and to spot the good and bad points of plans that you're shown.

Experiments Need to be **Carefully Planned**

Scientists solve problems by **suggesting answers** and then doing **experiments** that **test** their ideas to see if the evidence supports them. Being able to plan experiments that will give you **accurate** and **precise results** is an important part of this process. Here's how you go about it:

There's more about what accurate and precise results are on page 110.

1) State the **aim** of your experiment — what question are you trying to answer?
2) Make a **prediction** — a specific testable statement about what will happen in the experiment, based on observation, experience or a **hypothesis** (a suggested explanation for a fact or observation).
3) Identify the **independent**, **dependent** and other **variables** (see below) in your experiment.
4) Decide what **data** you need to collect.
5) Select **appropriate equipment** for your experiment.
6) Do a **risk assessment** and plan any safety precautions that you will need to take.
7) Write out a **detailed method** for your experiment.

After step 7), you can actually go ahead and do your experiment. Lucky you...

Make it a **Fair Test** — Control your **Variables**

You probably already know what the different kinds of **variable** are, but they're easy to mix up, so here's a recap:

Variable — A variable is a **quantity** that has the **potential to change**, e.g. temperature, mass, or volume. There are two types of variable commonly referred to in experiments:

- **Independent variable** — the thing that you **change** in an experiment.
- **Dependent variable** — the thing that you **measure** in an experiment.

As well as the independent and dependent variables, you need to think of all the **other variables** (sometimes called **control variables**) that could affect the result of the experiment and plan ways to keep each of them **the same**.

So, if you're investigating the effect of temperature on the rate of a reaction using this equipment, then the variables will be:

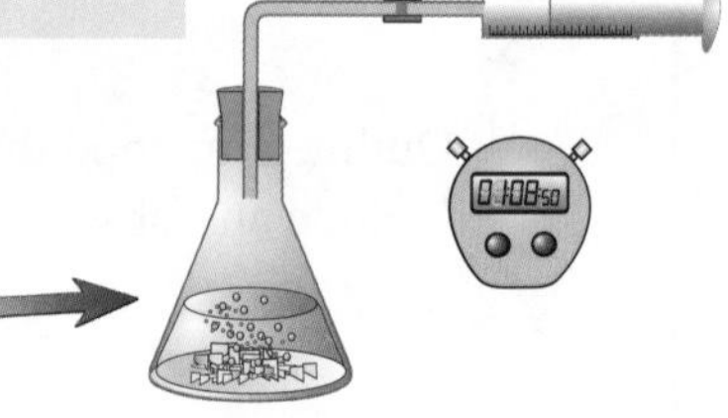

Independent variable	Temperature.
Dependent variable	Volume of gas produced in a set period of time.
Other variables — you MUST keep these the same	Concentration and volume of solutions, mass of solids, pressure, whether or not you use a catalyst, the surface area of any solid reactants, time over which the gas is collected.

Work **Safely** and **Ethically** — Don't Blow Up the Lab or Harm Small Animals

1) When you plan an experiment, you need to think about how you're going to make sure that you work **safely**.
2) The first step is to identify all the **hazards** that might be involved in your experiment (e.g. dangerous chemicals or naked flames).
3) Then you need to come up with ways to reduce the **risks** that these hazards pose.

   This means things like wearing **goggles** and a **lab coat** when you're handling acids (or any other hazardous chemicals), using a **fume cupboard** to do any reactions that produce nasty gases, or heating anything flammable with a **water bath** or **electric heater** (rather than over a flame).

4) You need to make sure you're working **ethically** too. This is most important if there are other people or animals involved. You have to put their welfare first.

Planning Experiments

Choose **Appropriate** Equipment — Think about **Size** and **Sensitivity**

Selecting the right equipment may sound easy but it's something you need to think carefully about.

1) The equipment has to be **appropriate** for the experiment.

   E.g. if you want to measure the amount of gas produced in a reaction, you need to make sure you use apparatus which will collect the gas, without letting any escape.

2) The equipment needs to be the right **size**.

   E.g. if you're using a gas syringe to measure the volume of gas produced by a reaction, it needs to be big enough to collect all the gas, or the plunger will be pushed out of the end. You might need to do some rough calculations to work out what size of equipment to use.

3) The equipment needs to have the right level of **sensitivity**.

   E.g. if you want to measure out 3.8 g of a substance, you need a balance that measures to the nearest tenth of a gram, not the nearest gram. If you want to measure out 6 cm^3 of a solution, you need to use a measuring cylinder that has a scale marked off in steps of 1 cm^3, not one that only has markings every 10 cm^3.

Moira was very sensitive to comments about the inappropriate size of her hat.

If you want to measure out a solution really accurately (e.g. 20.0 cm^3 of solution) you'll need to use a burette or a pipette.

Know Your Different Sorts of **Data**

Experiments always involve some sort of measurement to provide **data** and you need to decide what data to collect. There are different types of data — so it helps to know what they are.

Discrete — a discrete variable can only have **certain values** on a scale. For example the number of bubbles formed in a reaction is discrete (you can't have 1.77 bubbles). You usually get discrete data by **counting** things.

Continuous — a continuous variable can have **any value** on a scale. For example, the volume of gas produced or the mass of products from a reaction. You can never measure the exact value of a continuous variable.

Categoric — a categoric variable has values that can be sorted into **categories**. For example, the colours of solutions might be blue, red and green, or types of material might be wood, steel and glass.

Ordered (ordinal) — ordered data is similar to categoric, but the categories can be **put in order**. For example, if you classified reactions as 'slow', 'fairly fast' and 'very fast' you'd have ordered data.

Methods Must be **Clear** and **Detailed**

When **writing** or **evaluating** a method, you need to think about all of the things on these two pages. The method must be **clear** and **detailed** enough for **anyone** to follow — it's important that other people can recreate your experiment and get the **same** results. Make sure your method includes:

1) All the **substances** needed and what **quantity** of each to use.
2) How to **control** variables.
3) The exact **apparatus** needed (a **diagram** is often helpful to show the set-up).
4) Any **safety precautions** that should be taken.
5) What **data** to collect and **how** to collect it.

Presenting Results

Once you've collected the data from your experiment, it's not time to stop, put your feet up and have a cup of tea — you've got to present your results too. That might well mean putting them in a table or turning them into a graph.

Organise Your Results in a **Table**

It's a good idea to set up a table to **record** the **results** of your experiment. Make sure that you **include** enough **rows** and **columns** to **record all of the data** you need. You might also need to include a column for **processing** your data (e.g. working out an average).

Make sure each **column** has a **heading** so you know what's going to be recorded where.

The **units** should be in the **column heading**, not the table itself.

Temperature (°C)	**Time (s)**	**Volume of gas evolved (cm^3)**			**Average volume of gas evolved (cm^3)**
		Run 1	**Run 2**	**Run 3**	
20	**10**	8.1	8.4	8.1	(8.1 + 8.4 + 8.1) ÷ 3 = 8.2
	20	19.8	19.6	19.4	(19.8 + 19.6 + 19.4) ÷ 3 = 19.6
	30	29.8	29.9	30.0	(29.8 + 29.9 + 30.0) ÷ 3 = 29.9

You can find the **mean result** by **adding up** the data from each repeat and **dividing** by the number of repeats.

Graphs: **Line, Bar or Scatter** — Use the **Best Type**

When drawing graphs, the dependent variable should go on the y-axis, and the independent on the x-axis.

You'll often need to make a **graph** of your results. Not only are graphs **pretty**, they make your data **easier to understand** — so long as you choose the right type.

Scatter plots are great for showing how two sets of continuous data are related (or **correlated** — see page 108) Don't try to join all the points on a scatter plot — draw a straight or curved **line of best fit** to show the **trend**.

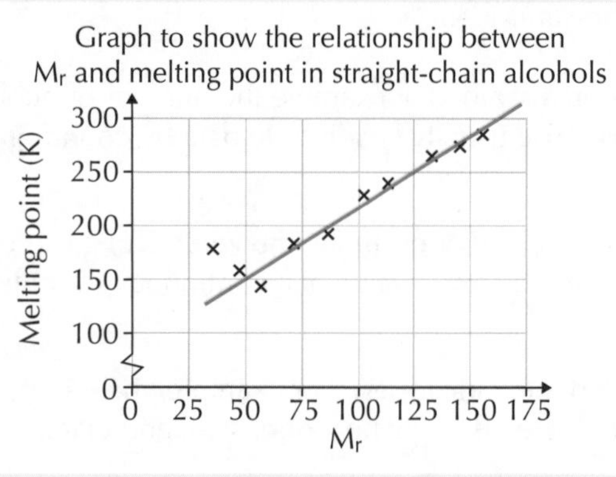

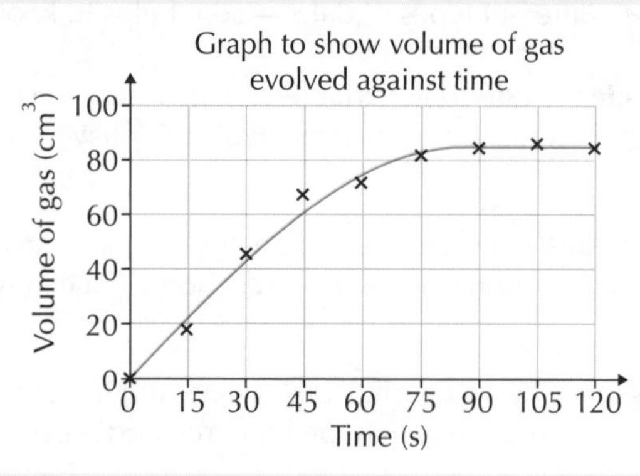

You should use a bar chart when one of your data sets is **categoric or ordered data**. For example:

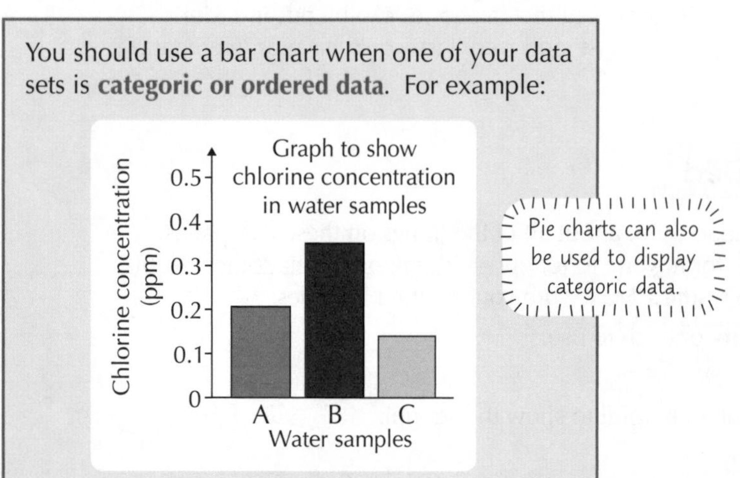

Pie charts can also be used to display categoric data.

Whatever type of graph you draw, you'll ONLY get full marks if you:

- Choose a sensible scale — don't draw a tiny graph in the corner of the paper.
- Label both axes — including units.
- Plot your points accurately — using a sharp pencil.

Presenting Results

Don't Forget About **Units**

Units are really important — 10 g is very different from 10 kg — so make sure you don't forget to add them to your **tables** and **graphs**. They're also important in **calculations**, particularly if you need to **convert** between two different units.

Here are some useful examples:

Volume can be measured in m^3, dm^3 and cm^3.

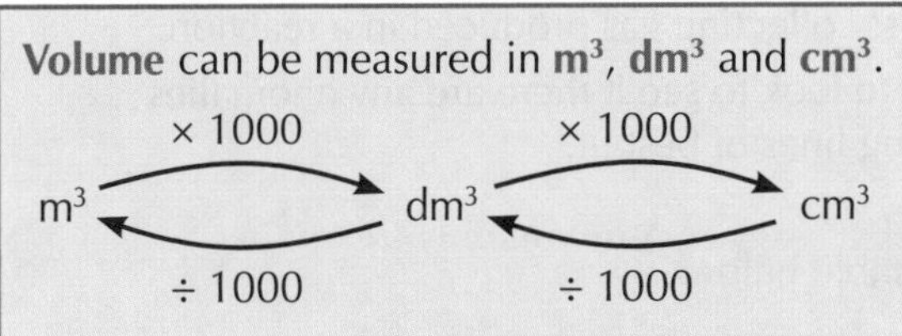

Example: Write 6 dm^3 in m^3 and cm^3.

First, to convert 6 dm^3 into m^3 you divide by 1000.

$6\ dm^3 \div 1000 = 0.006\ m^3 = \mathbf{6 \times 10^{-3}\ m^3}$

Then, to convert 6 dm^3 into cm^3 you multiply by 1000.

$6\ dm^3 \times 1000 = 6000\ cm^3 = \mathbf{6 \times 10^{3}\ cm^3}$

This is written in standard form. Standard form is a useful way to write very big or very small numbers neatly.

Temperature can be measured in **°C** and **K**.

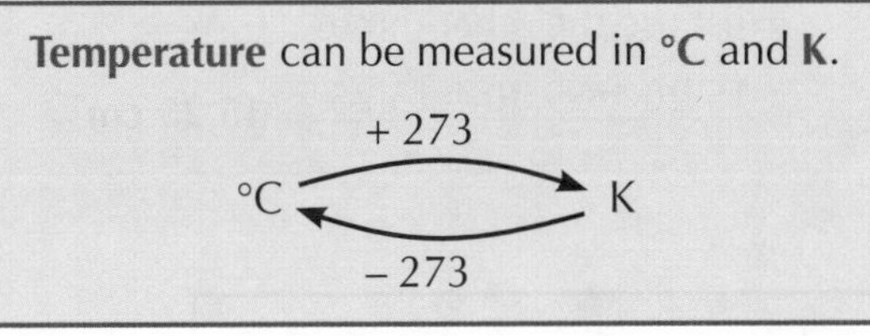

Example: Write 33 °C in K.

To convert 33 °C into K you add 273.

33 °C + 273 = **306 K**

Round to the **Lowest Number** of **Significant Figures**

The first **significant figure** (or s.f.) of a number is the **first digit that isn't a zero**. The second, third and fourth significant figures follow on immediately after the first (even if they're zeros). For example, the number **0.01072** is **0.01** to 1 s.f., **0.011** to 2 s.f., and **0.0107** to 3 s.f.

1) When you're doing a calculation, use the number of significant figures given in the data as a guide for how many you need to give in your answer.
2) Whether you're doing calculations with the results from an experiment or doing calculations in an exam, the rule is the same — round your answer to the **lowest number of significant figures** that's in your data.

Example: 13.5 cm^3 of a 0.51 mol dm^{-3} solution of sodium hydroxide reacts with 1.5 mol dm^{-3} hydrochloric acid. Calculate the volume of hydrochloric acid, in cm^3, required to neutralise the sodium hydroxide.

Moles of NaOH = 0.51 mol dm^{-3} × (13.5 cm^3 ÷ 1000) = 6.885 × 10^{-3} mol (0.51: 2 s.f.; 13.5: 3 s.f.)

Volume of HCl = (6.885 × 10^{-3}) mol ÷ 1.5 mol dm^{-3} = 0.00459 dm^3 (1.5: 2 s.f.)

= 0.00459 dm^3 × 1000 = 4.59 cm^3

= **4.6 cm^3 (2 s.f.)** ← Final answer should be rounded to 2 s.f.

You don't need to round intermediate answers. Rounding too early will make your final answer less accurate.

3) You should always **write down** the number of significant figures you've rounded to after your answer (as in the example above), so that other people can see what rounding you've done.
4) If you get told in an exam question **how many** significant figures you should give your answer to, make sure you follow those instructions — you'll **lose marks** if you don't.
5) If you're converting an answer into **standard form**, keep the same number of significant figures, e.g. 0.0060 mol dm^{-3} has the same number of significant figures as 6.0 × 10^{-3} mol dm^{-3}.

If you're ever asked to give an answer to "an appropriate degree of precision", this just means "to a sensible number of significant figures".

Analysing Results

You're not quite finished yet... there's still time to look at your results and try and make sense of them. Graphs are really useful for helping you to spot patterns in your data. There are lots of examples on these pages. Ooh, pretty...

Watch Out For **Anomalous** Results

1) **Anomalous results** are ones that **don't fit** in with the other values — this means they are likely to be wrong.
2) They're often caused by mistakes or problems with apparatus, e.g. if a drop in a titration is too big and puts you past the end point, or if a syringe plunger gets stuck whilst collecting gas produced in a reaction.
3) When looking at results in tables or graphs, you always need to look to see if there are any anomalies — you **ignore** these results when calculating means or drawing lines of best fit.

Example: Calculate the mean volume from the results in the table below.

Titration Number	1	2	3	4
Titre Volume (cm^3)	15.20	15.30	15.70	15.25

Titre **3** isn't **concordant** with (doesn't match) the other results, so you need to ignore that one and just use the other three.

$$\frac{15.20 + 15.30 + 15.25}{3} = \mathbf{15.25\ cm^3}$$

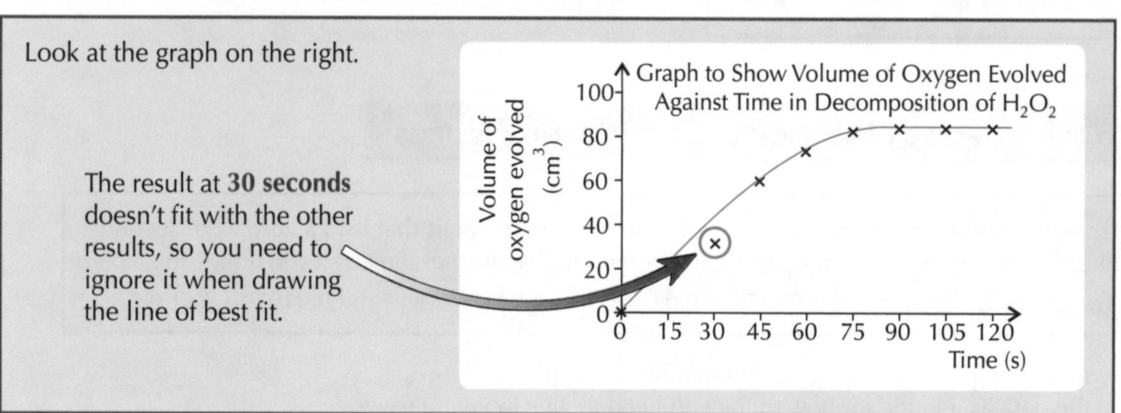

Look at the graph on the right.
The result at **30 seconds** doesn't fit with the other results, so you need to ignore it when drawing the line of best fit.
Graph to Show Volume of Oxygen Evolved Against Time in Decomposition of H_2O_2
Volume of oxygen evolved (cm^3)
0
20
40
60
80
100
0 15 30 45 60 75 90 105 120
Time (s)

Scatter Graphs Show How Two Variables Are **Correlated**

Correlation describes the **relationship** between two variables — the independent one and the dependent one. Data can show:

1) **Positive correlation** — as one variable **increases** the other **increases**.
2) **Negative correlation** — as one variable **increases** the other **decreases**.
3) **No correlation** — there is **no relationship** between the two variables.

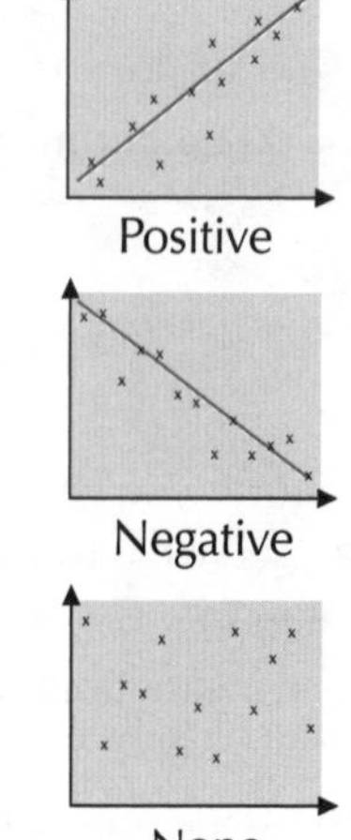

Look at the graph below.

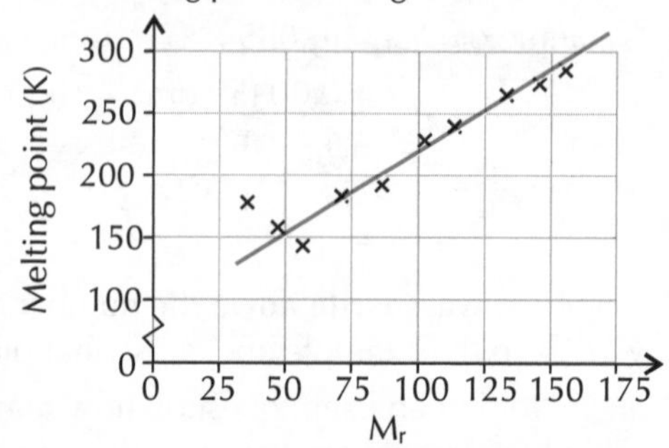

As the M_r of the straight-chain alcohols **increase**, their **melting points** also **increase** — so the two variables are **positively correlated**.

Analysing Results

Correlation **Doesn't** Mean **Cause** — Don't Jump to Conclusions

1) Ideally, only **two** quantities would **ever** change in any experiment — everything else would remain **constant**.
2) But in experiments or studies outside the lab, you **can't** usually control all the variables. So even if two variables are correlated, the change in one may **not** be causing the change in the other. Both changes might be caused by a **third variable**.

For example, some studies have found a correlation between **drinking chlorinated tap water** and the risk of developing certain cancers. Some people argue that this means water shouldn't have chlorine added.

BUT it's hard to control all the variables between people who drink tap water and people who don't. It could be many lifestyle factors.

Or, the cancer risk could be affected by something else in tap water — or by whatever the non-tap water drinkers drink instead...

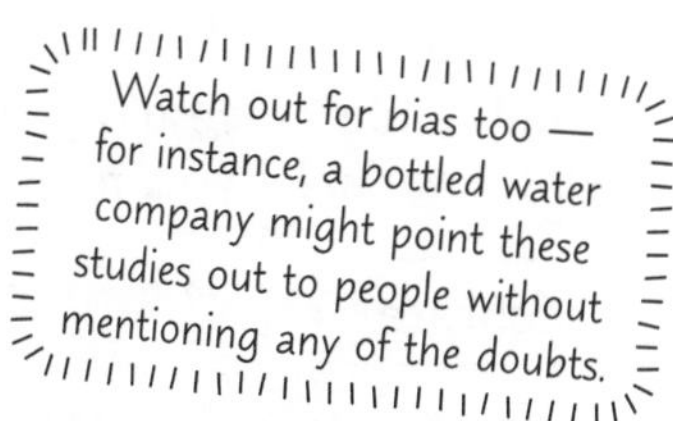

Watch out for bias too — for instance, a bottled water company might point these studies out to people without mentioning any of the doubts.

Don't Get **Carried Away** When Drawing Conclusions

The **data** should always **support** the conclusion. This may sound obvious but it's easy to **jump** to conclusions. Conclusions have to be **specific** — you can't make sweeping generalisations.

For example: the **rate** of a specific enzyme-controlled reaction was measured at **10 °C, 20 °C, 30 °C, 40 °C, 50 °C** and **60 °C**. All other variables were kept constant. The results of this experiment are shown in the graph below.

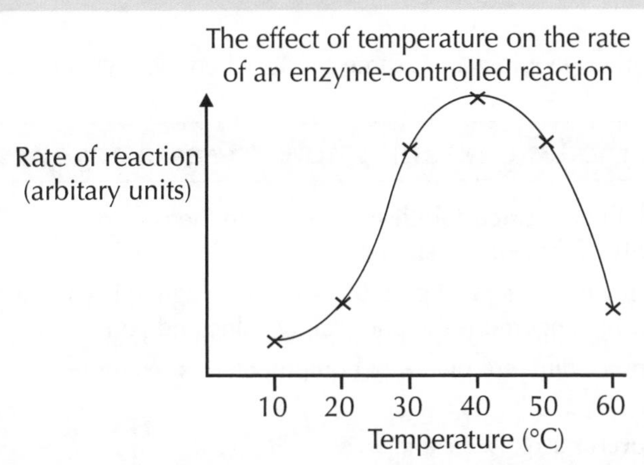

1) A science magazine **concluded** from this data that the enzyme used in the experiment works best at **40 °C**.
2) The data **doesn't** support this exact claim. The enzyme **could** work best at 42 °C or 47 °C, but you can't tell from the data because **increases** of **10 °C** at a time were used. The rate of reaction at in-between temperatures **wasn't** measured.
3) All you can say for certain is that it's faster at **40 °C** than at any of the other temperatures tested.
4) Also you can't be sure that if you did the experiment under **different conditions**, e.g. at a **different pressure**, you wouldn't get a **different optimum temperature**.
5) It's worth remembering that this experiment **ONLY** gives you information about this particular reaction too. You can't conclude that **all** enzyme-controlled reactions happen fastest at a particular temperature — only this one.

Evaluating Experiments

So you've planned an experiment, done the practical work, collected lots of data and plotted it all on a beautiful graph. Now it's time to sit back, relax and... work out everything you did wrong. That's science, I'm afraid.

You Need to Look **Critically** at Your Results

Here are a few terms that'll come in handy when you're evaluating how convincing your results are...

Valid

Valid results are results that answer the **original question**. For example, if you haven't **controlled all the variables** your results won't be valid, because you won't be testing just the thing you wanted to.

Accurate

Accurate results are results that are **really close** to the **true** answer.

You might see results that fulfil all of these being called reliable.

Precise

The smaller the amount of **spread** of your data around the **mean** (see page 106), the more **precise** it is. Calculating a **mean** (average) result from your repeats will **increase** the **precision** of your result, because it helps to reduce the effect of **random errors** on the answer (see page 111).

Repeatable

Your results are **repeatable** if **you** get the same results when you repeat the experiment using the same method and the same equipment. You really need to repeat your readings **at least three times** to demonstrate that your results really are repeatable.

Reproducible

Your results are **reproducible** if **other people** get the same results when they repeat your experiment.

You Need to Think About the **Uncertainty** Your **Measurements** Might Have

1) Any measurements you make will have **uncertainties** (or **errors**) in them, due to the limits of the **sensitivity** of the equipment.
2) Uncertainties are usually written with a ± sign, e.g ±0.05 cm. The ± sign tells you the **actual value** of the measurement lies between your reading **minus** the uncertainty value and your reading **plus** the uncertainty value.
3) The uncertainty will be different for different pieces of equipment. For example:

- The scale on a **50 cm³ burette** usually has marks every **0.1 cm³**. You should be able to tell which mark the level's closest to, so any reading you take won't be more than **0.05 cm³** out. So the **uncertainty** on each burette reading is **±0.05 cm³**.
- If a **mass balance** measures masses to the **nearest 0.1 g**, the real mass could be up to **0.05 g smaller or larger** (e.g. if the display says 1.7 g, the real mass could be anywhere between 1.65 g and 1.75 g.) So the **uncertainty** is **±0.05 g**.
- Pieces of equipment such as pipettes, volumetric flasks and thermometers will have uncertainties that depend on how well made they are. The manufacturers provide these **uncertainty values** — they're usually written on the equipment somewhere.

The level in this burette is between the 44.9 cm³ and 45.0 cm³ marks. It's closer to 45.0 — so the level is between 44.95 and 45.0. So a reading of 45.0 cm³ can't have an uncertainty of more than 0.05 cm³.

4) For any piece of equipment you use, the uncertainty will be **half** the **smallest increment** the equipment can measure, in either direction.
5) If you're **combining measurements**, you'll need to combine their **uncertainties**. For example, if you're calculating a temperature change by measuring an initial and a final temperature, the **total** uncertainty for the temperature change will be the uncertainties for both measurements added together.

Evaluating Experiments

You Can Calculate The **Percentage Uncertainty** in a Result

If you know the **uncertainty** (error) in a reading that you've taken using a certain piece of equipment, you can use it to calculate the **percentage uncertainty** in your measurement.

$$\text{percentage uncertainty} = \frac{\text{uncertainty}}{\text{reading}} \times 100$$

Example: 50.0 cm^3 of HCl is measured out in a pipette with an uncertainty of ±0.05 cm^3. Calculate the percentage uncertainty on this reading.

$$\text{percentage uncertainty} = \frac{0.05}{50.0} \times 100 = \mathbf{0.1\%}$$

If you're finding the uncertainty on a mean value, you'll need these formulas instead:

uncertainty on the mean = range ÷ 2

$$\%\ \text{uncertainty} = \frac{\text{uncertainty on the mean}}{\text{mean}} \times 100$$

Example: In a titration a burette with an uncertainty of ±0.05 cm^3 is used. The initial reading on the burette is 50.0 cm^3. The final reading is 28.8 cm^3. Calculate the percentage uncertainty on the titre value.

Titre value = 50.0 cm^3 – 28.8 cm^3 = 21.2 cm^3
Uncertainty on each burette reading = ±0.05 cm^3
Two burette readings have been combined to find the titre value.
So the total uncertainty on the measurement = 0.05 + 0.05 = ±0.1 cm^3

$$\text{Percentage uncertainty on titre value} = \frac{0.1}{21.2} \times 100 = 0.472\% = \mathbf{0.5\%\ (1\ d.p.)}$$

When you combine uncertainties, give the total uncertainty to the same number of decimal places as the measurement. (That's the titre value here.)

Percentage uncertainty is useful because it tells you how **significant** the uncertainty in a reading is compared to its **size**, e.g. ±0.1 g uncertainty is more significant when weighing out 0.2 g of a solid than when weighing out 100.0 g.

You Can **Minimise** the Percentage Uncertainty

1) One obvious way to **reduce uncertainties** in your measurements is to use the most **sensitive equipment** available. There's not much you can do about this at school or college though — you're stuck with whatever's available.
2) But there are other ways to **lower the uncertainty** in experiments. The **larger the reading** you take with a piece of equipment, the **smaller the percentage uncertainty** on that reading will be. Here's a quick example:
   - If you measure out **5.0 cm^3** of liquid in a burette with an uncertainty of **±0.05 ml** then the percentage uncertainty is (0.05 ÷ 5.0) × 100 = **1%**.
   - But if you measure **10.0 cm^3** of liquid in the same burette, the percentage uncertainty is (0.05 ÷ 10.0) × 100 = **0.5%**. Hey presto — you've just halved the percentage uncertainty.
   - So you can reduce the percentage uncertainty of this experiment by using a **larger volume** of liquid.
3) You can apply the same principle to other measurements too. For example, if you weigh out a small mass of a solid, the **percentage uncertainty** will be larger than if you weighed out a larger mass using the same balance.

Errors Can Be **Systematic** or **Random**

1) **Systematic errors** cause each reading to be different to the true value by the same amount, i.e. they shift all of your results. They may be caused by the **set-up** or the **equipment** you're using. If the 10.00 cm^3 pipette you're using to measure out a sample for titration actually only measures 9.95 cm^3, your sample will be 0.05 cm^3 too small **every time** you repeat the experiment.
2) **Random errors** cause readings to be spread about the true value due to the results varying in an **unpredictable** way. You get random error in all measurements and no matter how hard you try, you can't correct them. The tiny errors you make when you read a burette are random — you have to estimate the level when it's between two marks, so sometimes your figure will be **above** the real one and sometimes **below**.
3) **Repeating an experiment** and finding the mean of your results helps to deal with **random errors**. The results that are a bit high will be **cancelled out** by the ones that are a bit low, so your results will be more **precise**. But repeating your results won't get rid of **systematic errors**, so your results won't get more **accurate**.

This should be a photo of a scientist. I don't know what happened — it's a random error...

Synoptic Practice

So, you've revised every section, you've done every question in the book, and you're ready for the exam. Not quite... Examiners absolutely love throwing in a few 'synoptic questions'. These questions get you to pull together the chemistry you know from different parts of the course and apply it to one question. Often they use an unknown context — just to really get your brain cells working. There's no denying these questions are tricky, but luckily the next few pages are crammed full of synoptic practice. Enjoy.

1 This question is about the element boron.

1.1 Boron exists as two naturally occurring isotopes, ^{10}B and ^{11}B, in the ratio 1:4. Calculate the relative atomic mass of boron.

(1 mark)

1.2 Boron trifluoride reacts with a fluoride ion to form BF_4^-. The equation for the reaction is:

$$BF_3 + F^- \rightarrow BF_4^-$$

Give the shape of the BF_4^- ion. Name the type of bond that occurs between BF_3 and F^- and explain how it arises.

(3 marks)

1.3 Although not naturally occurring on Earth, boron can form compounds where it has an oxidation state of less than 3. One such compound has the same number of electrons as an N_2 molecule.

Give the formula of a molecule containing one atom of boron, combined with one atom of one other element, which has the same number of electrons as N_2.

(2 marks)

1.4 When the oxide of boron B_2O_3 is heated with carbon in a furnace it forms the ceramic material B_4C. The equation for the reaction is:

$$2B_2O_3 + 7C \rightarrow B_4C + 6CO$$

Each carbon atom in B_4C has donated four electrons.
State and explain whether boron is oxidised or reduced in this reaction.

(3 marks)

1.5 Suggest why the first ionisation energy of boron is lower than that of beryllium, but higher than that of aluminium.

(4 marks)

2 Fluorine is the most reactive element in Group 7. It reacts with water in a different way to chlorine. Oxygen, ozone (O_3) and hydrogen fluoride are produced when fluorine is added to water.

2.1 Write a balanced symbol equation for the reaction above.

(1 mark)

2.2 A student carried out some displacement reactions of aqueous halogens with aqueous solutions of metal halides. Suggest why fluorine was not used in these experiments.

(2 marks)

2.3 Hydrogen fluoride and water are molecules with similar masses.
Despite containing the same type of intermolecular force, the boiling point of water is significantly higher than that of hydrogen fluoride.

Suggest an explanation for the difference in the boiling points of hydrogen fluoride and water.

(3 marks)

Synoptic Practice

3 Butanoic acid reacts with ethanol to form an ester called ethyl butanoate.

$$CH_3CH_2CH_2COOH + CH_3CH_2OH \rightleftharpoons CH_3CH_2CH_2COOCH_2CH_3 + H_2O$$

A procedure for determining a value for the equilibrium constant, K_c, for the reaction is outlined below:

1. 0.500 mol of butanoic acid were added to 2.20 mol of ethanol in a boiling tube and the resulting mixture was sealed with a bung and gently heated in a water bath.
2. After reaching equilibrium, the contents of the boiling tube were poured into a volumetric flask and made up to 250 cm^3 with deionised water.
3. 25.0 cm^3 portions of the mixture were pipetted out and titrated against 0.200 mol dm^{-3} sodium hydroxide solution. Phenolphthalein indicator was used to detect the end point. This part of the experiment was repeated until concordant results were obtained.

The data obtained in the experiment are given in **Table 1**.

Table 1

	1	2	3
Initial burette reading / cm^3	0.20	13.80	27.60
Final burette reading / cm^3	13.80	27.60	41.50
Titre / cm^3	13.60	13.80	13.90

3.1 Use the information in the question and the average of the concordant titres to calculate a value for K_c for the reaction.

(7 marks)

3.2 Calculate a value for K_c for the reverse reaction.
If you have been unable to obtain a value for K_c in **3.1**, you should assume the value is 5.30, although this is not the correct answer.

(1 mark)

3.3 A concentrated sulfuric acid catalyst was used in the reaction.

Suggest one reason why the presence of concentrated sulfuric acid solution in the reaction mixture may lead to an inaccurate determination of a value for K_c.

(1 marks)

3.4 The enthalpy change of the reaction between butanoic acid and ethanol is –4 kJ mol^{-1}.
The standard enthalpies of formation of butanoic acid, ethanol and water are shown in **Table 2**.

Table 2

Compound	Butanoic acid	Ethanol	Water
$\Delta_f H^\circ$ / kJ mol^{-1}	–534	–276	–286

Using the enthalpy change of the reaction and the data in **Table 2**, calculate the enthalpy of formation of ethyl butanoate.

(3 marks)

3.5 Butanoic acid can be formed from an alcohol.
Draw the displayed formula of this alcohol and describe the method used to convert it to butanoic acid.

(3 marks)

Synoptic Practice

4 Organohalogen compounds are a group of compounds containing at least one carbon to halogen bond. They are formed from and can take part in reactions to produce compounds of different homologous series.

A student carries out the hydrolysis of three halogenoalkanes by reacting them with warm aqueous sodium hydroxide, resulting in the formation of an alcohol. The student suggested that the rate of hydrolysis of a halogenoalkane could depend upon either the bond polarity or bond enthalpy of the carbon to halogen bond.

Table 3 shows some data about three carbon to halogen bonds. You should refer to the information in **Table 3** to help you answer some of the following question parts.

Table 3

Bond	Difference in electronegativity between atoms	Bond enthalpy / kJ mol^{-1}
C – Cl	0.61	346
C – Br	0.41	290
C – I	0.11	228

4.1 Explain the difference in polarity between a carbon to chlorine bond and a carbon to bromine bond.

(2 marks)

The student hydrolysed 1-bromopropane, 1-iodopropane and 1-chloropropane.
Each halogenoalkane was added to a separate boiling tube and placed in a water bath.
The same volume of sodium hydroxide was then added to each tube at the same starting time.

4.2 Draw a mechanism for the hydrolysis of 1-bromopropane by a hydroxide ion, clearly showing the structure of the product.

(3 marks)

4.3 Suggest which of the three halogenoalkanes in the experiment has the fastest rate of hydrolysis. Explain your answer, referring to whether the rate hydrolysis of halogenoalkanes is determined by the bond polarity or the bond enthalpy of the carbon to halogen bond.

(3 marks)

4.4 Each of the halogenoalkanes tested have the structural formula $CH_3CH_2CH_2X$.
Suggest one change to this structural formula that could affect the rate of hydrolysis.

(1 mark)

4.5 Under different reaction conditions, bromopropane can react with hydroxide ions to form the alkene, propene. Propene can then undergo further reactions to produce a mixture of alcohols. This is done by first reacting propene with cold concentrated sulfuric acid. After adding water and warming the product, a further reaction occurs which produces a mixture of alcohols.

Describe how different reaction conditions produce the alkene propene.
Explain why the subsequent reactions of propene described above produce a mixture of alcohols.
You do not need to draw any mechanisms for the reactions occurring in your answer.

(6 marks)

4.6 At high temperatures, propene can be halogenated to form a halogenoalkene.
The halogenoalkene has a relative molecular mass of 76.5.

Deduce the molecular formula of the molecule and name the isomer that shows E/Z isomerism.
Draw the skeletal formula of an isomer that does not show E/Z isomerism.

(3 marks)

Answers

Unit 1: Section 1 — Atomic Structure

Page 3 — The Atom

1 a) Similarity — They've all got the same number of protons/electrons *[1 mark]*.
Difference — They all have different numbers of neutrons *[1 mark]*.
b) 1 proton, 1 neutron (2 – 1), 1 electron *[1 mark]*.
c) $^{3}_{1}H$ *[1 mark]*

2 a) i) Same number of electrons. $^{32}S^{2-}$ has 16 + 2 = 18 electrons. ^{40}Ar has 18 electrons too *[1 mark]*.
ii) Same number of protons. Each has 16 protons (the atomic number of S must always be the same) *[1 mark]*.
iii) Same number of neutrons. ^{40}Ar has 40 – 18 = 22 neutrons. ^{42}Ca has 42 – 20 = 22 neutrons *[1 mark]*.
b) **A** and **C** *[1 mark]*. They have the same number of protons but different numbers of neutrons *[1 mark]*.
It doesn't matter that they have a different number of electrons because they are still the same element.

Page 7 — Relative Mass and the Mass Spectrometer

1 a) First multiply each relative abundance by the relative mass:
120.8 × 63 = 7610.4, 54.0 × 65 = 3510.0
Next add up the products:
7610.4 + 3510.0 = 11 120.4 *[1 mark]*
Now divide by the total abundance (120.8 + 54.0 = 174.8)
A_r(Cu) = 11 120.4 ÷ 174.8 ≈ **63.6** *[1 mark]*
You can check your answer by seeing if A_r(Cu) is in between 63 and 65 (the lowest and highest relative isotopic masses).
b) A sample of copper is a mixture of 2 isotopes in different abundances *[1 mark]*. The average mass of these isotopes isn't a whole number *[1 mark]*.

2 a) Mass spectrometry *[1 mark]*
b) You use pretty much the same method here as for question 1 a).
93.11 × 39 = 3631.29, (0.12 × 40) = 4.8, (6.77 × 41) = 277.57
3631.29 + 4.8 + 277.57 = 3913.66 *[1 mark]*
This time you divide by 100 because they're percentages.
A_r(K) = 3913.66 ÷ 100 = **39.1** (3 s.f.) *[1 mark]*
Again check your answer's between the lowest and highest relative isotopic masses, 39 and 41. A_r(K) is closer to 39 because most of the sample (93.11%) is made up of this isotope.

3 a) So that they can be accelerated *[1 mark]* and detected *[1 mark]*.
b) Positive ions are accelerated by an electric field *[1 mark]* to a constant kinetic energy *[1 mark]*. Lighter ions will end up moving faster *[1 mark]*. The faster ions arrive first at the detector *[1 mark]*.
c) B Gallium *[1 mark]*.
The percentage isotope abundance is around 60-40.

Page 9 — Electronic Structure

1 a) K atom: $1s^2\ 2s^2\ 2p^6\ 3s^2\ 3p^6\ 4s^1$ *[1 mark]*
K^+ ion: $1s^2\ 2s^2\ 2p^6\ 3s^2\ 3p^6$ *[1 mark]*
b) Oxygen atom: 1s [↑↓] 2s [↑↓] 2p [↑↓][↑][↑]
Correct number of electrons in each sub-shell *[1 mark]*.
Having spin-pairing in one of the p orbitals and parallel spins in the other two p orbitals *[1 mark]*.
A box filled with 2 arrows is spin pairing — 1 up and 1 down. If you've put the four p electrons into just 2 orbitals, it's wrong.

2 a) $1s^2\ 2s^2\ 2p^6\ 3s^2\ 3p^6\ 3d^5\ 4s^2$ *[1 mark]*
b) Al^{3+} ion: 1s [↑↓] 2s [↑↓] 2p [↑↓][↑↓][↑↓]
Correct number of electrons in each sub-shell *[1 mark]*.
One arrow in each box pointing up, and one pointing down *[1 mark]*.
c) Germanium ($1s^2\ 2s^2\ 2p^6\ 3s^2\ 3p^6\ 3d^{10}\ 4s^2\ 4p^2$) *[1 mark]*
d) Ar (atom) *[1 mark]*, K^+ (positive ion) *[1 mark]*, Cl^- (negative ion) *[1 mark]*. You also could have suggested Ca^{2+}, S^{2-} or P^{3-}.

Page 11 — Ionisation Energy

1 a) $C_{(g)} \rightarrow C^+_{(g)} + e^-$
Correct equation *[1 mark]*. Both state symbols showing gaseous state *[1 mark]*.
b) First ionisation energy increases as nuclear charge increases *[1 mark]*.
c) As the nuclear charge increases there is a stronger force of attraction between the nucleus and the electron *[1 mark]* and so more energy is required to remove the electron *[1 mark]*.

2 a) Group 3 *[1 mark]*
There are three electrons removed before the first big jump in energy.
b) The electrons are being removed from an increasingly positive ion *[1 mark]* so the force of attraction that has to be broken is greater *[1 mark]*.
c) When an electron is removed from a different shell there is a big increase in the energy required (since that shell is closer to the nucleus) *[1 mark]*.
d) There are 3 shells *[1 mark]*.
You can tell there are 3 shells because there are 2 big jumps in energy. There is always one more shell than big jumps.

Page 13 — Trends in First Ionisation Energy

1 a) The shielding from the electrons is the same in these atoms *[1 mark]* but there is an increase in the number of protons in the nucleus / nuclear charge *[1 mark]*. So it takes more energy to remove an electron from the outer shell *[1 mark]*.
b) i) Boron has the configuration $1s^2\ 2s^2\ 2p^1$ compared to $1s^2\ 2s^2$ for beryllium *[1 mark]*. The 2p orbital is at a slightly higher energy level than the 2s orbital. The extra distance and partial shielding by the 2s electrons make it easier to remove the outer electron *[1 mark]*.
ii) Oxygen has the configuration $1s^2\ 2s^2\ 2p^4$ compared to $1s^2\ 2s^2\ 2p^3$ for nitrogen *[1 mark]*. Electron repulsion in the shared 2p sub-shell in oxygen makes it easier to remove an electron *[1 mark]*.

2 As you go down Group 2, it takes less energy to remove an electron *[1 mark]*. This is evidence that the outer electrons are increasingly distant from the nucleus *[1 mark]* and additional inner shells of electrons exist to shield the outer shell *[1 mark]*.

3 a) D Neon *[1 mark]*
b) Ionisation energy increases across a period *[1 mark]* so the Group 0 elements have the highest first ionisation energies of the elements in their period. Ionisation energy decreases down a group *[1 mark]* so neon has a higher ionisation energy than krypton.

4 a) A Sodium *[1 mark]*
b) E.g. in sodium, the first electron is removed from the third shell but the second is removed from the second shell *[1 mark]*. The second shell electron is nearer to the nucleus and experiences less shielding, which means it is much more strongly attracted to the nucleus *[1 mark]*. In all of the other elements given, the second electron is being removed from the same shell as the first one *[1 mark]*.

Unit 1: Section 2 — Amount of Substance

Page 15 — The Mole

PQ1 6.02×10^{23}
This is just Avogadro's constant.
PQ2 Number of atoms = 0.500 × (6.02×10^{23}) = $\mathbf{3.01 \times 10^{23}}$
PQ3 concentration = 0.100 moles ÷ 0.500 dm^3 = **0.200 mol dm^{-3}**

1 M_r of $CaSO_4$ = 40.1 + 32.1 + (4 × 16.0) = 136.2
number of moles = $\frac{34.05}{136.2}$ = **0.2500 moles** *[1 mark]*

2 M_r of CH_3COOH = (2 × 12.0) + (4 × 1.0) + (2 × 16.0) = 60.0
Mass = 60.0 × 0.360 = **21.6 g** *[1 mark]*

3 number of moles = 0.250 × $\frac{50.0}{1000}$ = **0.0125 moles** *[1 mark]*

4 number of moles = 0.250 × $\frac{60.0}{1000}$ = 0.0150 moles *[1 mark]*
M_r of H_2SO_4 = (2 × 1.0) + (1 × 32.1) + (4 × 16.0) = 98.1
Mass = 0.0150 × 98.1 = **1.48 g** *[1 mark]*

Answers

5 M_r of HCl = 1.0 + 35.5 = 36.5
number of moles = $\frac{3.65}{36.5}$ = 0.100 ***[1 mark]***
Volume of water in dm^3 = 100 ÷ 1000 = 0.100 dm^3
Concentration = $\frac{\text{moles}}{\text{volume}} = \frac{0.100}{0.100}$ = **1.00 mol dm^{-3}** ***[1 mark]***

6 M_r of C_3H_8= (3 × 12.0) + (8 × 1.0) = 44.0
number of moles of C_3H_8 = $\frac{88.0}{44.0}$ = 2.00 moles ***[1 mark]***
p = 100 × 10^3 Pa, T = (25 + 273) = 298 K ***[1 mark]***
V = nRT ÷ p = (2 × 8.31 × 298) ÷ (100 × 10^3)
= **0.0495 m^3 (3 s.f.)** ***[1 mark]***
You get the mark if you wrote the answer in standard form here — that would be 4.95 × 10^{-2} m^3.

7 B 100 kPa ***[1 mark]***
M_r of CO_2 = 12.0 + (2 × 16.0) = 44.0
number of moles of CO_2 = (35.2 ÷ 44.0) = 0.800
p = nRT ÷ V
n = 0.800 moles, R = 8.31 J K^{-1} mol^{-1}, T = 301 K,
V = 20.0 × (1 × 10^{-3}) = 0.0200 m^3
p = (0.800 × 8.31 × 301) ÷ 0.0200
= 100052.4 Pa = 100 kPa (to 3 s.f.)

Page 17 — Equations and Calculations

PQ2 a) $Cl_2 + 2KBr \rightarrow 2KCl + Br_2$
b) $Cl_2 + 2Br^- \rightarrow 2Cl^- + Br_2$

1 M_r of C_2H_5Cl = (2 × 12.0) + (5 × 1.0) + (1 × 35.5) = 64.5
Number of moles of C_2H_5Cl = $\frac{258}{64.5}$ = 4.00 moles ***[1 mark]***
From the equation, 1 mole C_2H_5Cl is made from 1 mole C_2H_4, so 4 moles C_2H_5Cl is made from 4 moles C_2H_4 ***[1 mark]***.
M_r of C_2H_4 = (2 × 12.0) + (4 × 1.0) = 28.0
mass of 4 moles C_2H_4 = 4 × 28.0 = **112 g** ***[1 mark]***

2 a) M_r of $CaCO_3$ = 40.1 + 12.0 + (3 × 16.0) = 100.1
Number of moles of $CaCO_3$ = $\frac{15.0}{100.1}$ = 0.150 moles ***[1 mark]***
From the equation, 1 mole $CaCO_3$ produces 1 mole CaO, so 0.150 moles of $CaCO_3$ produces 0.150 moles of CaO ***[1 mark]***
M_r of CaO = 40.1 + 16.0 = 56.1
mass of 0.15 moles of CaO = 56.1 × 0.150 = **8.42 g** ***[1 mark]***
b) From the equation, 1 mole $CaCO_3$ produces 1 mole CO_2, so 0.150 moles of $CaCO_3$ produces 0.150 moles of CO_2 ***[1 mark]***
T = 25.0 + 273 = 298 K and p = 100 × 10^3 Pa ***[1 mark]***
V = nRT ÷ p
Volume of CO_2 = $\frac{0.150 \times 8.31 \times 298}{100 \times 10^3}$ = 0.00371 m^3
= **3.71 × 10^{-3} m^3** ***[1 mark]***

3 **2**KI + $Pb(NO_3)_2$ → PbI_2 + **2**KNO_3 ***[1 mark]***
The LHS needs 2 Is, so pop a 2 in front of KI. Then the RHS needs 2 Ks, so put a 2 in front of KNO_3. Once you've done that, everything balances.

Page 20 — Titrations

1 Moles of NaOH = 0.500 × $\frac{14.6}{1000}$ = 0.00730 ***[1 mark]***
From the equation, 1 mole of NaOH neutralises 1 mole of CH_3COOH, so 0.00730 moles NaOH must neutralise 0.00730 moles of CH_3COOH ***[1 mark]***.
Concentration CH_3COOH = 0.00730 ÷ $\frac{25.4}{1000}$
= **0.287 mol dm^{-3}** ***[1 mark]***

2 M_r of $CaCO_3$ = 40.1 + 12.0 + (3 × 16.0) = 100.1 ***[1 mark]***
Moles of $CaCO_3$ = $\frac{0.75}{100.1}$ = 0.0075 ***[1 mark]***
From the equation, 1 mole $CaCO_3$ reacts with 1 mole H_2SO_4 so, 0.0075 moles of $CaCO_3$ must react with 0.0075 moles of H_2SO_4 ***[1 mark]***.
Volume needed = $\frac{0.0075}{0.25}$ = **0.030 dm^3** (or **30 cm^3**) ***[1 mark]***
If the question mentions concentration, you can bet your last clean pair of underwear that you'll need to use this formula: number of moles = conc. × volume (dm^3)

3 a) Titration 3 (42.90 cm^3) is anomalous. It is not concordant with / is significantly different to the other three results ***[1 mark]***.
b) Mean titre = $\frac{45.00 + 45.10 + 44.90}{3}$ = **45.00 cm^3** ***[1 mark]***
c) Moles of NaOH = 0.400 × $\frac{45.00}{1000}$ = 0.01800 ***[1 mark]***
From the equation, 1 mole of NaOH reacts with 1 mole of HNO_3, so 0.01800 moles NaOH must react with 0.0180 moles of HNO_3 ***[1 mark]***.
Moles of HNO_3 = 0.01800 ÷ $\frac{50.0}{1000}$ = **0.3600 mol dm^{-3}** ***[1 mark]***

Page 23 — Formulas, Yield and Atom Economy

1 Start by working out how many moles of carbon and hydrogen there would be in 100 g of the hydrocarbon:
Number of moles of C = $\frac{92.3}{12.0}$ = 7.69 moles ***[1 mark]***
Number of moles of H = $\frac{7.70}{1.0}$ = 7.70 moles ***[1 mark]***
Divide both by 7.69: C: 7.69 ÷ 7.69 = 1. H: 7.70 ÷ 7.69 = 1.00.
So ratio C : H = 1 : 1
Empirical formula = CH ***[1 mark]***
Empirical mass = 12.0 + 1.0 = 13.0
Number of empirical units in molecule = $\frac{78.0}{13.0}$ = 6
So the molecular formula = 6 × CH = **C_6H_6** ***[1 mark]***

2 a) Moles PCl_3 = $\frac{\text{mass}}{M_r} = \frac{0.275}{137.5}$ = **0.00200 mol** ***[1 mark]***
From the formula, 1 mole of PCl_3 reacts with Cl_2 to form 1 mole of PCl_5, so 0.00200 moles of PCl_3 will react to form 0.00200 moles of PCl_5 ***[1 mark]***.
M_r of PCl_5 = 31.0 + (5 × 35.5) = 208.5
Theoretical yield = 0.00200 × 208.5 = **0.417 g** ***[1 mark]***
b) percentage yield = (0.198 ÷ 0.417) × 100 = **47.5%** ***[1 mark]***
c) 100% ***[1 mark]***. Since the equation shows that this reaction has only one product, its atom economy must be 100% ***[1 mark]***.

Unit 1: Section 3 — Bonding

Page 25 — Ionic Bonding

1 a) E.g.

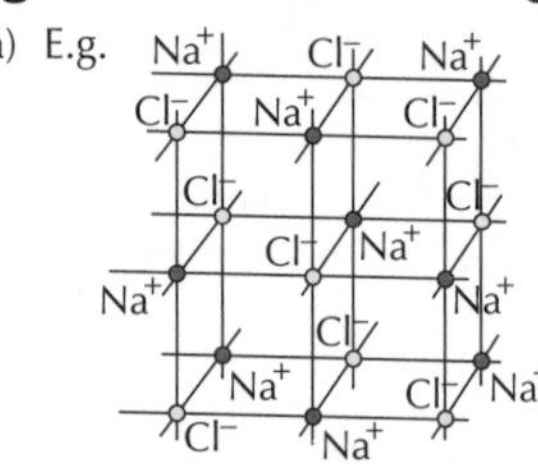

Your diagram should show the following:
- cubic structure with ions at corners ***[1 mark]***
- sodium ions and chloride ions labelled ***[1 mark]***
- alternating sodium ions and chloride ions ***[1 mark]***

b) giant ionic lattice ***[1 mark]***
c) You'd expect it to have a high melting point because the electrostatic attraction between ions ***[1 mark]*** is strong ***[1 mark]*** so a lot of energy is needed to overcome this attraction ***[1 mark]***.

2 $MgCO_3$ ***[1 mark]***
Magnesium is in group 2 of the periodic table, so a magnesium ion has a charge of 2+. A carbonate ion has a charge of 2–.

3 In a solid, ions are held in place by strong ionic bonds ***[1 mark]***. When the solid is heated to melting point, the ions gain enough energy to overcome these forces and move ***[1 mark]***, carrying charge (and so electricity) through the substance ***[1 mark]***.

Page 27 — Covalent Bonding

1 a) A shared pair of electrons between two atoms ***[1 mark]***
b) A single covalent bond only contains one pair of shared electrons, A double covalent bond contains two pairs of shared electrons ***[1 mark]***.

2 a) Dative covalent/coordinate bonding ***[1 mark]***
b) One atom donates a pair of electrons to the bond. / Both the electrons in the bond come from one atom. ***[1 mark]***.

Answers

3 a) Macromolecular/giant covalent ***[1 mark]***

b) Diamond Graphite

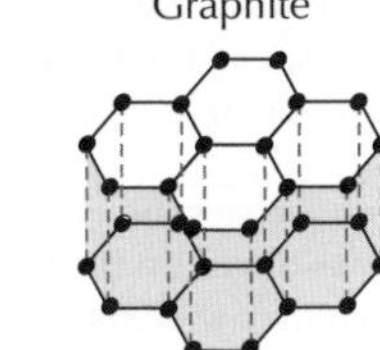

[1 mark for each correctly drawn diagram]

Diamond's a bit awkward to draw without it looking like a load of ballet dancing spiders — just make sure each carbon is connected to four others.

c) Diamond only has electrons in covalent bonds ***[1 mark]***, so is a poor electrical conductor ***[1 mark]***. Graphite has some delocalised electrons which can flow within the sheets ***[1 mark]***, making it an electrical conductor ***[1 mark]***.

Page 29 — Shapes of Molecules

1 a) NCl_3:

xx
N
Cl Cl 107° Cl ***[1 mark]***

shape: (trigonal) pyramidal ***[1 mark]***,
bond angle: 107° (accept between 105° and 109°) ***[1 mark]***

b) BCl_3:

Cl Cl
B 120°
Cl ***[1 mark]***

shape: trigonal planar ***[1 mark]***, bond angle: 120° exactly ***[1 mark]***

c) BCl_3 has three bonding electron pairs around B which repel each other equally ***[1 mark]***. NCl_3 has three bonding electron pairs and one lone pair ***[1 mark]***. The lone pair repels the bonding pair more strongly than the bonding pairs repel each other ***[1 mark]***.

Page 32 — Polarisation and Intermolecular Forces

1 Decene has a higher boiling point. Decene is a larger molecule than octene, so it has more electrons/a larger surface area ***[1 mark]***. This means that the van der Waals forces between molecules of decene will be stronger ***[1 mark]***, so it will take more energy to overcome them ***[1 mark]***.

The more energy you need to overcome the intermolecular forces between the molecules, the higher the boiling point of the compound will be.

2 a) The C–Cl bond will be polar, because chlorine has a much higher electronegativity than carbon ***[1 mark]***.

b) The molecule CCl_4 is not polar. Each of the C–Cl bonds in the CCl_4 molecule is polar ***[1 mark]***, but the polar bonds are arranged symmetrically all around the molecule, so the charges cancel out ***[1 mark]***.

3 a) E.g.

δ–
O
δ+ H H δ+
δ– O H δ+
H δ+

Your diagram should show the following:

- A hydrogen bond, shown as a dotted line, between an H atom on one molecule and an O atom on the other ***[1 mark]***.
- Two lone pairs on each oxygen atom ***[1 mark]***.
- Partial charges on all the atoms ***[1 mark]***.

b) Hydrogen bonding is present in water but not in any of the other group 6 hydrides ***[1 mark]***. Hydrogen bonds are stronger than other intermolecular forces ***[1 mark]***, so more energy is needed to break the intermolecular forces between water molecules than for other group 6 hydride molecules ***[1 mark]***.

Page 35 — Metallic Bonding and Properties of Materials

1 a) E.g.

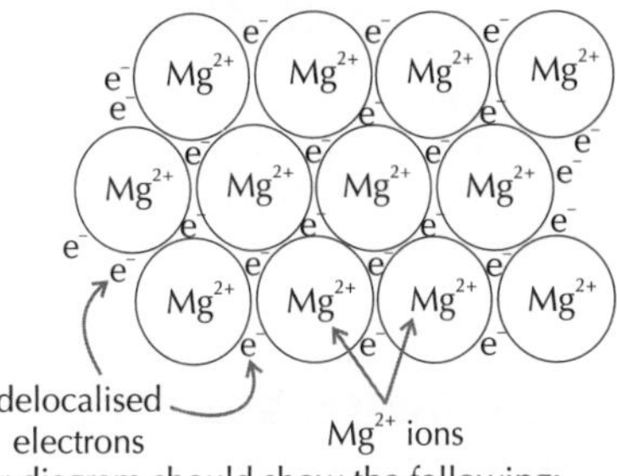

Your diagram should show the following:

- Closely packed Mg^{2+} ions ***[1 mark]***.
- Delocalised electrons ***[1 mark]***.

b) Metals contain delocalised electrons, which can move through the structure to carry a current ***[1 mark]***.

2 A = ionic ***[1 mark]***, B = simple molecular/covalent ***[1 mark]***, C = metallic ***[1 mark]***, D macromolecular/giant covalent ***[1 mark]***.

3 Iodine is a simple molecular substance ***[1 mark]***. To boil iodine, you only need to break the weak intermolecular forces holding the molecules together, which doesn't need much energy ***[1 mark]***. Graphite is a giant covalent substance ***[1 mark]***. To boil graphite, you need to break the strong covalent bonds between atoms, which needs a lot of energy ***[1 mark]***.

Unit 1: Section 4 — Energetics

Page 37 — Enthalpy Changes

1 a) Total energy required to break bonds = (4 × 435) + (2 × 498) = 2736 kJ mol^{-1} ***[1 mark]***

Energy released when bonds form = (2 × 805) + (4 × 464) = 3466 kJ mol^{-1} ***[1 mark]***

Enthalpy change = 2736 – 3466 = **–730 kJ mol^{-1}** ***[1 mark]***

b) The reaction is exothermic, because the enthalpy change is negative / more energy is given out than is taken in ***[1 mark]***.

2 a) $CH_3OH_{(l)} + 1\frac{1}{2}O_{2(g)} \rightarrow CO_{2(g)} + 2H_2O_{(l)}$ ***[1 mark]***

It's fine to use halves to balance equations. Make sure you've only got 1 mole of CH_3OH being burned, since the question is asking for the standard enthalpy of combustion.

b) $C_{(s)} + 2H_{2(g)} + \frac{1}{2}O_{2(g)} \rightarrow CH_3OH_{(l)}$ ***[1 mark]***

Again, make sure you're only forming 1 mole of CH_3OH, since the question is asking for the standard enthalpy of formation.

3 The standard enthalpy change of combustion is the enthalpy change when 1 mole of a substance is burned. This equation shows 2 moles of propane being burned ***[1 mark]***.

You really need to know the definitions of the standard enthalpy changes by heart. There's loads of teeny little details they could ask you about.

Page 39 — Calorimetry

1 ΔT = 25.5 – 19.0 = 6.50 °C = 6.50 K ***[1 mark]***

25.0 + 25.0 = 50.0 cm^3 of solution which has a mass of 50.0 g ***[1 mark]***

$q = mc\Delta T$ = 50.0 × 4.18 × 6.50 = 1358.5 J ***[1 mark]***

1358.5 J ÷ 1000 = 1.3585 kJ

moles of HCl = concentration (mol dm^{-3}) × volume (dm^3)

1.00 × (25.0 ÷ 1000) = 0.0250 ***[1 mark]***

Enthalpy change = –1.3585 ÷ 0.0250 = **–54.3 kJ mol^{-1}** (3 s.f.) ***[1 mark]***

It's important that you remember to add a minus sign to the enthalpy change here (because the reaction's exothermic).

2 Heat produced by reaction = $mc\Delta T$ = 50.0 × 4.18 × 2.60 = 543.4 J ***[1 mark]***

543.4 J ÷ 1000 = 0.5434 kJ

moles of $CuSO_4$ = concentration (mol dm^{-3}) × volume (dm^3) = 2.00 × (50.0 ÷ 1000) = 0.0100 mole ***[1 mark]***

From the equation, 1 mole of $CuSO_4$ reacts with 1 mole of Zn. So 0.0100 mole of $CuSO_4$ reacts with 0.0100 mole of Zn ***[1 mark]***.

Enthalpy change = –0.5434 ÷ 0.0100 = **–54.3 kJ** ***[1 mark]***

Once again, you can tell this reaction is exothermic, because it releases heat — so remember to add the minus sign to the enthalpy change.

Answers

Page 41 — Hess's Law

PQ3 $\Delta_r H^\circ = -965 + 890 = \mathbf{-75\ kJ\ mol^{-1}}$

1 $\Delta_r H^\circ$ = sum of $\Delta_f H^\circ$(products) – sum of $\Delta_f H^\circ$(reactants) ***[1 mark]***
$= [0 + (3 \times -602)] - [-1676 + 0]$
$= \mathbf{-130\ kJ\ mol^{-1}}$ ***[1 mark]***

Don't forget the units — if you leave them out, you might well lose marks.

2 $\Delta_r H^\circ = \Delta_c H^\circ(C_2H_4) + \Delta_c H^\circ(H_2) - \Delta_c H^\circ(C_2H_6)$ ***[1 mark]***
$= (-1400) + (-286) - (-1560)$
$= \mathbf{-126\ kJ\ mol^{-1}}$ ***[1 mark]***

Unit 1: Section 5 — Kinetics, Equilibria and Redox Reactions

Page 43 — Reaction Rates

1 The molecules don't always have enough energy to react ***[1 mark]***.

2

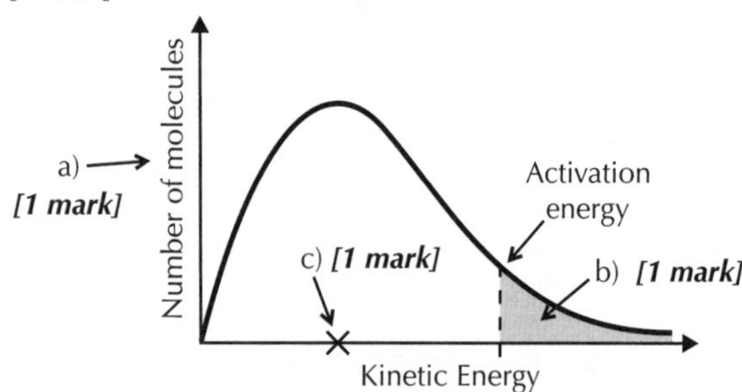

For part c), the important thing is to get your mark on the axis as close to the peak of the curve as possible.

Page 46 — More on Reaction Rates

1 a)

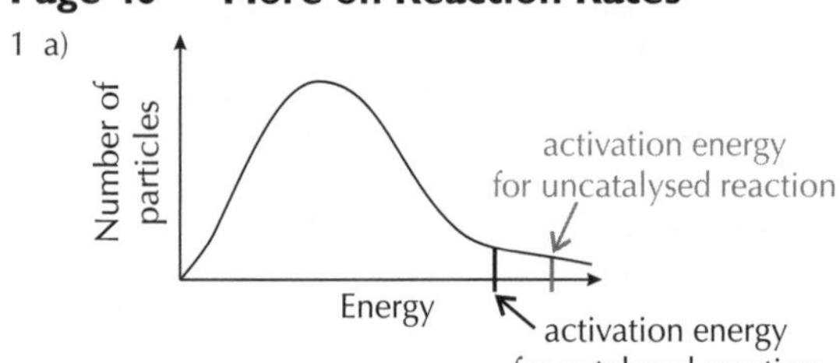

It doesn't matter exactly where you put the line showing the activation energy for the catalysed reaction here — as long as it's a bit lower than the one for the uncatalysed activation energy.

b) Manganese(IV) oxide lowers the activation energy of the reaction by providing an alternative reaction pathway ***[1 mark]***.

c) Raising the temperature will increase the rate of reaction ***[1 mark]***. When you raise the temperature you increase the kinetic energy of the molecules ***[1 mark]***. This means that more molecules will have at least the activation energy/enough energy to react ***[1 mark]***. Since the molecules are moving faster, it also means that collisions will occur more frequently ***[1 mark]***.

Page 49 — Reversible Reactions

1 a) If a reaction at equilibrium is subjected to a change in concentration, pressure or temperature, the position of equilibrium will move to counteract the change ***[1 mark]***.
You could well be asked to give definitions of things like this in an exam, so make sure you learn them — they're relatively easy marks.

b) i) There are the same number of molecules/moles on each side of the equation ***[1 mark]***, so the position of equilibrium will not move ***[1 mark]***.
ii) The reverse reaction is exothermic ***[1 mark]*** so the position of equilibrium will shift to the left to increase the temperature ***[1 mark]***.
iii) The position of equilibrium will shift to the right ***[1 mark]*** to increase the concentration of nitrogen monoxide ***[1 mark]***.

c) No effect ***[1 mark]***.
Catalysts don't affect the equilibrium position. They just help the reaction to get there sooner.

2 a) The forward reaction is exothermic ***[1 mark]***. If you decrease the temperature, the position of equilibrium will move to the right/the forward reaction will speed up in order to produce heat ***[1 mark]***. This will increase the amount of ethanol/product that is made ***[1 mark]***.

b) i) Increasing pressure increases the yield of ethanol ***[1 mark]***. There are fewer moles of gas on the right hand side of the equation so equilibrium is shifted to the right ***[1 mark]***.
ii) E.g. producing a high pressure is expensive. / The equipment needed to produce a high pressure is expensive. / The cost of producing the extra pressure is greater than the value of the extra yield ***[1 mark]***.

Page 51 — The Equilibrium Constant

1 $K_c = \frac{[H_2][I_2]}{[HI]^2}$ ***[1 mark]***

At equilibrium, $[H_2] = [I_2]$ ***[1 mark]***

$[HI]^2 = \frac{[H_2][I_2]}{K_c} = \frac{0.770 \times 0.770}{0.0200} = 29.6$ ***[1 mark]***

$[HI] = \sqrt{29.6} = \mathbf{5.44\ mol\,dm^{-3}}$ ***[1 mark]***

2 a) i) mass ÷ M_r = 34.5 ÷ [14.0 + (2 × 16.0)] = 34.5 ÷ 46.0
= **0.750 mol** ***[1 mark]***

ii) moles of O_2 = mass ÷ M_r = 7.04 ÷ (2 × 16.0) = **0.220** ***[1 mark]***
moles of NO = 2 × moles of O_2 = 2 × 0.220 = **0.440** ***[1 mark]***
moles of NO_2 = 0.750 – 0.440 = **0.310** ***[1 mark]***

b) Concentration of O_2 = 0.220 ÷ 9.80 = 0.0224 mol dm^{-3}
Concentration of NO = 0.440 ÷ 9.80 = 0.0449 mol dm^{-3}
Concentration of NO_2 = 0.310 ÷ 9.80 = 0.0316 mol dm^{-3}
[1 mark for all three concentrations correct]

$K_c = \frac{[NO]^2[O_2]}{[NO_2]^2}$ ***[1 mark]***

$= \frac{0.0449^2 \times 0.0224}{0.0316^2} = 0.0452$

Units $= \frac{[mol\,dm^{-3}]^2[mol\,dm^{-3}]}{[mol\,dm^{-3}]^2} = mol\,dm^{-3}$

So $K_c = \mathbf{0.0452\ mol\,dm^{-3}}$
[1 mark for the correct value of K_c, 1 mark for units.]

Page 53 — Redox Reactions

1 a) Oxidation is the loss of electrons ***[1 mark]***.
b) i) 0 ***[1 mark]***
ii) +1 ***[1 mark]***
c) Oxygen is being reduced ***[1 mark]***.
$O_2 + 4e^- \rightarrow 2O^{2-}$ ***[1 mark]***

2 a) An oxidising agent accepts electrons and gets reduced ***[1 mark]***.
b) $In \rightarrow In^{3+} + 3e^-$ ***[1 mark]***
c) $2In + 3Cl_2 \rightarrow 2InCl_3$ ***[2 marks — 1 mark for correct reactants and products, 1 mark for correct balancing.]***

Extra Exam Practice for Unit 1: Sections 1-5

Pages 54-55

2.1

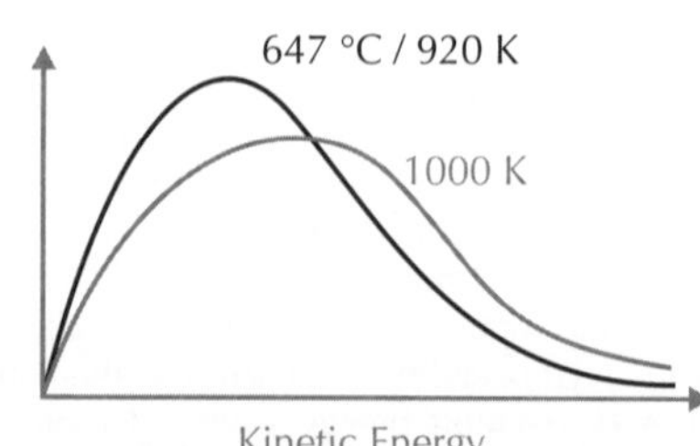

[1 mark for the peak of the new curve being displaced to the left of the original curve and 1 mark for all of the following: curve starts at origin, the peak is higher than the original, the new curve only crosses the original curve once, the new curve does not touch the energy axis or diverge from the original curve in this region.]

Answers

2.2 A small proportion of molecules will have very high kinetic energies *[1 mark]*.

2.3 E.g. moles of CO formed = (67.2 ÷ (12.0 + 16.0)) = 2.40 mol
Theoretical yield = (actual yield ÷ percentage yield) × 100
Theoretical yield of CO = (2.40 ÷ 85.6) × 100 = 2.803... mol
1 mole of CO is produced from 1 mole of CH_4,
so theoretical moles of CH_4 that reacted = 2.803... mol.
Mass of CH_4 at the start =
2.803... × (12.0 + (4 × 1.0)) = 44.8598... = **44.9 g**
[4 marks for correct answer, otherwise 1 mark for correct number of moles of CO formed, 1 mark for correct theoretical yield of CO, 1 mark for correct total number of moles of CH_4 at the start.]

3.1 Ammonia has hydrogen bonding which is stronger than the van der Waals forces between nitrogen molecules and between hydrogen molecules *[1 mark]*. So, ammonia has a higher boiling point and will condense/turn into a liquid first upon cooling *[1 mark]*.

3.2 $4NH_3 + 5O_2 \rightarrow 4NO + 6H_2O$
$\Delta_r H^\ominus$ = sum of $\Delta_f H^\ominus$ (products) – sum of $\Delta_f H^\ominus$ (reactants)
$\Delta_r H^\ominus = 4\Delta_f H^\ominus [NO] + 6\Delta_f H^\ominus [H_2O] - 4\Delta_f H^\ominus [NH_3]$
[3 marks — 1 mark for identifying NO, 1 mark for a correctly balanced equation and 1 mark for a complete equation for calculating the enthalpy change of the reaction.]

3.3 $pV = nRT \Rightarrow n = \frac{pV}{RT}$
$n = \frac{mass}{M_r}$ so $\frac{mass}{M_r} = \frac{pV}{RT}$
Therefore, $M_r = \frac{mass \times RT}{pV}$
sub in density $= \frac{mass}{V}$ so $M_r = \text{density} \times \frac{RT}{p} = 770 \times \frac{RT}{p}$
Therefore $M_r = 770 \times \left(\frac{8.31 \times 273}{1.0 \times 10^5}\right) = 17.468 = $ **17 (2 s.f.)**
[4 marks for correct answer, otherwise 1 mark for rearrangement of the ideal gas equation, 1 mark for substituting in $n = \frac{mass}{M_r}$ and rearrangement and 1 mark for using density = $\frac{mass}{V}$.]

3.4 A high voltage is applied and each molecule gains a proton/H^+ ion *[1 mark]*. The mass/charge value of the most abundant ion will be 29 *[1 mark]*.

Unit 2: Section 1 — Periodicity

Page 57 — Periodicity

1 Magnesium ions have a 2+ charge whereas sodium ions only have a 1+ charge *[1 mark]*. Magnesium also has more delocalised electrons as sodium *[1 mark]*. So the metal-metal bonds are stronger in magnesium than in sodium and more energy is needed to break them *[1 mark]*.

2 a) Si has a macromolecular (or giant molecular) structure *[1 mark]* consisting of very strong covalent bonds *[1 mark]*.
b) Sulfur (S_8) molecules are larger than phosphorus (P_4) molecules *[1 mark]*, which results in stronger van der Waals forces of attraction between molecules *[1 mark]*.

3 The atomic radius decreases across the period from left to right *[1 mark]*. The number of protons increases, so nuclear charge increases *[1 mark]*. Electrons are pulled closer to the nucleus *[1 mark]*.

Unit 2: Section 2 — Group 2 and Group 7 Elements

Page 59 — Group 2 — The Alkaline Earth Metals

1 a) Mg: $1s^2\ 2s^2\ 2p^6\ 3s^2$ *[1 mark]*
Ca: $1s^2\ 2s^2\ 2p^6\ 3s^2\ 3p^6\ 4s^2$ *[1 mark]*
b) First ionisation energy of Ca is lower *[1 mark]* because Ca has an extra electron shell *[1 mark]*. This reduces the attraction between the nucleus and the outer electrons because it increases the shielding effect and because the outer electrons of Ca are further from the nucleus *[1 mark]*.

2 a) Y *[1 mark]*
b) Y has the largest radius *[1 mark]* so it will have the smallest ionisation energy/lose its outer electrons more easily *[1 mark]*.

3 Barium *[1 mark]* is oxidised from 0 to +2 *[1 mark]*.

4 The melting points decrease from calcium to strontium to barium. This is because the metallic ions get bigger *[1 mark]* but the number of delocalised electrons per atom doesn't change *[1 mark]*. This means there's reduced attraction of the positive ions to the delocalised electrons, so it takes less energy to break the bonds *[1 mark]*.

Page 61 — Uses of the Group 2 Elements

1 Add acidified barium chloride solution to both.
Zinc chloride would not change/no reaction.
Zinc sulfate solution would give a white precipitate *[1 mark]*.
$BaCl_{2(aq)} + ZnSO_{4(aq)} \rightarrow BaSO_{4(s)} + ZnCl_{2(aq)}$
OR $Ba^{2+}_{(aq)} + SO_4^{2-}{}_{(aq)} \rightarrow BaSO_{4(s)}$ *[1 mark]*

2 a) D barium *[1 mark]*
b) B calcium *[1 mark]*
c) A magnesium *[1 mark]*

3 Patients can swallow a suspension of barium sulfate which will coat the tissues of the digestive system *[1 mark]*. This will make them show up on the X-rays so any problems can be diagnosed *[1 mark]*.

Page 63 — Group 7 — The Halogens

1 a) $I_2 + 2At^- \rightarrow 2I^- + At_2$ *[1 mark]*
b) The astatide *[1 mark]*

2 a) i) Boiling point increases down the group *[1 mark]* because the size and relative mass of the molecules increases *[1 mark]*, so the van der Waals forces holding the molecules together get stronger *[1 mark]*.
ii) Electronegativity decreases down the group *[1 mark]* because the atoms get larger *[1 mark]*, and the shielding effect of the inner electrons increases *[1 mark]*.
b) Fluorine *[1 mark]*

3 a) $Cl_2 + H_2O \rightarrow 2H^+ + Cl^- + ClO^-$ *[1 mark]*
b) Chlorine (or the chlorate(I) ions) kill bacteria *[1 mark]*.
Too much chlorine would be dangerous as it's toxic *[1 mark]*.

Page 65 — Halide Ions

1 First, separately dissolve each solid in water *[1 mark]*.
Add dilute nitric acid each solution. Then add a few drops of aqueous $AgNO_3$ *[1 mark]*. With sodium chloride, the silver nitrate gives white precipitate *[1 mark]* which dissolves in dilute ammonia solution *[1 mark]*. With sodium bromide, the silver nitrate gives cream precipitate *[1 mark]* which is only soluble in concentrated ammonia solution *[1 mark]*.

2 a) C $NaHSO_{4(aq)}$, $At_{2(s)}$, $H_2S_{(g)}$, $2H_2O_{(l)}$ *[1 mark]*
b) AgAt would not dissolve *[1 mark]*. E.g. AgI is insoluble in concentrated ammonia solution and the solubility of halides in ammonia solution decreases down the group *[1 mark]*.

Question 2 is the kind of question that could throw you if you're not really clued up on the facts. If you really know page 64, then in part a) you'll go, "Ah - ha! Reactions of halides with H_2SO_4 — reducing power increases down the group..." If not, you basically won't have a clue. The moral is, it really is just about learning all the facts. Boring, but true.

Page 67 — Tests for Ions

1 D Iodide *[1 mark]*

2 $BaCO_3$ ***[2 marks — 1 mark for correct cation, 1 mark for correct anion]***

3 Add a few drops of sodium hydroxide to a sample of the solution Warm the mixture and test any gas that is given off using damp red litmus paper *[1 mark]*. If the solution contained ammonium ions, the litmus paper will turn blue *[1 mark]*. Take another sample of the solution and add dilute hydrochloric acid followed by barium chloride solution *[1 mark]*. If the solution contained sulfate ions, a white precipitate will form *[1 mark]*.

Answers

Extra Exam Practice for Unit 2: Sections 1 and 2

Pages 68-69

2.1 Fizzing / bubbles of gas/CO_2 given off would be observed on the addition of dilute nitric acid (due to reaction with the carbonate) ***[1 mark]***. A white precipitate would be formed on the addition of barium nitrate (due to the formation of barium sulfate) ***[1 mark]***.

2.2 For the reaction between nitric acid and sodium hydroxide:
$H^+ + OH^- \rightarrow H_2O$ ***[1 mark]***
For the reaction between silver nitrate and sodium chloride:
$Ag^+ + Cl^- \rightarrow AgCl$ ***[1 mark]***

2.3 A mixture of sodium chloride and sodium iodide ***[1 mark]***. A pale yellow precipitate is a result of a mix of a yellow and a white precipitate ***[1 mark]***. The precipitate partly dissolves in concentrated ammonia solution because silver chloride is soluble, but silver iodide is insoluble in dilute ammonia solution ***[1 mark]***.

3.1 Chlorine is a simple molecule / has a simple molecular structure ***[1 mark]***. There are only weak van der Waals forces between molecules, which require little energy to overcome, therefore it is a liquid at 200 K ***[1 mark]***. Argon exists as single atoms / is monatomic ***[1 mark]***. Therefore it has a lower melting point and boiling point than chlorine because it has weaker van der Waals forces between the atoms, so it is a gas at 200 K ***[1 mark]***. Sulfur is also a simple molecule, but sulfur exists as S_8 and is therefore a larger molecule than chlorine with more electrons ***[1 mark]***. This means that the van der Waals forces between S_8 molecules are stronger than in chlorine and so S_8 is a solid at 200 K ***[1 mark]***.

3.2 Any temperature between 230 K and 350 K ***[1 mark]***.
Phosphorus exists as P_4 and therefore the melting point should be higher than Cl_2, but lower than the melting point for sulfur which exists as S_8. The actual melting point of phosphorus is 317 K.

3.3 The atomic radius of magnesium would be larger than the atomic radius of argon ***[1 mark]***. Magnesium has fewer protons in its nucleus/a lower nuclear charge so the electrons are not held as tightly to the nucleus. / Argon has more protons in its nucleus/a higher nuclear charge so the electrons are held more tightly to the nucleus ***[1 mark]***.

3.4 Magnesium hydroxide is sparingly soluble, so most of this product will be left on the filter paper ***[1 mark]***. Magnesium sulfate is very soluble so it will all pass through the filter paper in solution and so none of this product will be observed on the filter paper ***[1 mark]***.

Unit 3: Section 1 — Introduction to Organic Chemistry

Page 72 — Basic Stuff

1 a)
```
    H  H  H  H
    |  |  |  |
 H-C- C- C- C-Br
    |  |  |  |
    H  H  H  H
```
[1 mark]

b) Halogenoalkanes ***[1 mark]***

c) but-1-ene ***[1 mark]***

2 a) A group of compounds that have the same functional group ***[1 mark]***.

b) i) C_5H_{12} ***[1 mark]***

ii) Pentane ***[1 mark]***

3 a) 1,2-dichloroethane ***[1 mark]***

b)
```
    H   H
    |   |
 H— C — C —H
    |   |
    Cl  Cl
```
[1 mark]

c) Cl–CH₂CH₂–Cl (skeletal formula) ***[1 mark]***

Page 75 — Isomerism

1 a) 1-chlorobutane, 2-chlorobutane, 1-chloro-2-methylpropane, 2-chloro-2-methylpropane ***[1 mark for each correct isomer]***

b) 1-chloro-2-methylpropane and 2-chloro-2-methylpropane OR 1-chlorobutane and 2-chlorobutane ***[1 mark]***

c) 1-chlorobutane and 1-chloro-2-methylpropane OR 2-chlorobutane and 2-chloro-2-methylpropane ***[1 mark]***

2 a)
```
 Br      H
   \    /
    C=C
   /    \
 H       CH3
```
E-1-bromopropene ***[1 mark]***

b)
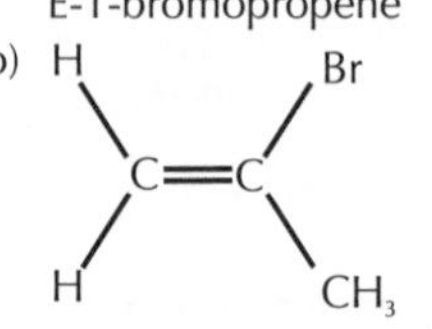

2-bromopropene ***[1 mark]***

```
 H       CH2Br
   \    /
    C=C
   /    \
 H       H
```
3-bromopropene ***[1 mark]***

If one of the C=C carbons has the same two groups attached, then the alkene won't have E/Z isomers.

3 a)
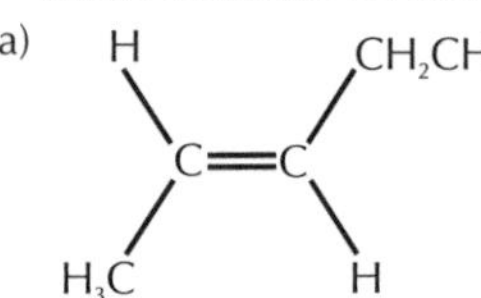

E-pent-2-ene ***[1 mark]***

```
 H3C      CH2CH3
    \    /
     C=C
    /    \
  H       H
```
Z-pent-2-ene ***[1 mark]***

b) E/Z isomers occur because atoms can't rotate about C=C double bonds ***[1 mark]***. Alkenes contain C=C double bonds and alkanes don't, so alkenes can form E/Z isomers and alkanes can't ***[1 mark]***.

Unit 3: Section 2 — Alkanes and Halogenoalkanes

Page 77 — Alkanes and Petroleum

1 a) As a mixture, crude oil is not very useful, but the different alkanes it's made up of are useful ***[1 mark]***.

b) Boiling point ***[1 mark]***.

c) i) C_8H_{18} ***[1 mark]***

ii) Near the top. This is because the molecules in petrol have a relatively low boiling point ***[1 mark]*** and the fractionating column is cooler at the top than the bottom ***[1 mark]***.

2 a) There's greater demand for the smaller fractions ***[1 mark]***.

b) $C_{12}H_{26} \rightarrow C_6H_{14} + C_4H_8 + C_2H_4$ ***[1 mark]***.

Page 79 — Alkanes as Fuels

1 a) $C_7H_{16} + 11O_2 \rightarrow 7CO_2 + 8H_2O$ ***[1 mark]***

b) i) carbon monoxide ***[1 mark]***

ii) By fitting a catalytic converter ***[1 mark]***.

2 a) The high pressures and temperatures in the engine of a car ***[1 mark]*** cause nitrogen and oxygen from the air to react together ***[1 mark]***.

b) Powdered calcium carbonate is mixed with water to make an alkaline slurry ***[1 mark]***. When the flue gases mix with the alkaline slurry, the acidic sulfur dioxide gas reacts with the calcium carbonate to form a salt/calcium sulfate ***[1 mark]***.

Page 81 — Chloroalkanes and CFCs

1 $Cl\bullet + O_3 \rightarrow O_2 + ClO\bullet$ ***[1 mark]***
$ClO\bullet + O_3 \rightarrow 2O_2 + Cl\bullet$ ***[1 mark]***

Answers

2 a) Free radical substitution ***[1 mark]***

b) Initiation: $Cl_2 \xrightarrow{UV} 2Cl\bullet$ ***[1 mark]***

Propagation: $C_2H_6 + Cl\bullet \rightarrow C_2H_5\bullet + HCl$ ***[1 mark]***

$C_2H_5\bullet + Cl_2 \rightarrow C_2H_5Cl + Cl\bullet$ ***[1 mark]***

Termination: $C_2H_5\bullet + Cl\bullet \rightarrow C_2H_5Cl$ /

$C_2H_5\bullet + C_2H_5\bullet \rightarrow C_4H_{10}$ ***[1 mark]***

You can't have a termination reaction where two chlorine radicals react together to form Cl_2 here, because the question asked for one that forms an organic compound.

Page 84 — Halogenoalkanes

1 a) Reaction 1:

Reagent — NaOH/KOH ***[1 mark]***
Solvent — Water/aqueous solution ***[1 mark]***

Reaction 2:

Reagent — Ammonia/NH_3 ***[1 mark]***
Solvent — Ethanol/alcohol ***[1 mark]***

Reaction 3:

Reagent — NaOH/KOH ***[1 mark]***
Solvent — Ethanol/alcohol ***[1 mark]***

b) The reaction would be faster ***[1 mark]*** because the C–I bond is weaker than C–Br/C–I bond enthalpy is lower ***[1 mark]***.

2 B ***[1 mark]***

Unit 3: Section 3 — Alkenes and Alcohols

Page 87 — Alkenes

1 a) Shake the alkene with bromine water ***[1 mark]***. The solution goes from orange to colourless if a double bond is present ***[1 mark]***.

b) Electrophilic addition ***[1 mark]***

c) i)

```
H        CH2CH3              H  CH2CH3               H  CH2CH3
 \      /                    |   |                   |   |
  C==C        ------>    H—C———C—H     ------>   H—C———C—H
 /    \                      |   +                   |   |
H    H(δ+)—H                 H   :Br⁻                H   Br
     |
     Br(δ-)                                          2-bromobutane
```

[1 mark for each correct curly arrow and 1 mark for the product being correctly named.]

Check that your curly arrows are exactly right, or you'll lose marks. They have to go from exactly where the electrons are from, to where they're going to.

ii) The secondary carbocation OR the carbocation with the most attached alkyl groups ***[1 mark]*** is the most stable intermediate and so is the most likely to form ***[1 mark]***.

2 A ***[1 mark]***

Page 89 — Addition Polymers

1 a)

```
H       H
 \     /
  C==C
 /     \
H       CH3
```

[1 mark]

b)

```
    H   H
    |   |
 —— C — C ——
    |   |
    H   CH3
```

[1 mark]

2 a)

```
    H   H
    |   |
 —— C — C ——
    |   |
    H   Cl
```

[1 mark]

b) When you add a plasticiser, PVC becomes more flexible ***[1 mark]***. This is because the plasticisers get between the polymer chains and push them apart ***[1 mark]***. This reduces the strength of the intermolecular forces between the chains, so they can slide over each other more easily ***[1 mark]***.

c) Any two from: e.g. electrical cable insulation / flooring tiles / clothing ***[1 mark for each]***.

Page 91 — Alcohols

1 a) i) Primary ***[1 mark]***
ii) Tertiary ***[1 mark]***
iii) Secondary ***[1 mark]***
iv) Primary ***[1 mark]***

b) i)

```
    H   H   H
    |   |   |    H
H — C — C — C = C
    |   |        H
    H   H
```

[1 mark]

ii)

```
        H
        |
     H—C—H
    H   |
    |   |    H
H — C — C = C
    |        H
    H
```

[1 mark]

iii)

```
    H   H   H                        H       H   H
    |   |   |    H                   |       |   |
H — C — C — C = C        or      H — C — C = C — C — H
    |   |        H                   |   |       |
    H   H                            H   H       H
```

[1 mark]

iv)

```
       H   H
        \ /
         C
    H    ||   H
    |    ||   |
H — C —— C —— C — H
    |         |
    H         H
```

[1 mark]

2 Each liquid in a mixture has a different boiling point ***[1 mark]***. Collecting only the liquid (fraction) that boils at a particular temperature will separate it from the mixture ***[1 mark]***.

Page 93 — Ethanol Production

1 a) $C_6H_{12}O_{6(aq)} \rightarrow 2C_2H_5OH_{(aq)} + 2CO_{2(g)}$ ***[1 mark]***

b) In the presence of yeast ***[1 mark]***, at a temperature of between 30 and 40 °C ***[1 mark]***, anaerobic conditions / air/oxygen excluded ***[1 mark]***.

c) Fractional distillation ***[1 mark]***

2 a) E.g. as they grow, the plants used to produce bioethanol take in the same amount of carbon dioxide as burning the fuel you produce from them gives out. ***[1 mark]***.

b) E.g. fossil fuels will need to be burned to power the machinery used to make fertilisers for the crops / harvest the crops / refine and transport the bioethanol ***[1 mark]***. Burning the fuel to power this machinery produces carbon dioxide ***[1 mark]***.

Page 95 — Oxidation of Alcohols

1 a) i) Acidified potassium dichromate(VI) ***[1 mark]***

ii)

```
          H
     H    |
H     \   C=O
  \    C /
   C  /
H /  \ 
    H  H
```

[1 mark]

b) i) Warm with Fehling's/Benedict's solution: turns from blue to brick-red ***[1 mark]***.
OR warm with Tollens' reagent: a silver mirror is produced ***[1 mark]***.

ii) Propanoic acid ***[1 mark]***

iii) $CH_3CH_2CH_2OH + [O] \rightarrow CH_3CH_2CHO + H_2O$ ***[1 mark]***
$CH_3CH_2CHO + [O] \rightarrow CH_3CH_2COOH$ ***[1 mark]***

iv) Distillation ***[1 mark]***

c) i) (skeletal formula of 2-methylpropan-2-ol) OH ***[1 mark]***

ii) 2-methylpropan-2-ol is a tertiary alcohol ***[1 mark]***.

Answers

Unit 3: Section 4 — Organic Analysis

Page 98 — Tests for Functional Groups

1 D ***[1 mark]***
Propanone is a ketone and so nothing happens when it is warmed with Fehling's solution.

2 B ***[1 mark]***
Cyclohexene is an alkene so it decolourises bromine water.

3 E.g. put a sample of the solution that you want to test in a test tube and add some sodium carbonate ***[1 mark]***. If the solution is a carboxylic acid, the mixture will fizz ***[1 mark]***. If you collect the gas produced and bubble it through limewater, the limewater should turn cloudy ***[1 mark]***.

4 E.g. add excess alcohol to acidified potassium dichromate solution ***[1 mark]*** in a round bottomed flask. Set up the flask as part of distillation apparatus, gently heat it and collect the product ***[1 mark]***. Place some Fehling's solution/Benedict's solution/Tollens' reagent in a test tube and add a few drops of the product ***[1 mark]***. Put the test tube in a hot water bath to warm it for a few minutes ***[1 mark]***. If the blue solution gives a brick red precipitate/if a silver mirror forms on the inside of the tube, the alcohol was a primary alcohol. If there is no change, the alcohol was a secondary alcohol ***[1 mark for a correct observation that matches the reagent used]***.

Page 101 — Analytical Techniques

1 a) C ***[1 mark]***
The relative molecular mass of the compound = the m/z value of the molecular ion, so calculate the precise M_r of each possible molecular formula:
A: (3 × 12.0000) + (6 × 1.0078) + (2 × 15.9990) = 74.0448
B: (4 × 12.0000) + (10 × 1.0078) + 15.9990 = 74.077
C: (3 × 12.0000) + (10 × 1.0078) + (2 × 14.0064) = 74.0908
D: (2 × 12.0000) + (6 × 1.0078) + (2 × 14.0064) + 15.9990 = 74.0586

b) The four options given in part a) all have the same M_r to the nearest whole number, so their molecular ions would all have the same m/z value on a low resolution mass spectrum ***[1 mark]***.

c) 64.0364 – [(2 × 12.0000) + (5 × 1.0078) + 15.9990] = 64.0364 – 45.038 = **18.9984** ***[1 mark]***
The m/z value of the molecular ion is equal to the molecular mass of the compound, so to find the precise atomic mass of F you can just subtract the precise atomic masses of the other elements:

2 a) A is caused by an O–H bond in an alcohol ***[1 mark]***. B is caused by a C–O bond ***[1 mark]***.

b) E.g. the molecule must be an alcohol ***[1 mark]***. An O–H group has a mass of 17, so the rest of the molecule must be a hydrocarbon chain with a mass of 57 ***[1 mark]***. So the molecule is probably C_4H_9OH ***[1 mark]***.
You can tell that the molecule is an alcohol because the spectrum has peaks caused by an O–H bond in an alcohol and a C–O bond.

Extra Exam Practice for Unit 3: Sections 1-4

Pages 102-103

2.1 Product Y:
[1 mark]
High molecular weight substance:
[1 mark]
2-chloropropane undergoes an elimination reaction to form Product Y/propene ***[1 mark]***, which opens up its double bond and joins together with other molecules of Product Y/propene to form the high molecular weight substance/poly(propene) ***[1 mark]***.

2.2 A hydrogen ion is regenerated in the reaction, showing the acid is a catalyst. ***[5 marks — 1 mark for the correct structure of the alkene, 1 mark for a curly arrow from the double bond to a hydrogen ion, 1 mark for a curly arrow from a lone pair on H_2O to the C^+ atom in the carbocation, 1 mark for a curly arrow from the O-H bond to the O^+ atom and 1 mark for an explanation of the hydrogen ion as a catalyst.]***

2.3 Add an excess amount of each sample to separate samples of acidified potassium dichromate(VI) ***[1 mark]***. For each sample, distil the mixture and collect the product ***[1 mark]***. Add a few drops of the product to a test tube of Fehling's solution/Benedict's solution/Tollens' reagent ***[1 mark]*** and gently warm the test tube in a water bath for a few minutes ***[1 mark]***. If the substance is Compound W, the blue solution will give a brick red precipitate / a silver mirror will form on the inside of the tube. If the sample is Product X then nothing will happen. ***[1 mark for both correct observations which match the reagent used]***.

2.4 The IR spectrum of Product X would show a peak between 3230 cm^{-1} and 3550 cm^{-1} for the O–H bond and the IR spectrum of Product Z would show a peak between 3300 cm^{-1} and 3500 cm^{-1} for the N–H bond ***[1 mark]***. This means that both spectra would have peaks in the same regions and so the data in Table 1 could not be used to differentiate between the two spectra ***[1 mark]***.

2.5 The salt formed is ammonium chloride.
[5 marks — 1 mark for a curly arrow from the NH_3 lone pair to the correct C atom, 1 mark for a curly arrow from the C–Cl bond to the Cl atom, 1 mark for a curly arrow from the NH_3 lone pair to the H atom, 1 mark for a curly arrow from the N^+–H bond to the N^+ atom and 1 mark for the salt formed.]

Synoptic Practice

Pages 112-114

1.1 A 1:4 ratio is 20% : 80% and there is 80% of the ^{11}B isotope.
$A_r = \frac{(80 \times 11) + (20 \times 10)}{100}$ = **10.8** ***[1 mark]***

1.2 BF_4^- ion is tetrahedral (4 bond pairs and 0 lone pairs) ***[1 mark]***. The bond between BF_3 and F^- is a coordinate bond ***[1 mark]*** and arises because F^- provides both the electrons in the bonding pair ***[1 mark]***.

1.3 An N_2 molecule has 7 + 7 = 14 electrons.
Boron has 5 electrons. So the other element in the compound has 14 – 5 = 9 electrons ***[1 mark]***. Fluorine has 9 electrons so BF has the same number of electrons as N_2 ***[1 mark]***.

1.4 Boron is reduced. Carbon has donated four electrons, so it must have an oxidation state of –4 in B_4C ***[1 mark]***. So boron must have an oxidation state of +1 in B_4C ***[1 mark]***. Oxygen has a fixed oxidation state of –2, so boron must start with an oxidation state of +3 in B_2O_3 and is therefore reduced ***[1 mark]***.

1.5 In boron the outer electron is removed from a 2p orbital ***[1 mark]***, which is further away from the nucleus than the outermost 2s electron of beryllium ***[1 mark]***. Aluminium has an extra electron shell and inner electron shells provide shielding ***[1 mark]***.
The outermost electron is further from the nucleus than in boron and requires less energy to remove ***[1 mark]***.

Answers

2.1 $5F_2 + 5H_2O \rightarrow O_2 + O_3 + 10HF$ ***[1 mark]***

2.2 The displacement reactions of halogens use the halogen dissolved in water (chlorine water, bromine water or iodine water) ***[1 mark]***. It is not possible to produce fluorine water / fluorine water does not exist since fluorine reacts with water ***[1 mark]***.

2.3 One molecule of water can participate in up to four hydrogen bonds with other water molecules (one to each oxygen lone pair and one to each hydrogen atom) ***[1 mark]***, whereas one molecule of hydrogen fluoride can only participate in hydrogen bonds with up to two other molecules (one to the fluorine atom and one to the hydrogen atom) ***[1 mark]***. This means that more energy is needed to overcome the intermolecular forces in water than in hydrogen fluoride ***[1 mark]***.

3.1 Average of concordant titres = (13.80 + 13.90) ÷ 2 = 13.85 cm^3
Moles sodium hydroxide = (13.85 ÷ 1000) × 0.200 = 2.77×10^{-3}
$CH_3CH_2CH_2COOH + NaOH \rightarrow CH_3CH_2CH_2COONa + H_2O$
So, moles of butanoic acid in 25.0 cm^3 = 2.77×10^{-3}
and moles of butanoic present in 250 cm^3 of equilibrium mixture = $(2.77 \times 10^{-3}) \times 10$ = 0.0277
Moles of butanoic acid used up = 0.500 – 0.0277 = 0.4723
= moles of ester and moles of water formed
Moles of ethanol present in equilibrium mixture = 2.20 – 0.4723 = 1.7277

$$K_c = \frac{[\text{ethyl butanoate}][\text{water}]}{[\text{butanoic acid}][\text{ethanol}]}$$

concentration = moles ÷ volume, therefore,

$$K_c = \frac{(0.4723 \div V)(0.4723 \div V)}{(0.0277 \div V)(1.7277 \div V)} = \frac{(0.4723)(0.4723)}{(0.0277)(1.7277)}$$

= 4.6610... = **4.66 (3 s.f.)**

[7 marks for correct answer, otherwise 1 mark for an average of concordant titres, 1 mark for moles of NaOH, 1 mark for moles of butanoic acid in equilibrium mixture, 1 mark for moles of ethyl butanoate and water formed, 1 mark for moles of ethanol in equilibrium mixture and 1 mark for K_c equation.]

3.2 K_c (reverse reaction) = $\frac{[\text{butanoic acid}][\text{ethanol}]}{[\text{ethyl butanoate}][\text{water}]}$

K_c (reverse reaction) = 1 ÷ K_c (forward reaction)
= 1 ÷ 4.66... = **0.215 (3 s.f.)**
or 1 ÷ 5.30 = **0.189 (3 s.f.)** (using the value given in the question)
[1 mark]
If you correctly used an incorrect answer from part 3.1, you would still get the mark.

3.3 The sulfuric acid present would also react with the sodium hydroxide leading to a larger titre. / The sulfuric acid solution contains water, which would not be accounted for in the K_c calculation. ***[1 mark]***

3.4 $\Delta_r H^\ominus = \Delta_f H^\ominus(\text{products}) - \Delta_f H^\ominus(\text{reactants})$
$\Delta_f H^\ominus(\text{products}) = \Delta_f H^\ominus(\text{reactants}) + \Delta_r H^\ominus$
= (–534 + –276) + (–4) = –814 kJ mol^{-1}
$\Delta_f H^\ominus$(ethyl butanoate) = $\Delta_f H^\ominus$(products) – $\Delta_f H^\ominus$(water)
= –814 – (–286) = **–528 kJ mol^{-1}**

[3 marks for the correct answer, otherwise 1 mark for stating the formula and 1 mark for rearranging the formula to find $\Delta_f H^\ominus$(ethyl butanoate).]
You would also get the marks if you correctly substituted the enthalpy change for the reaction and the standard enthalpy of formation values straight into $\Delta_r H^\ominus = \Delta_f H^\ominus(\text{products}) - \Delta_f H^\ominus(\text{reactants})$ to find $\Delta_f H^\ominus$(ethyl butanoate).

3.5
```
   H  H  H  H
   |  |  |  |
H—C—C—C—C—OH
   |  |  |  |
   H  H  H  H
```
[1 mark]
The alcohol (butan-1-ol) is mixed with an excess of an oxidising agent / acidified potassium dichromate(VI) ***[1 mark]*** and heated under reflux ***[1 mark]***.

4.1 There is a greater difference in electronegativity between carbon and chlorine than between carbon and bromine ***[1 mark]***. This means that the carbon to chlorine bond is more polar ***[1 mark]***.

4.2
```
   H  H  H                       H  H  H
   |  |  |δ+   δ-                |  |  |
H—C—C—C—Br        ——>      H—C—C—C—OH    :Br⁻
   |  |  |                       |  |  |
   H  H  H  :OH⁻                 H  H  H
```
[1 mark for the curly arrow from lone pair on the OH^- ion to the δ+ C atom, 1 mark for the curly arrow from the C–Br bond to the Br atom and 1 mark for the correct structure of the product.]

4.3 The rate of hydrolysis will be fastest in 1-iodopropane ***[1 mark]***. This is because hydrolysis involves breaking the carbon-halogen bond, so it's the enthalpy (strength) of the bond that determines the rate ***[1 mark]***. The C–I bond has a lower bond enthalpy than the C–Cl and C–Br bonds so it will break the most easily, leading to a faster reaction ***[1 mark]***.

4.4 E.g. if the halogen was attached to the second carbon atom in any of the halogenoalkanes this would result in a secondary halogenoalkane, which may hydrolyse at a different rate to a primary halogenoalkane ***[1 mark]***.

4.5 How to grade your answer:
Level 0: There is no relevant information. ***[No marks]***
Level 1: One stage is covered well OR two stages are covered, but they are incomplete and not always accurate. The answer is not in a logical order or shows confused reasoning. ***[1 to 2 marks]***
Level 2: Two stages are covered well OR all 3 stages are covered but they are incomplete and not always accurate. The answer is mostly in a logical order. ***[3 to 4 marks]***
Level 3: All three stages are covered and are complete and accurate. The answer is coherent and is in a logical order. ***[5 to 6 marks]***
Indicative content:
Stage 1: Production of propene
Use warm sodium hydroxide dissolved in ethanol with no water present.
Heat the mixture under reflux.
An elimination reaction takes place.
A carbon to carbon double bond forms.
Stage 2: Reaction mechanism
Alkenes undergo electrophilic addition reactions.
Propene is an unsymmetrical alkene.
There are two possible products because the δ+ H atom on sulfuric acid can add on to the carbon atom either side of the double bond when the double bond breaks.
This results in two possible carbocation intermediates.
One is primary and one is secondary.
Secondary carbocations are more stable than primary carbocations because they have one more alkyl group which feeds electrons towards the positive charge and stabilises it.
A secondary carbocation is therefore much more likely to form.
An alkyl hydrogen sulfate forms where OSO_3H is attached to the first or middle carbon atom in the chain.
On addition of water an alcohol forms.
Stage 3: Products
The secondary carbocation results in the product propan-2-ol.
The primary carbocation results in the product propan-1-ol.
Propan-2-ol is the major product and propan-1-ol is the minor product.

4.6 The molecular formula of the molecule is $C_3H_{(6-x)}Cl_x$.
76.5 = (3 × 12) + [(6 – x) × 1) + 35.5x
76.5 = 36 + 6 – x + 35.5x
34.5 = 34.5x
1 = x
So the molecular formula is C_3H_5Cl ***[1 mark]***.
1-chloroprop-1-ene will show E/Z isomerism ***[1 mark]***.

(3-chloroprop-1-ene) OR (2-chloroprop-1-ene)
[1 mark for the skeletal formula of either 3-chloroprop-1-ene or 2-chloroprop-1-ene].

Specification Map

This specification map tells you where each bit of the AQA specification is covered in this book.

3.1 — Physical Chemistry

3.1.1 — Atomic structure

3.1.1.1	p.2, p.4
3.1.1.2	p.3, p.5-7
3.1.1.3	p.8-13

3.1.2 — Amount of substance

3.1.2.1	p.5
3.1.2.2	p.14
3.1.2.3	p.15, p.17
3.1.2.4	p.21
3.1.2.5	p.16-20, p.22, p.23

3.1.3 — Bonding

3.1.3.1	p.24, p.25
3.1.3.2	p.26, p.27
3.1.3.3	p.33
3.1.3.4	p.25-27, p.31-35
3.1.3.5	p.28, p.29
3.1.3.6	p.30
3.1.3.7	p.30-32

3.1.4 — Energetics

3.1.4.1	p.36, p.37
3.1.4.2	p.38, p.39
3.1.4.3	p.40, p.41
3.1.4.4	p.36, p.37

3.1.5 — Kinetics

3.1.5.1	p.42
3.1.5.2	p.43-45
3.1.5.3	p.42, p.44-46
3.1.5.4	p.44
3.1.5.5	p.44, p.45

3.1.6 — Chemical equilibria, Le Chatelier's principle and K_c

3.1.6.1	p.47-49
3.1.6.2	p.50, p.51

3.1.7 — Oxidation, reduction and redox equations
p.52, p.53

3.2 — Inorganic Chemistry

3.2.1 — Periodicity

3.2.1.1	p.56
3.2.1.2	p.56, p.57

3.2.2 — Group 2, the alkaline earth metals
p.58-61

3.2.3 — Group 7(17), the halogens

3.2.3.1	p.62, p.64, p.65
3.2.3.2	p.62, p.63, p.66, p.67

3.3 — Organic Chemistry

3.3.1 — Introduction to organic chemistry

3.3.1.1	p.70, p.71
3.3.1.2	p.72
3.3.1.3	p.73-75

3.3.2 — Alkanes

3.3.2.1	p.76
3.3.2.2	p.77
3.3.2.3	p.78-79
3.3.2.4	p.80

3.3.3 — Halogenoalkanes

3.3.3.1	p.82-84
3.3.3.2	p.83, p.84
3.3.3.3	p.81

3.3.4 — Alkenes

3.3.4.1	p.85
3.3.4.2	p.85-87
3.3.4.3	p.88, p.89

3.3.5 — Alcohols

3.3.5.1	p.92, p. 93
3.3.5.2	p.90, p.94, p.95
3.3.5.3	p.90, p.91

3.3.6 — Organic analysis

3.3.6.1	p.96-98
3.3.6.2	p.99
3.3.6.3	p.100, p.101

Index

Index

CAR54